BIBLE KEY WORDS

VOLUME IV

Previously Published:

BIBLE KEY WORDS—Volume I

four books in one:

BIBLE KEY WORDS—Volume II

four books in one:

BIBLE KEY WORDS—Volume III

two books in one:

BIBLE KEY WORDS

Volume IV

from **GERHARD KITTEL'S**

**THEOLOGISCHES WÖRTERBUCH
ZUM NEUEN TESTAMENT**

A ONE-VOLUME EDITION CONTAINING
TWO BOOKS:

I. LAW

by Hermann Kleinknecht *and* W. Gutbrod

II. WRATH

by Hermann Kleinknecht, J. Fichtner,
G. Stählin, *and* others

TRANSLATED AND EDITED BY
DOROTHEA M. BARTON AND P. R. ACKROYD

HARPER & ROW, PUBLISHERS

New York and Evanston

LAW

BY

HERMANN KLEINKNECHT
and W. GUTBROD

EDITOR'S PREFACE

THIS book is a translation of the article Νόμος in the *Theologisches Wörterbuch zum Neuen Testament* (TWNT), begun by G. Kittel and now edited by G. Friedrich, Vol. IV pp. 1016-1084, and written by Drs Kleinknecht and W. Gutbrod (1911-1941). Apart from some abbreviation in Chapter I and some curtailing of footnotes, the whole text is here translated. The retaining of references to many German works in an English translation may seem unnecessary to some readers. But while it is clear that those who read German easily will turn to the original rather than to a translation, there are many among those who read theological books who have a little German and who may wish to follow up a particular point without the labour of searching the original for an elusive reference. Nor does it seem altogether inappropriate that statements should be supported by the authority for them, since the weightiness or the bias of that authority may well influence the reader's judgement of what is here said.

The article on Law was published in 1942. Its text here is translated unchanged, but some additions have been made to the Bibliography and by way of footnotes. References to more recent works may be found in the newer Theologies of Old and New Testaments, and in other books to which reference has now been included. A special note may, however, be made here of a field of study entirely unavailable to the original authors, that of the Qumran documents. A fuller understanding of the background to the New Testament interpretation of Law will be one of the contributions which this new field may be expected to bring.

The reader may be referred to Millar Burrows, *New Light on the Dead Sea Scrolls* (1958), for much bibliographical information, and especially there to chapter XXXII.

The still common antithesis between Law and Gospel—narrowly interpreted—has tended to simplify in the minds of many the relationship between Old and New Testaments, and also that between Judaism and Christianity. Some parts of this present work may perhaps help to enlarge the understanding of the term Law as it appears in the Old Testament and in Judaism—and here the Qumran material may be able to fill in some of the gaps, and dialogue between Christians and Jews may also help to clarify the issues. The understanding of the nature of Law is a matter which vitally affects the understanding of the Gospel; and the relationship between Gospel and Law, Gospel and Ethic, is one in which clear and constructive thinking—related to sound exegesis of biblical material—is an ever present necessity.[1]

All Hebrew words have been transliterated and, where necessary, translated. Greek words are not transliterated. Where quotations are given from elsewhere than the New Testament (or Septuagint), a translation has been given, except where the meaning is evident or where the actual Greek word used is of particular importance. In a number of cases translations have been given of crucial Greek words, but these are to be taken only as rough guides to the meaning, since, as will appear from their contents, these are words which are deserving of full and separate study. Such of them as appear in the New Testament are, of course, so treated in other volumes of TWNT.

[1] Cf. G. A. F. Knight, *Law and Grace* (1962) for a fresh discussion of these issues.

CONTENTS

BIBLIOGRAPHY

CHAPTER I

In Plato's *Laws* (*Leges*) the reflexions on law and the concept of it which had developed during the course of history were expressed in an exalted form. Amongst the rich literature on νόμος, of which only a small part has been preserved, the following may be mentioned:

PSEUD.-PLATO: *Minos*.

PSEUD.-DEMOSTHENES: *Orationes* 25, 15 ff.

CHRYSIPPUS: fr. 314 ff. (III, pp. 77 ff. von Arnim).

CICERO: *De Legibus*.

DIO CHRYSOSTOM: *Orationes* 58 (Budé).

STOBAEUS: *Eclogae* IV.115-83.

Orphic Hymns (ed. W. Quandt, *Orphei Hymni* [²1955]), 64.

Modern Studies

U. VON MILAMOWITZ: 'Aus Kydathen, Excursus 1: Die Herrschaft des Gesetzes', PhU, 1 (1880), pp. 47 ff.

R. HIRZEL: *Themis, Dike und Verwandtes* (1907), pp. 133 ff.

—— '*ΑΓΡΑΦΟΣ ΝΟΜΟΣ*', Abhandlungen Sächsische Akademie der Wissenschaften, 20 (1900), pp. 65 ff.

V. EHRENBERG: *Die Rechtsidee im frühen Griechentum* (1921), pp. 103 ff.

W. JAEGER: 'Die griechische Staatsethik im Zeitalter des Plato' (1924), *Humanistische Reden und Vorträge* (1937), pp. 96 ff.

—— *Paideia* (1934), pp. 152 ff.

H. E. STIER: '*ΝΟΜΟΣ ΒΑΣΙΛΕΥΣ*', Philol., 83 (1928), pp. 225 ff.

H. BOGNER: 'Der griechische Nomos. Die Zersetzung des griechischen Nomos', *Deutsches Volkstum*, 13 (1931), pp. 745ff., 854 ff.

M. MUHL: 'Untersuchungen zur altorientalischen und althellenischen Gesetzgebung', *Klio*, Beiheft 29 (1933), pp. 85 ff.

U. GALLI: *Platone e il Nomos* (1937).

A. BILL: *La morale et la loi dans la philosophie antique* (1928), especially pp. 261 ff., where the most important ancient texts for νόμος are brought together.

K. KERENYI, *Die antike Religion* (1940), pp. 77 ff.

CHAPTERS II-IV

Reference may be made to the general Theologies of the Old and
New Testaments

CHAPTER II

A. ALT: *Die Ursprünge des israelitischen Rechts* (1934), = *Kleine Schriften*, I (1953), pp. 278-332.

J. BEGRICH: 'Die priesterliche Thora', *Werden und Wesen des AT*, edited by Volz, Stummer, Hempel (1936), pp. 63 ff.

A. JEPSEN: *Untersuchungen zum Bundesbuch* (1927).

O. PROCKSCH: *Die Elohimquelle* (1906), pp. 225 ff., 263 ff.

L. KÖHLER: 'Der Dekalog', ThR (1929), pp. 161 ff.

G. VON RAD: *Das Gottesvolk im Deuteronomium* (1929).

H. H. SCHAEDER: *Esra der Schreiber* (1930).

J. B. PRITCHARD: *Ancient Near Eastern Texts* (^{2}1955) for ancient legal texts.

CHAPTER III

BOUSSET-GRESSMANN = W. Bousset, *Die Religion des Judentums im späthellenistischen Zeitalter*, ed H. Gressmann (^{3}1926).

M. NOTH: *Die Gesetze im Pentateuch* (1940), reprinted in *Gesammelte Studien zum AT* (1957), pp. 9-141.

G. ÖSTBORN: *Torah in the OT* (1945).

L. COUARD: *Die religiösen und sittlichen Anschauungen der alttestamentlichen Apokryphen und Pseudepigraphen* (1907).

S. KAATZ: *Die mündliche Lehre und ihr Dogma* (1921/22).

M. LÖWY: 'Die paulinische Lehre vom Gesetz', *Monatsschrift für Geschichte und Wissenschaft des Judentums* (1903 f.).

E. STEIN: *Die allegorische Exegese des Philo aus Alexandreia* (1929).

—— *Philo und der Midrasch* (1931).

J. WOHLGEMUTH: 'Das jüdische Religionsgesetz in jüdischer Beleuchtung', *Beilage zum Jahresbericht* (1918/19) *des Rabbinerseminars Berlin* (1919).

D. DAUBE: *Studies in Biblical Law* (1947).

G. F. MOORE: *Judaism* 3 vols. (1927-30).

CHAPTER IV

K. BENZ: 'Die Stellung Jesu zum alttestamentlichen Gesetz', *Biblische Studien*, XIX, 1 (1914).

W. BRANDT: *Das Gesetz Israels und die Gesetze der Heiden be Paulus und im Hebräerbrief* (1934).

B. H. BRANSCOMB: *Jesus and the law of Moses* (New York, 1930).

R. BULTMANN: 'Die Bedeutung des geschichtlichen Jesus für die Theologie des Paulus', *Glauben und Verstehen* (1933).

H. CREMER: *Biblisch theologisches Wörterbuch des nt.lichen Griechisch,* W. J. Kögel ([11]1923).

E. GRAFE: *Die paulinische Lehre vom Gesetz* ([2]1893).

A. HARNACK: 'Hat Jesus das alttestamentliche Gesetz abgeschafft?, *Aus Wissenschaft und Leben,* II (1911), pp. 225 ff.

J. HERKENRATH: *Die Ethik Jesu in ihren Grundzügen* (1926).

A. JUNCKER: *Die Ethik des Apostels Paulus,* I (1904), II (1919).

G. KITTEL: 'Die Stellung des Jakobus zu Judentum und Christentum', ZNW, 30 (1931), 145 ff.

E. LOHMEYER: *Grundlagen paulinischer Theologie* (1929), chapter I.

O. MICHEL: *Paulus und seine Bibel* (1929).

A. W. SLATEN: 'The qualitative use of "nomos" in the Pauline Epistles', *American Journal of Theology,* XXIII (1919), 213 ff.

E. BRUNNER: *Der Mensch im Widerspruch* (1937), pp. 150 ff., 532 ff. E.T. *Man in Revolt* (1939), pp. 155 ff., 516 f.

T. W. MANSON: *Ethics and the Gospel* (1960), esp. ch. III.

W. D. DAVIES: *Paul and Rabbinic Judaism* (1948), esp. ch. 7.

—— *Torah in the Messianic Age and for the Age to Come* (JBL Monograph Series VII, 1952).

D. DAUBE: *The NT and Rabbinic Judaism* (1956).

ABBREVIATIONS

BZAW   *Beihefte der Zeitschrift für die alttestamentliche Wissenschaft*

Diels   H. Diels, *Die Fragmente der Vorsokratiker*, ed. W. Kranz (I, ⁷1954; II, III, ⁶1952); cf. K. Freeman, *Ancilla to the PreSocratic Philosophers. A complete translation of the fragments in Diels . . .* (1948).

Ditt Or   W. Dittenberger, *Orientis Graeci Inscriptiones Selectae*, I-II (1903-5).

Ditt Syll   W. Dittenberger, *Sylloge Inscriptionum Graecarum*, I-IV, 1, 2 (³1915-24).

ET   English translation.

EVV   English versions.

IEJ   *Israel Exploration Journal.*

MGWJ   *Monatsschrift für Geschichte und Wissenschaft des Judentums.*

Philol   *Philologus, Zeitschrift für das klassische Altertum.*

PhU   *Philologische Untersuchungen.*

TGF   *Tragicorum Graecorum Fragmenta*, ed. A. Nauck (²1899).

ThR   *Theologische Rundschau.*

ThStKr   *Theologische Studien und Kritiken.*

TWNT   *Theologisches Wörterbuch zum Neuen Testament*, ed. G. Friedrich.

ZAW   *Zeitschrift für die alttestamentliche Wissenschaft.*

ZNW   *Zeitschrift für die neutestamentliche Wissenschaft.*

Works which appear in the Bibliography are referred to in the text and footnotes by the author's name either alone or with an abbreviated title. References to classical texts are in some cases followed by the name of the editor whose text has been used.

I. *ΝΟΜΟΣ* IN THE GREEK AND HELLENISTIC WORLD

1. *The meaning of the word* νόμος

(a) νόμος belongs by its etymology to νέμω, *deal out* or *dispense*, and corresponding to this it had in early times a comprehensive range of meaning as 'the characteristic quality which is dealt out to each one',[1] in so far as, in the first instance, this is understood in general to mean *every kind of existing or valid standard, order, practice, usage, custom*. νόμος is everything that is accepted and usual (cf. Pseud.-Plat. *Min.* 313b; cf. Aristoph. *Nu.* 1185 f., 1420 ff.; Xenoph. *Mem.* IV.4, 19). The concept is religious in origin and plays an important part in the cult. The connexion between νόμος and *worship of the gods* is expressed linguistically in the regular phrase νομίζειν θέους (Hdt. 1.131, 4.59; Aristoph. *Nu.* 329, 423), i.e. to honour the gods according to the cultic usage of the city-state by taking part in the (civic) public worship[2] (cf. Hes. fr. 221 (Rzach.), Plat. *Crat.* 400 e). νόμος covers such matters as marriage, procreation (Plat. *Leg.* IX.720 e ff.), love (Plat. *Symp.* 182 a), communal meals, schools for physical training,

---

[1] Walde-Pokorny 2 (1927), 330. Greek philosophy expounding the νόμος concept had special delight in alluding to this etymological origin (Plat. *Leg.* IV.714a; Pseud.-Plat. *Min.* 317d; M. Ant. 10.25; Plut. *Quaest. Conv.* 2.10 (II.644c)). This basic concept of νέμειν explains the fact that νόμος in the course of its development occurs with the meaning of 'connected by close kinship', and frequently as almost synonymous with or equivalent to *right* (cf. *Righteousness* in this series), order, reason, mind.

[2] So still in the formal accusation against Socrates (Xenoph. *Mem.* I.1.1 f.) νομίζειν is first transferred in Plat. *Apol.* 26c ff. to the intellectual meaning of *acknowledge, believe* (cf. Aristoph. *Nu.* 819; Eur. *Suppl.* 732). Cf. A. Menzel, *Hellenika* (1938), pp. 17 f.; J. Tate, *Class. Rev.* 51 (1937), pp. 3 ff.

the use of arms (Plat. *Leg.* I.625 c), above all the honouring and burial of the dead (Thuc. 2.35; Eur. *Suppl.* 563; Isoc. *Or.* 2.169). The arrangement and 'rules' for the Nemean games (Pind. *Nem.* 10.28, cf. *Isthm.* 2.38) can be designated νόμος just as easily as a political organisation and 'constitution' (Pind. *Pyth.* 2.86, 10.70). The gods too have νόμοι (Pind. *Pyth.* 2.43, *Nem.* 1.72; cf. Hes. *Theog.* 66). This wide use of the word has always been preserved.

(*b*) As the Greek world became organised politically, νόμος was used in addition especially in the sphere of the law and the state: the *judges' rule*, the *legal usage*, became a consciously settled and binding νόμος, the *law*. At the same time the political and the absolute law are not differentiated (Heracl. fr. 114 (I.176.5 ff. Diels⁵); Aesch. *Prom.* 150 f.; Pind. fr. 169; Soph. *Oed. Tyr.* 865). νόμος is expanded into the (divine) *universal law* (Plat. *Leg.* IV.716a; Callim. *Hymn* 5.100, M.Ant. 7.9), into the '*natural*' *law* (Plat. *Gorg.* 483 e; Dio Chrys. *Or.* 58.5 (Budé); Porphyr. *Abst.* 2.61), into the (philo-sophical) *moral law* (Epict. *Diss.* I.26.1; Muson. p. 87, 5 ff. (Hense)).

(*c*) Not until the fifth century, when we might say that the νόμος is written down in the individual νόμοι, does there arise in connexion with the development of democracy the particular meaning of *written law*, the *expression fixed in writing of the legal system and political constitution of the democratic city-state* (or *polis*) (Aristot. *Resp. Ath.* 7.1; Andoc. *Myst.* 83). Xenophon in *Mem.* I, 2, 42 ff. gives the definition of constitutional law: *Laws are all the rules approved and enacted by the majority in the assembly.* νόμος becomes the *compulsory order* and *command* by the state and punishment is involved if it is not obeyed (Antiphon *Or.* 6.4; Democr. fr. 181 (II.181.11 ff. Diels⁵); Pseud.-Aristot. *Rhet. Al.* 2p. 1422a, 2 ff.).

(d) When νόμος was understood in contrast to the divine nature (φύσις) essentially as a variable *human ordinance* (Hippocr. *Vict.* 1.11; Diod. S. Excerpta Vaticana 7.26 [p. 26 Dindorf 7], it could finally when used by the Sophists at the end of the fifth century acquire the debased meaning of a *contract* or an *agreement* (Aristoph. *Av.* 755 ff.); especially in the formula νόμῳ/φύσει (Democr. fr. 9 [II.139.10 ff.]; Hippias in Plat. *Prot.* 337c), a meaning which is by no means originally to be found in νόμος.

(e) The fundamental meaning of νόμος = *order* (τάξις) led in music to a technical term: *mode, manner of singing, melody, Nomos* (Alcman fr. 93 Diehl; Hom. *Hymn Ap.* 20; Aesch. *Prom.* 576). Since Plato the twofold meaning in politics and music of the 'mode of the law' was used again and again as a play on the word (Plat. *Leg.* IV.722d f.; 800a; Archytas Pythagoraeus in Stob. *Ecl.* IV.1.138 (p. 88, 2 ff. Hense); Max. Tyr. 6, 7).

If we have John vii.51 and Rom. iii.19 in view, it is not unimportant that νόμος too, like various other characteristic concepts of the Greek world, is personified and appears as a divine figure in poetry (Eur. *Hec.* 799 f.; Plat. *Crito* 50a ff.) and later in theology (Procl. in *Rem. Publ.* II.307.20 ff. (Kroll)). This is the place too for the expressions *the law regulates, declares, says* (Inscrip. Magn. 92a, 11; b 16; Plat. *Resp.* V.451b; Callim. *Hymn* 5.100)[1] as well as for the designation of the νόμος as δεσπότης (Hdt. 7.104), τύραννος (Plat. *Prot.* 337e), βασιλεύς[2] (Pind. fr. 169 *et passim*), and finally even as θεός (Plat. *Ep.* VIII.354e; TGF fr. adesp 471). Dio Chrys. (*Or.* 58.8 (Budé)) praises the νόμος in a mythical form as *actually the son of Zeus.* It

---

[1] cf. W. Schubart, 'Das Gesetz und der Kaiser in griech. Urkunden', *Klio* 30 (1937), pp. 56 ff.

[2] cf. *Basileia* in this series (1957).

occurs also in Orphism as assistant of Zeus (*Orph. Fr.* 160 (Kern)) with Δικαιοσύνη as the daughter of itself and of Εὐσέβεια (*Orph. Fr.* 159), and among the Orphic songs there is even a hymn addressed to law as a cosmic power (*Hymn Orph.* (ed. Quandt, 1941) 64).

2. *The nature and development of the νόμος concept in the Greek world*

νόμος was originally, before it was written down, rooted in religion as the embodiment of all that was valid in the affairs of the community. In the expressions τὰ νομιζόμενα, νομίζειν Θεούς (cf. p. 1) its relationship to the cult and to the worship of the gods has been permanently kept alive (cf. the Pythagorean precept in *Carmen Aureum* 1 f.; Jambl. *Vit. Pyth.* 144; (Diog. L.8.33)). Even the written νόμος in the city-state is considered to be the expression of the will of the deity who holds sway over the city (Aristot. *Pol.* 3.16, p. 1287a, 28 ff., cf. Plat. *Leg.* IV.712b). Its deep roots in the divine, which it always preserved, give to the Greek concept of νόμος its characteristic meaning and its real centre.

This is true particularly with reference to its origin: it is part of the nature of the νόμος to have an originator. Either it has been given by the gods, or it is the creation of a great personage, the lawgiver, one who is the kind of man gifted with understanding in a particularly high degree by the gods or of himself. By this means the νόμος becomes a work of the highest 'art' and wisdom. This does not prevent the laws, given to the people mythically or historically, from being often also traced back indirectly to particular gods or to the religious authority of Delphi. When finally the νόμοι in the city-state are brought about by mutual agreement and men's votes (Xenoph. *Mem.* I.2.42 f.), that is the beginning of their decline: soon they are no longer νόμοι, but only decrees (ψηφίσματα) (Demosth. *Or.* 20, 89 ff.).

(*a*) In the earliest period the νόμος as a creation and manifestation of Zeus βασιλεύς is firmly attached to a divine being who inspires belief.

Already myth refers the lawgiving of king Minos (βασιλεὺς καὶ νομοθέτης, Plut. *Thes.* 16 (I.7)) back to his association with Zeus (cf. Plat. *Leg.* I.624). The god is the original archetype of royal power and wisdom which express themselves in the νόμος. In Hesiod *Theogn.* 901 ff. the θεῶν βασιλεύς (886) after his victory over the Titans enters into a marriage with Themis, out of which springs in addition to Δίκη and Εἰρήνη, also Εὐνομίη, i.e. the 'correct order', the 'good νόμος'.[1] When Pindar in fr. 169 extols the νόμος as *monarch of mortal men and of the Immortals*, one who *leads on violence with a high hand dressing it as justice*, it can be recognised from the form of the wording as well as from the connexion of thought that here the νόμος occupies the position of him who is plainly the πάντων βασιλεύς (Democr. fr. 30 (II.151, 14 Diels[5]); Hes. fr. 195 (Rzach), cf. Theog. 923), and holds power and law together in his hand, namely Zeus.[2] He established the νόμος that the animals should devour each other by force (βία), but that mankind should live according to the δίκη which he gave them (Hes. *Op.* 276 ff.). The lawgiver Solon prided himself on the fact that he joined in marriage βία and δίκη (fr. 24.15 f. Diehl)

[1] Kingship and the establishment of εὐνομίη belonged in the early Greek world generally to a large extent together (cf. Hdt. 1.97 ff.; Plut. *Num.* 4); cf also Plato *Polit.* 300c/e).

[2] So now also K. Kerenyi, p. 78. For the history of Pindar's often quoted and misinterpreted saying (Hdt. 3.38; Anonym. Jambl. 6.1 (II.402.28 f. Diels[5]); Plat. *Gorg.* 484b, *Leg.* III.690b/c, IV.714c; Chrysipp. fr. 314 [III.77.34 ff. v. Arnim]) cf. H. E. Stier, pp. 225 ff.

by the power of law (κράτει νόμου), i.e. as a result of the complete power of such a *divine standard*, of a *determination for order* and of a personal *sense of what is right*—all this is involved in νόμος.

In accordance with its nature νόμος has developed into *justice*, as a result of its struggle for the right within the organisation of human life (Plut. *Princ. Inerud.* 3 (II.780e) cf. p. 1, no. 1). But *right* (δίκη) and also *reverence* (αἰδώς, expressed in the νόμος) rest with Zeus (Plat. *Prot.* 322d; Ael. Arist. *Or.* 43, 20 (344 Keil)); couched in terms which combine myth and religion: the goddess Dike in the retinue of the supreme ruler (βασιλεύς, Plut. *Exil.* 5 [II.601b]) keeps watch over the θεῖος νόμος (*Orph. Fr.* 21 (Kern); Plat. *Leg.* IV.716a). Thus νόμος always remained into the later ancient period linked in a special way with Zeus (cf. p. 3).

In the city-state the customs inherited from early days continued to develop into a permanent constitution and became the embodiment of all legal standards of what is right. At this point the concept reaches its characteristic elaboration and position of supremacy. For the state in its spiritual form is called by the Greeks νόμος (Aristot. of Demosth. in Stob. *Ecl.* IV.1.144 (p. 90 Hense); Aristot. *Pol.* 4.4, p. 1292a, 32). Therefore the people must fight for its νόμος as for its walls (Heracl. fr. 44 (I.160, 13 f. Diels[5])). It is the sovereign power which as βασιλεύς or δεσπότης (cf. p. 14) gives orders in the city-state and so, for instance, bids the Spartans conquer or die in the battle (Hdt. 7.104).

(*b*) The new understanding of existence in the sixth century changes the content of νόμος correspondingly. It is not yet dissociated from the divine; now what was formerly Zeus is merely given a fresh form as the divine principle. The idea of the cosmos creates the idea that

the νόμος is an image of the universe in which the same
δίκη rules as in political life. Terrestrial law is only a
particular case of the divine law in the cosmos (Heracl.
fr. 114 (I.176.5 ff. Diels⁵)). Man is not able to exist
without the νόμος of his city-state, but he is even less
able to exist without the νόμος of the cosmos.

The Stoics, who based themselves upon Heraclitus,
later looked on this as the earliest form in which their
cosmopolitanism appeared (cf. Cleanthes fr. 537
(I.121.34 f. v. Arnim); Dio Chrys. Or. 58.2 (Budé)).
In contrast to this, Heraclitus maintains the sense of
being rooted in the concrete νόμος πόλεως. In fact
the laws of the state are such a 'strong' standard (cf.
fr. 44 (I.160.13 f. Diels⁵)) that Heraclitus uses them
as the basis from which to understand the universe:
the νόμος of the city-state is 'something held in common' (ξυνόν or κοινόν (common) Pseudo-Demosth.
Or. 25.15 f.¹; cf. Plat. Crito 50a, Leg. I.645a; Plut.
Quaest. Conv. II.10.2 (II.644e, 7); i.e. in a life κατὰ
νόμον the citizen lives, as it were, the κοινὸς βίος in
contrast with the private existence of each individual.
Corresponding to this there is in the cosmos τὸ ξυνὸν
πάντων which is explained by the image of the city-state
and its νόμος: it is the divine law of the universe which
must be grasped by the mind (νοῦς, ξὺν νόῳ) and
'followed' like the λόγος and the deity (fr. 2 [I.151.1 ff.
Diels⁵]). Perception means here perception of a
universal law and thus at the same time the performance of it. Both of these together are in Greek
φρονεῖν: for *the thinking faculty* (φρονέειν) *is common to all*
(fr. 113 (I.176.4 Diels⁵)); the ξυνόν is the law of the
universe.

(c) The problem raised by the existence of a νόμος
which is contrary to another νόμος (cf. Democr. fr. 259
(II.198.2 ff. Diels⁵)) and is therefore 'not unambigu-

¹ cf. M. Pohlenz in NGG (1924), pp. 19 ff.

ously clear',[1] and so the problem of whether it can be carried out, dawned upon the Greeks for the first time in tragedy. Whilst criticism of the νόμος was opening up new aspects on every side in the most varied forms (cf. p. 9 f.), Sophocles in the *Antigone* once more lets 'the νόμος triumph in its double form'.[2] Although the law of the state was founded originally on that of the gods, yet in Antigone's speech in her defence (450 ff.) an unwritten, divine law is set up against the written law of the city-state: neither Zeus nor Δικἡ who *enacted not these human laws* (452) dictated her action to Antigone, but the *immutable unwritten laws of heaven* (459 f.).[3] There springs from an ancient source above the law of the state and originating in the divine world another law, equally divine. But where the law originating with God can no longer be reconciled with God, there arises the dilemma for the individual: the tragic end of Antigone and the downfall of Creon. Nothing is so characteristic of the way the Greek understood human existence as the fact that when he came up against that aspect of the law as a whole which had a twofold interpretation and could not be carried out (in so far as the performance of one part of it necessarily involved the breach of another part), it did not occur to him to recognise in himself the man who is by nature utterly incapable of obeying the law. He interprets the conflict which caused Antigone to perish as the eternal tragic conflict of a law originating with God, which can no longer be reconciled with God, and thereby he transferred it to the deity itself.

---

[1] R. Bultmann, 'Polis und Hades in der Antigone des Sophokles', in *Theol. Aufs. K. Barth zum 50. Geburtstag* (1936), p. 80.

[2] W. Schadewaldt, 'Sophokles' Aias und Antigone', in *Neue Wege zur Antike* 8 (1929), p. 114.

[3] These are the same νόμοι the divine origin of which is proclaimed in Soph. *Oed. Tyr.* 865 ff.

In so far as the Greeks felt this impracticability to be a problem at all, they gave it a tragic solution and did not regard it from the point of view of man being a sinner in the sight of the law.[1]

As a result of this antithesis, and as a supplement to the written law of the city-state, the ἄγραφος νόμος acquired from the fifth century a greater importance (Thuc. II.37.3; Pseud.-Aristot. *Rhet. Al*, 2, p. 1421b, 35 ff.).[2] It is conceived differently in detail: as an old traditional national νόμος of this or that city-state (Diog. *L*. 3.86), but usually as a natural or divine law, valid amongst all men (Xenoph. *Mem*. IV.4.19 f.; Demosth. *Or*. 18, 275, 23, 61.85; Plat. *Resp*. VIII.563d). Thus in a vague way it could be equated partly with the 'natural' law of the Sophists, partly with the universal law of the Stoics (Max. Tyr. 6, 7). Amongst the chief ἄγραφοι or ἱεροὶ νόμοι which repeatedly recur in the tradition, there are found beside the rules of religious ritual the precepts of social ethics which are already grouped together in Xenoph. *Mem*. IV.4, 20 under the designation θεοῦ νόμος. The fullest list is given in Plut. *Lib. Educ*. 10 (II.7e) (cf. Aesch. *Eum*. 545 ff.; Eur. fr. 853; Ditt Syll³ 1268). It is in line with the high regard enjoyed throughout the ages by the ἄγραφοι νόμοι that they are called by Plato the *bonds in every constitution* (Plat. *Leg*. VII.793b), and were later even regarded as the original source of all earthly laws (Archytas in Stob. *Ecl*. IV.1.132 (p. 79 Hense)).

(*d*) In the fifth century the authority of the νόμος was severely shaken, at first by the discovery of different kinds of νόμοι in the world. It is true that Herodotus still describes them with a certain respect and admiration (3.38). For he recognises in the laws of

---

[1] cf. G. Kittel, *Die Religionsgeschichte und das Urchristentum* (1932), pp. 118 ff.

[2] cf. R. Hirzel, *ΑΓΡΑΦΟΣ ΝΟΜΟΣ*, pp. 29 ff.

the nations their *wisdom* (σοφίη), and at the same time
the break-up of an original σοφίη (Hdt. 1.196 f., 7.102;
cf. Heracl. fr. 114). But soon in the ruthless struggle
for existence the subject began to make himself the
criterion of absolute validity (cf. Eur. fr. 433; Plat.
Ep. VIIII.354c). 'Human nature gained the ascendancy over the laws and became stronger than justice'
says Thucydides of the Peloponesian War (III.84,
cf. III.45.7). In Sophism the νόμος is then pushed
aside in theory too and man now sees himself only
confronted with φύσις (cf. Eur. fr. 920). A gulf is
opened up between what is just according to the law
(νόμῳ) and according to nature (φύσει) (Plat. *Gorg.*
483 ff., *Leg.* X. 889e). For the regulations of the law
are merely arbitrary, brought about by the agreement
of men (Antiphon fr. 44, col. 1.23 ff. (II.346 f. Diels[5])).
On the other hand nature has its own law which is
now the only one still to be recognised (in ethics and
politics too) as the true standard, namely the νόμος τῆς
φύσεως (Callicles in Plat. *Gorg.* 483e). Thus νόμος
remains firmly anchored to something higher. Only
this is no longer a divine being in whom one believes,
but that which has been put in its place: the φύσις
(cf. Hippocr. *Vict.* i.11).

A conception of nature, deprived of the divine
element, in which all fight against all and covetousness
(πλεονεξία) rules as the only law (Plat. *Gorg.* 483, cf.
Leg. IX.875b), was not only bound to undermine the
old law of the state which was directed towards community life, but also inevitably undermined religion
at the same time. For belief in the gods stands and
falls with reverence for the νόμος.

*Yet are the gods strong, and their order strong, even Law;
for by this Law we know gods are* (Eur. *Hec.* 799 f., cf.
Antiphon *Or.* 6.4). This means that if the gods refuse
to obey the law which holds sway over them (namely

that all misdeeds must be expiated [791 f.]), they have
by this act forfeited their being as gods (cf. Eur. *Ion.*
442 f.). On the other hand if they secure respect for
the just νόμος, they demonstrate the justification for
their own existence. Therefore man believes in God
and justice because of the νόμος (cf. Plat. *Menex.* 237d).
In Sophism religion is seen not only in tension with the
νόμος, but finally is unmasked as a fiction of the lawgiver (Critias fr. 25, 5 ff. [II.386 f. Diels⁵]). The νόμοι
are the clumsy handiwork of men and would not be
kept if there were no witnesses. Therefore some clever
fellow invented the punishing gods as permanent over-
seers and guarantors, particularly for secret offences.[1]
Thus according this view there are really no gods at
all; it is only the νόμος which enjoins belief in them
(cf. Plat. *Leg.* X.889e-890a).

Two things follow from this: (i) In the last resort
the νόμος can only be overthrown by an attack on
religion; such is the extent to which both are involved
with each other by their nature and their origin.
(ii) The crisis of νόμος arises from and culminates in
the world's abolishing the gods, a process which the
fifth century as it comes to an end brings with it: *this
overthrow of religion substituted the name of Nature (for God)*
(Lact. *Inst.* III.28.3). This is how Plato described it.
For him the repudiation of the sovereignty of the laws
is equivalent to apostasy from God (Plat. *Leg.* IV.701b/c
Ep. VII.336b; in the myth of the inhabitants of Atlantis
it is said: *as long as the inherited nature of the god remained
strong in them, they were submissive to the laws and kindly
disposed to their divine kindred* [*Critias* 120e]). For he
maintains that the law expresses by its actual nature

---

[1] To deal with secret sinning (cf. fr. 181 [II.181.11 ff. Diels⁵])
Democritus demands that the νόμος should stand in front of a
man's soul, i.e. that his own inner disposition should itself be
determinative for his actions (cf. fr. 264 [II.199.6 ff. Diels⁵]).

(cf. Plat. *Leg.* XII.966c) the manner of the gods'
existence and activity (*Leg.* X.885b, cf. *Resp.* II.365e,
Leg. X.904a). The νόμος determines how they are to
be worshipped and conceived (Plat. *Leg.* X.890a/b).
This Platonic association of 'theology' and legality is
simply the philosophical expression of that which was
conveyed to the early Greek world by the fact of
νομίζειν θεούς (cf. p. 1).

Plato therefore undertakes to preserve the νόμος
firstly by proving the existence of the gods, secondly by
asserting that the νόμος being an offspring of νοῦς is
related to the soul and for that reason is 'of nature'
(φύσει)[1] like the latter (*Leg.* 982a ff., cf. also *Leg.*
X.890d, 891b. Jambl. *Vit. Pyth.* 171, 223). By setting
up the νόμος finally as divine[2] (*Ep.* VIII.354e), he
defeated the Sophists' criticism of the νόμος at its
crucial point.

(*e*) Socrates, in contrast to the Sophists, starts in all
his thought from the νόμος as that which is the most
vital constituent of the city-state. The νόμος τῆς πόλεως
is so much the rule of his life that not only does he not

[1] In this connexion Plato develops the concept, aimed at
Sophism, of a *proper nature* (ἔμφρων φύσις) (to use the words of a
parallel passage in *Timaeus* 46d) which he here almost merges in
his concept of ψυχή (*Leg.* X.891c ff.). On Plato's attitude to the
law cf. A. Capelle, *Platos Dialog Politikos* (Diss., Hamburg, 1939),
pp. 53 ff.

[2] *Men of sound sense have Law for their god, but men without sense
Pleasure.* Here νόμος and ἡδονή are thought of on the plane of the
divine as the two opposing powers. Plato, like Thucydides
(II.53, III.82.8), has again and again indicated ἡδονή as the basis
on which the decline of the νόμος is to be understood (*Leg.* IV.714a;
Resp. VIII.548b, IV.429c). Life in accordance with the law is the
most complete contrast to ἡδέως ζῆν (*Leg.* II.662c/663a f.). The
art of the Muses, which was too much under the influence of
ἡδονή, gave rise to the general lawlessness in the Athenian state
(*Leg.* III.700/701a). The final result is that the νόμος βασιλεύς is
succeeded by the rule of ἡδονή and λύπη (*grief. Resp.* X.607a).

act contrary to the laws, but he will go so far as to die
at their command when they are manipulated un-
justly by men. (cf. Xenoph. *Mem.* IV.4.4). Plato has
expressed this conviction of Socrates in noble fashion
in the *Crito*, when he describes the appearance of the
time-honoured Athenian Νόμοι καὶ τὸ κοινὸν τῆς πόλεως
as a kind of epiphany to Socrates in prison. A dialogue
ensues concerning the right of the individual to re-
pudiate the νόμος (*Crito* 50a ff.). In this the νόμοι
come forward as parents, providers and educators
(51c). Man is their *offspring* and *servant* (50e) and
stands in a relationship of dependence on them quite
different from that which he has on his physical
parents. These νόμοι have 'brothers in Hades' (54c),
i.e. they are valid also in the face of death and beyond.

(*f*) The relationship of Socrates to the laws of the
state provides a conspicuous example of the significance
of the νόμος for Greek ethics. Socrates does not draw
a distinction between his clear conscience and the
debased morality of the state. For the classical world
of Greece has no knowledge of a personal moral
conscience (συνείδησις),[1] but is well aware objectively
of what is right and wrong.[2] This knowledge acquires
a form in the law. Obedience to the law is righteousness (cf. Aristot. *Eth. Nicom.* 5.1, p. 1129a, 33 ff., cf.
Xenoph. *Mem.* IV.4.13 ff.). Now righteousness includes every virtue.[3] It is impossible to account in
detail for the whole of the content of the νόμος which
embraces the whole of life (cf. Aristot. *Pol.* 3.15, p.

---

[1] cf. C. A. Pierce, *Conscience in the NT* (1955).

[2] 'Conscience has no rights in the state, legality alone has them.
If conscience is to be of the right mind, it is necessary that what it
regards as right should be objective . . . and should not merely
dwell within . . .' (Hegel, *Werke* (ed. Lasson), XIII.2 (1927),
p. 127 [*Vorlesungen über die Philosophie der Religion*]), ET *Lectures on
the Philosophy of Religion*, II (1895), p. 233).

[3] cf. *Righteousness* in this series (1951), esp. pp. 9 ff.

1286a, 9 ff.), unless it is described in more general terms as in Aristot. *Eth. Nicom.* 5.4, p. 1130a, 18 ff.

The aim of all education is therefore education in the spirit and ethos of the laws (Plat. *Leg.* II.659d, cf. *Leg.* VI.751c, *Prot.* 326c/d). Indeed, the law is itself an educator, even though in a completely different sense from that of Paul in Gal. iii.24. (Plat. *Leg.* VII.809a, cf. Aristot. *Pol.* 3.16, p. 1287b, 25 f.; Archytas Pyth. in Stob. *Ecl.* IV.1.135 [p. 82, 16 f. Hense]).

Obedience to the law goes so far that it is possible to speak of *serving* (δουλεύειν) *the laws* (Plat. *Leg.* 698c, 700a, IV.715d; cf. Paul in Rom. vii.25) without any trace of the idea of disparagement which is usually connected with the term. This almost paradoxical usage enables us to realise that the νόμος exercises authority.[1] The law 'rules' (Aristot. *Pol.* 4.4 p. 1292a, 32, cf. Plat. *Leg.* IV.715d), even, according to circumstances, as δεσπότης, τύραννος (Plat. *Prot.* 337d) or βασιλεύς (Alcidamas in Aristot. *Rhet.* 3.3 p. 1406a, 23, cf. Anonym. Jambl. 6.1 [II.402.29 Diels⁵]; Plat. *Epis.* VIII.354c). He who lives according to the law, as Aristotle says (*Eth. Nicom.* x, ix.11, p. 1180a, 17 ff.), lives *by a certain intelligence and by a right system, invested with adequate sanctions*, i.e. according to an order determined by the mind which at the same time has authority to impose itself. The νόμος has coercive power (*ib.* a 21, cf. Antiphon *Or.* 6.4) which far exceeds that of an individual man (as that of a father), unless he be a βασιλεύς or similar personage. His 'servitude' to the law makes the man in the city-state (as later in the cosmos) a citizen and gives him his freedom: *it makes servants of us all only to set us free* (Cic. *Pro Cluent.* 53.146;

---

[1] It is said that Pittacus answered the question of king Croesus concerning the greatest authority by pointing to the νόμοι (Diod. S. *Excerpta Vaticana* 7.27; Diog. L. 1.77).

cf. Plat. *Leg.* III.701b; Aristot. *Pol.* 5.9, p. 1310a 34 ff.),
distinguishing him from the slave who by his very
nature has no part in the νόμοι (TGF fr. adesp. 326).

Apart from the νόμοι, there is no question of a servitude (δουλεία) in the positive sense except with regard
to the gods (especially Apollo of Delphi) (cf. Soph.
Oed. Tyr. 410; Eur. *Orest.* 418, *Ion*, 309; Plat. *Phaedr.*
85b). For to be subject to the laws means at the same
time to serve the gods (Plat. *Leg.* VI.762e, cf. Plat.
Ep. VIII.354e). The νόμιμος is not only the δικαίος,[1]
but also the εὐσεβής (Xenoph. *Mem.* IV.6.2). This
seems to be the Delphic view of religion in particular,
to which Socrates also adhered (Xenophon *Mem.*
I.3.1, cf. IV.3.16). Amongst the various traditional
instructions attributed to Apollo of Delphi, the saying
is found[2]: *Follow God: obey the law* (Stob. *Ecl.* III.1.173
[125.5 Hense]). Following God and obeying the law
are placed side by side without any interrelationship.[3]

For the sovereignty of the law, together with the
blessing of the gods, guarantees the stability of the
state and the possibility of existence for man (Plat.
Leg. IV.715d). This 'soteriological function remained
a permanent characteristic of the νόμος (cf. Pseud.-
Plat. *Min.* 314d; Aristot. *Rhet.* 1.4, p. 1360a 19 f.; Dio
Chrys. *Or.* 58.1 [Budé]; Porphyr. *Marc.* 25; Letter of
Aristeas 240; Just. *Apol.* 1.65.1). But it is only when it
is obeyed from conviction that *it shows* to them *their
own particular virtue* (Democr. fr. 248 [II.194.18 ff.
Diels[5]]). Without the νόμος mankind would have to
lead a life of the beasts (Plut. *Col.* 30.1 [II.1124d]
from Plat. *Leg.* IX.874e).

(*g*) Plato interprets the death of Socrates, obediently

---

[1] cf. *Righteousness* in this series, p. 13.

[2] cf. W. H. Roscher, *Philol.*, 59 (1900), pp. 37 f.

[3] M. Ant. (7.31) took up the saying of Apollo about following
God by way of the law, but gave it a Stoic interpretation.

defying the law, as the transition of that which was the norm and the law from the institutions of the state to the ψυχή of Socrates, i.e. to the mind.

Within the human ψυχή, as it was disclosed to the Greeks by the example of Socrates, Plato seeks and finds a κόσμος and a τάξις (using a medical analogy). Medicine clearly possessed for the normal condition of the body no single name, but spoke of health, strength, beauty and the like. But for the κόσμος and the τάξις of the soul Plato used one word only: νόμος (cf. Plat Gorg. 504c, Crito 53c, Phileb. 266).

Here we have the foundation of the 'state' and the ideal legislation of the 'Νόμοι' by Plato (cf. Leg. XII.960d). Its new, inner νόμος is that of which the τάξις is determined by the standard of the ψυχή, i.e. δικαιοσύνη and σωφροσύνη.[1] In Plato this law is 'begotten'[2] anew out of a generally valid principle, knowledge (Plat. Leg. X.890d; cf. I.645a/b; IV.712a). That which manifests itself through the νόμοι is the mind. In an etymological play upon words, which always reveals a real relationship of ideas, Plato calls the νόμος the *reason's ordering* (τοῦ νοῦ διανομή Leg.

---

[1] The opposite of this is found in Plat. *Leg.* V.728a/b: violation and neglect of the laws make the soul bad.

[2] cf. Plat. *Symp.* 209d: *Solon is highly esteemed among you for begetting his laws.* The use of this metaphor places Plato in a venerable tradition. Sophocles lets the eternal νόμοι likewise be 'engendered' (*Oed. Tyr.* 865 ff.) and 'live' (*Ant.* 457); their begetter is Olympus and no dead human native has 'brought them forth' (*Oed. Tyr.* 869 ff.). The laws which Lycurgus left are called in Plat. *Symp* 209e 'children' and the νόμοι which appear to Socrates in prison refer to their 'brothers in Hades' (Plat. *Crito* 54c). The growing up of the νόμοι in Heraclitus (cf. fr. 114 (176.7 f. Diels⁵)) also belongs in this biological realm of ideas. The continuing influence of the Platonic formulation is seen in Josephus (*Ant.* 4.319) who otherwise knows nothing of a begetting (cf. TWNT, I, p. 667) by God, but says of the Jewish laws: *laws which he* (i.e. God), *the begetter of them, presented to you himself.*

IV.714a; cf. XII.967c II.674b). According to Aristotle the dominion of the νοῦς is embodied in the coercive power of the νόμος (*Eth. Nic.* 10, p. 1180a 21). To make νόμος rule in the state is to make God and the reason alone to be the sovereign (Aristot. *Pol.* III.xi.4, p. 1287a 28 ff.). By being firmly anchored to the νοῦς the Greek concept of law once more acquires in a philosophic form an absolute validity. For it is thereby tied afresh to the divine (Plat. *Leg.* IV.713a/c).

Contrasted with this it is a revolutionary idea, pointing towards the future of Hellenism, when the same Plato advances for the first time the thesis that the ideal is not the rule of the law, which necessarily always lags behind progress, but the rule of the just and royal person who possesses true knowledge (*Pol.* 294a/b; cf. Plat. *Leg.* IX.875c/d). In Aristotle too (*Pol.* 3.13, p. 1284a 3 ff.) there appears the man who towers above all others by his excellence (ἀρετή), no longer bound by any law. He does not only stand above the νόμος, but he is, as a god among men (10 f.), himself the law for himself and for others (13 f.; cf. *Eth. Nic.* 14, p. 1128a 32; Plut. *Alex.* 52 (I.694 f.)).

3. νόμος in Hellenism

(*a*) In Hellenism this philosophical theory became historical reality. The νόμος no longer rules in the city-state as 'king', but the will and the person of the βασιλεύς has itself become νόμος (Dio Chrys. *Or.* 3.43 [Budé]; cf. Anaxarch. in Plut. *Alex.* 52.I.694 f.). The god-king is the new divine source of the νόμος which is connected with him in a special manner (Themist. *Or.* 9, p. 123a (Dindorf); cf. Isoc. *Demonax* 36; Isis hymn from Andros 4 f. (p. 15 Peek)) and is in part expressly called after him βασιλικὸς νόμος (Pseud.-Plat. *Min.* 317a/c; Ditt. *Or* II.483.1 [Pergamon]; cf. I.329.14

James ii.8).[1] Corresponding to his worship as living image (Ditt. *Or.* 90.3) and imitator of Zeus (Muson. p. 37, 3 ff. [Hense]) the king, or alternatively the philosopher, is himself even considered to be the visible manifestation of the eternal law in the cosmos, as a νόμος ἔμψυχος (Muson. p. 37, 2 ff.; Archytas Pyth. in Stob. *Ecl.* IV.1.135 [p. 82, 20 f. Hense]; Diotogenes Pyth. in Stob. *Ecl.* IV.7.61 [p. 263, 19 Hense]; Philo *Vit. Mos.* 2.4).[2]

(*b*) In Stoicism, where the 'law' is a fundamental concept, the place of the πολιτικὸς νόμος of the classical period which had grown up historically, is taken by a cosmic and universal νόμος. The designation νόμος in its proper sense is no longer appropriate to the laws of the state[3]; they have sunk to be false ideas (δόξαι ψευδεῖς) [Max. Tyr. 6.5 (Hobein)]. The individual in Hellenism now seeks and finds the only true and divine νόμος in the cosmos alone (cf. Plut. *De Exilio* 5 [II.601b]). The world is his 'state'. Here a homogeneous law holds sway (Chrysipp. fr. 323 [III.79.38 ff. von Arnim]; Plut. *Alex. Fort. Virt.* 1.6 [II.329a]; Philo *Op. Mund.* 143), and this, as the foundation of all communal life, also unites men and gods (Chrysipp. fr. 335 [III.82.18 von Arnim]). Since it is the universal supreme reason (M. Ant. 7.9), this νόμος pervades the whole of nature just as it determines the moral conduct of men (Chrysipp. fr. 314 [III.77.34 ff. von Arnim]). The world order, as determined by the mind, is identical with the concept of law. This in its turn is founded in the last resort on the religious sense, whether the νόμος

[1] cf. Eus. *De Laude Constantini* (p. 201, 27) of Constantine.

[2] cf. E. R. Goodenough, 'The Political Philosophy of Hellenic Kingship', in *Yale Class. Studies*, 1 (1928), pp. 55 ff.

[3] The νόμος of the city-state is used only for purposes of comparison: God is for the world what the law is in the state, as is explained by Pseud.-Aristot. *Mund.* 6, p. 400b 7 ff. (cf. Epictet. *Diss.* I.12.7 *et passim*).

is set up directly as a θεός (II.315.23 v. Arnim) or the deity is identified with the law of the cosmos, itself unmoved[1] yet moving all things (Pseud.-Aristot. *Mund.* 6, p. 400b 28 ff.). This is accommodated with popular religion by giving the world-νόμος the name of Zeus (Zeno fr. 162 [I.43 von Arnim = Diog. *L.* 7.88]). In the hymns of Cleanthes too (fr. 537 [I.121 ff. von Arnim]), it is the almighty Zeus who on the one hand guides the universe by means of the νόμος (v.2), and on the other is placed in the final verses on an equality with the world-order itself, and the right to glorify this is the highest honour for men and gods (v. 38 f. [I.123.4 f. von Arnim]).[2]

Thus man must make a decision, by virtue of the νοῦς or λόγος which dwells within him, for the νόμος and a life in conformity with it (Plut. *Stoic. Rep.* 1 [II.1033b]). But in doing so he does not obey an absolute demand approaching from without or from another world, but he comes to himself and gains his freedom (Chrysipp. fr. 360 [III.87.43 f. von Arnim], cf. Max. Tyr. 33.5; M. Ant. 10.25). Therefore it is not fundamentally impossible to fulfil the law; on the contrary it is that to which the striving and destiny of man is directed by nature. Thus the *law of nature and of God* or the *divine law*, which Epictetus proclaims (*Diss.* I.29.13/19) is as regards its content simply the moral law of philosophy[3] (cf. *Diss.* II.16.28, cf. I.29.4). For Epictetus it is the laws which issue thence (*Diss.* IV.3.11/12), which alone lead to the life of bliss. When the philosopher follows them of his own accord,

---

[1] For the immutability of the law cf. Plat. *Leg.* XII.960d; Pseud.-Plat. *Min.* 321b; Max. Tyr. 11.12; Plut. *Vit. Lycurg.* 29 (I.57d); Philo *Op. Mund.* 61. Cf. M. Mühl, pp. 88 ff.

[2] cf. also Heracl. fr. 114 (v. 24 f. [I.122, 20 f. von Arnim]).

[3] cf. A. Bonhoeffer, 'Epiktet und das NT', in RVV 10 (1911), pp. 154 f.

he is free and a friend of God (*Diss.* IV.3.9). For in
doing so, he follows God.[1] This is made clear if we
combine the sayings of Plutarch in *Ad Principem
Ineruditum* 3.1(II.780c) and in *Aud.* 1 (II.37d).

Thus whilst on the one hand the νόμος has undergone
an expansion into the cosmic order, on the other hand it
has been given a markedly inward quality. It is now, as
it were, written within the man, on his soul (Max. Tyr.
6),[2] so that M. Ant. X.13.2 names it beside πίστις,
αἰδώς, ἀλήθεια and ἀγαθὸς δαίμων amongst the most
valuable elements in human nature.

(*c*) Neo-Platonism added no more new features to
the Greek concept of law. Other basic motifs had replaced in it the fundamental Platonic and Stoic ideas
about the law. In Plotinus the νόμος plays only a
subordinate role in ethics and the doctrine of the soul.
A life of bliss cannot be bestowed on those who have
not done what makes them worthy of bliss (Plot.
Enn. III.2.4 towards the end). This is the will of οἱ ἐν
τῷ παντὶ νόμοι (*Enn.* III.2.8). Plotinus recognises in
this the operation of the divine will which by the νόμος
of providence maintains man in existence (Plot. *Enn.*
III.2.9). The Gnostic teaching is reproached with dis-
paraging together with divine foreknowledge also 'all
the lawfulness of the world' and bringing ἀρετή into
ridicule (*Enn.* II.9.15). For all wrongdoing is punished
and nothing can escape that which is settled ἐν τῷ τοῦ
παντὸς νόμῳ (*Enn.* III.2.4). This applies also in the
case of the various reincarnations of the soul.[3] The
Neo-Platonist Porphyry then developed in addition

[1] In Muson. (p. 86, 19 ff. Hense) the ideal life for a Stoic sage
appears as the law of Zeus.

[2] cf. Jul. *Or.* 7, p. 209c (cf. Paul in Rom. ii.15); cf. Plot. *Enn.*
V.3.4; Procl. in *Rem. Publ.* II.307.7 ff. (Kroll).

[3] With reference to Plat. *Phaedr.* 248c, *Tim.* 41e; in the Her-
metic literature cf. Stob. *Ecl.* I.49.49 (=p. 418, 6 Hense), I.49.69
(=p. 463, 23 Hense).

a detailed doctrine in three stages concerning the νόμος
(*Ad Marc.* 25/27).

(*d*) The later ancient world goes back in the main
to the 'Orphic' and Platonic conceptions of νόμος
(especially Plat. *Leg.* IV.716a = *Orph. Fr.* 21 [Kern];
Gorg. 523a; *Phaedr.* 248c; *Tim.* 41e *et passim*), but gives
them a cosmic theological interpretation (Procl. in
Rem. Publ. II.307.20 ff. [Kroll], cf. in *Tim.* I.203.28 f.).
Beside the one world-creating νόμος which ranks as god
and associate of Zeus (*Orph. Fr.* 160 [Kern], cf. Procl.
in *Tim.* I.156.9 ff., cf. *Orph. Fr.* 159 [Kern]) there is
an elaborately organised system of cosmic νόμοι (Procl.
in *Tim.* I.136.13 ff., 397.22 ff.) which are given a comprehensive unity in Adrasteia (Nemesis, cf. Hermias
in Plat. *Phaedr.* 248c [p. 161, 15 ff. Couvr] = *Orph. Fr.*
105 [Kern]).

4. *The Greek concept of* νόμος *and the New Testament*

In contrast to every law derived from revelation,
νόμος for the Greeks originated in the mind (νοῦς). So
the genuine νόμος is no mere obligatory law, but something in which an entity valid in itself is discovered and
appropriated (Pseud.-Plat. *Min.* 315a, cf. Plat. *Polit.*
300c/e). It is 'the order which exists (from time im-
memorial), is valid and is put into operation. It does
not simply set in order, but orders, does not simply
command, demand and forbid, but rules. This order
as it were brings its own fulfilment and in the event of
non-fulfilment imposes its will or is upheld'.[1] This
aspect of the nature of the νόμος has something in
common with the Greek gods.[2] This is the only ex-

---

[1] cf. H. Cremer, *Biblisch-theologisches Wörterbuch des nt.lichen
Griechisch*, rev. by J. Kögel ([11]1923), p. 749. Cf. Xenoph. *Mem.*
IV.4.24; Plat. *Leg.* IV.716a; Plot. *Enn.* IV.3.13/24.

[2] This is often stated by way of comparison, e.g. by Aristot.
Pol. e.13, p. 1284a 10; Pseud.-Aristot. *Mund.* 6. p. 400b 7 ff.

planation of the command: *we must keep to the laws of our country just as though they were some gods of second rank* (Hierocles Stoicus in Stob. *Ecl.* III.39.36 [p. 733, 10 f.]). The νόμος, like the gods, has a supreme and terrible power over all those who wish to evade it. At the same time it is like them surrounded by a supremely ideal quality because it is the only σωτηρία (cf. p. 15) for all who obey it (Eur. *Ba.* 890 ff.). It is a simple logical consequence that the νόμος of the city-state as well as that of the cosmos, now appears in fact again and again also as 'god' (TGF fr. adesp. 471, cf. Plat. *Ep.* 8.354e; Pind. fr. 169; Aristot. *Pol.* 3.16, p. 1287a 28 ff.; Procl. in *Rem. Publ.* II.307.20 [Kroll]; Philodem. Philos. *Pietat.*11 [II.315.23 von Arnim]), called in mythological theology Zeus (Plut. *Ad Principem Ineruditum* 4.2 [II.781b], cf.Zeno fr. 162 ([I.43 von Arnim = Diog. *L.* 7.88]; cf. p. 3 f.).

By understanding the concept of law in this way the Greek world, from the point of view of the NT, concealed from itself the true meaning of the law. For a Greek never thought of the law as something which, when correctly understood, would destroy him or make him despair of himself, because it makes a man conscious of the fact that he cannot keep it.[1] On the contrary the later ancient world was in the end brought to despair[2] because it no longer possessed an objective historical νόμος and even philosophy could no longer give it one.

[1] No Greek could speak, as Paul does in Rom. ii.23, of νόμος τῆς ἁμαρτίας (cf. I Cor. xv.56). For to Greek eyes the law cannot be at the same time a cause of transgressing the law (Chrysipp. fr. 1125 [II.326.35 v. Arnim]).

[2] cf. the pious wish of Celsus in Orig. *Cels.* 8.72: *Would that it were possible to unite under one law the inhabitants of Asia, Europe and Libya, both Greeks and barbarians even at the furthest limits* (cf. H. Chadwick, *Origen: Contra Celsum* (1953), p. 507, n. 1). The νόμος Christi (cf. Just. *Dial.* 11) has taken the place of the individual national νόμοι of the ancient world as well as of much of the Stoic ideal of the homogeneous and all-embracing νόμος. Cf. E. Peterson, *Der Monotheismus als politisches Problem* (1935), pp. 62 f.

II. LAW IN THE OLD TESTAMENT

1. *Early Israelite law*

LITERARY and form criticism have made it possible to
pick out from amongst the whole stock of the OT legal
literature the earliest corpora of Israelite law so as to
reveal the fundamental features of early Israelite law.[1]
Particular examples of these old legal corpora are the
groups of five-unit sayings,[2] probably originally twelve
in number, in each case with the ending *shall surely be
put to death*[3]; in addition, the groups of four-unit sayings, also twelve originally, beginning with *cursed*[4]
and the so-called Decalogue which was historically
the most influential.[5] This last has indeed abandoned
complete symmetry of form for the sake of its contents, but on the other hand it enables the essentials
of those ancient laws to be perceived all the more
distinctly.

The situation in life of these Israelite laws was that
act which was performed regularly at the central
shrine[6] to renew and commemorate Yahweh's covenant

---

[1] For the following see especially Alt, *Die Ursprünge des israelitischen Rechts*, pp. 33 ff.

[2] i.e. sayings consisting of a poetic line with five 'stresses'.

[3] Exod. xxi.12, 15-17, xxii.18 f., xxxi.14 f.; Lev. xx.2, 9-16, 27,
xxiv.16, xxvii.29. The original precepts can be recovered in part
only by reconstruction, cf. Alt pp. 45 f.

[4] Deut. xxvii.15-26 with small emendations.

[5] Exod. xx.2 ff.; Deut. v.6 ff. On the question of the original
form of the decalogue cf. L. Köhler, 'Der Dekalog', ThR (1929),
pp. 161 ff.

[6] cf. M. Noth, *Das System der 12 Stämme Israels* (1930), (cf.
History of Israel (ET ²1960), pp. 100 ff. Possibly the essential cult-
object was the ark of Yahweh in which were perhaps preserved
simply the laws of the covenant. Cf. P. Volz, *Mose und sein Werk*

with Israel. For the origin of these laws we must look
to Sinai and to a special event there, the details of
which will certainly be difficult to elucidate.[1]

These statements about the presumed situation in
life of these laws in the period of the judges must
correspond to and be interpreted by what they themselves reveal about their theological situation in Israel's
belief in God. Now this 'situation' of the law is the
conception of the covenant.[2] Yahweh has chosen Israel
to be his people, Israel has acknowledged this Yahweh
to be its God. This basic proposition of the whole
OT[3] is the immediate foundation of these laws. They
are an expression of Yahweh's claim to reign over the
whole life of the people belonging to him in virtue of
his choice. This is declared as clearly as possible by
the first commandment of the Decalogue.

Thus these laws are not understood as an equitable
adjustment of men's vital interests, perhaps with
divine sanction. Nor when they are obeyed is this an
achievement which Israel of its own accord offers to its
God in thanks for covenant and election. It is certainly
not an achievement by means of which the people
would come to belong to the deity. These laws are in
the strict sense demands made by the God to whom
this people belongs because he has revealed himself to

([2]1932), pp. 100 ff.; Galling in RGG[2] III, cols. 1449 f. Cf. the
discussion by M. Haran in IEJ 9 (1959), pp. 30 ff., 89 ff.

[1] Although it seems that it was the priests who recited the law
(Deut. xxxi.11, xxxiii.10), tradition points to Moses, who was not
a priest, for the Decalogue. There is no decisive reason against
this tradition. Cf. Volz, pp. 20 ff.; Köhler, pp. 178 ff., 18.4

[2] W. Eichrodt, *Theologie des AT*, I ([2]1939), pp. 26 ff., ET
Theology of the OT (1961), pp. 70 ff.; Volz, pp. 73 f. It must
be admitted that the conception of election was not yet present in
its later theological form. [Cf. also H. H. Rowley, *The Biblical
Doctrine of Election* (1950).]

[3] Contrary to e.g. L. Köhler, *Theologie des AT* (1936), p. 12
(ET 1953), p. 30.

it by bringing it out of Egypt and because he has shown himself in every way, both up till then and for the future, to be its God. So the motive for keeping this law is simply obedience, although in fact it is hardly possible to detect that conscious thought has been given to the motive for fulfilling the law.

Now the nature of the law in detail is in line with all this:

(a) *Its demand is absolute.* This is shown in the style of these series of laws, in their forcefulness, in their uncompromising wording, which estimates the deed as such and gives no place to hidden difficulties or particular circumstances. Moreover this can be seen in the punishment threatened which can only be death, that is, being rooted out from the people of God, or cursing, which hands the wrongdoer over to God's destructive power, when the deed concerned is beyond the reach of men. It is even more evident in the fact that this law can also be formulated without the mention of any punishment for its transgression; it appears not even in the imperative or jussive form, elsewhere usual, but simply as the indicative: *Thou shalt not kill.*[1]

(b) *The negative character of these commands or, consequently rather, of these prohibitions.* In this way again it is distinctly confirmed that the theological situation of this law is the covenant of election. It is not a matter of commanding that which makes a man belong to God, but of forbidding that which abolishes this relationship.

(c) *But the laws are not thereby prevented from displaying an element of encouragement to obey.* This is shown in the manner by which it is intended to impress the proclamation of the law on the will of the hearer and to make its infringement impossible from within the man by the reminder of Yahweh's deeds. But the encouragement consists by no means in the promise

[1] For this whole subject cf. Alt pp. 37 ff.; Volz p. 26.

of a reward simply because the covenant precedes the prohibition. The 'reward' can thus consist only in remaining in this positive relationship to Yahweh.[1] In consequence mention is made of the judgement for transgression, but not of a special reward for observing the law.

(*d*) *Furthermore in spite of its brevity this law is comprehensive.* It is not only the cult of Yahweh, but the whole of life which stands under the law. The claim of this God to rule leaves no neutral zone. And yet it is not in the nature of these laws to deal in detailed casuistry, however much in the course of time more precise catalogues became necessary, to a certain extent as regulations for carrying out particular instances of these basic prohibitions.[2]

(*e*) *Finally it is in the nature of these laws that they are addressed to Israel as a whole.* The individual is treated as a member of the nation, and the neighbour whom the law indicates is the member of the nation. Thus the punishment too in the event of the law being violated is the affair of the whole body. Hence the method of inflicting death is stoning, in which all take part (Deut. xiii.9 f.),[3] and in the case of a murder which has not been cleared up the nearest community is under the obligation to make atonement (Deut. xxi.1 ff.).

With this the object of the law has already been described. The intention is to guarantee that the nation and the individual are bound to Yahweh alone. Hence *thou shalt have no other gods beside me.* Hence the dissociation from all magic and sorcery.[4] The rest is

---

[1] e.g. the promise (admittedly perhaps secondary) in the commandment concerning honouring parents.

[2] Detailed evidence in Alt pp. 49 ff.

[3] [For another interpretation of stoning, cf. Köhler, *Hebrew Man* (1956), p. 112.]   [4] cf. Volz pp. 27 ff., 40 ff.

connected with this: the shaping of the nation as the people of God, the exclusion of those actions which disturb the dealings of the members one with another and endanger the life of the whole community. But at the same time it must be kept firmly in mind that the validity of the law is not based on its suitability for social purposes, but on the will of the God of the covenant who stands behind it. Thus the object of the law is to settle the relationship of the covenant-nation and of the individual to the God of the covenant and to the members of the nation who belong to the same God. Because this nation has been chosen by this God this is to be done by excluding those things which invalidate or disturb the relationship.[1]

2. *The understanding of law in the earlier historical books*

The understanding of law which we find expressed in the early Israelite corpora is in line with the interpretation of Israel's history given by the 'Yahwist' and 'Elohist' sources, particularly with regard to the position assigned to the law. Even though J and E are not brought to an end until the promise that Palestine will be conquered by Israel has been fulfilled,[2] yet in both of them the period when the law was given is the culmination. The preparation for it is made by presenting the history up till then from the point of view of the wholly undeserved election of Israel from among the nations. So it is made abundantly clear how little this election depends on the part played by the nation.[3] It is just this story of the merciful dealings of God with

[1] cf. the awakening of the consciousness of being Israel (Judges xix f.); Noth pp. 100 ff., Volz p. 500.

[2] cf. H. Holzinger, *Einleitung in den Hexateuch* (1893), pp. 71 ff.

[3] Neither naturally (since Ishmael and Esau were the firstborn) nor morally (cf. the story of Jacob, the journey through the wilderness).

the often rebellious people which reaches its climax in
the fact that Yahweh reveals himself to the whole
nation, makes himself to be its God, the nation to be
his people (Exod. xix). This event gives to the law its
meaning as the divine gift intended to show the people
what conduct is appropriate to its position as a people
in God's possession, and alternatively what undermines
this position. Thus the law is a demonstration of his
mercy by showing how the people lives in the sight of
God, because it lives through Him. Since 'God the
deliverer gives the law' in this way, 'obedience has
been made the proof of faith'.[1]

As regards its contents, the law accepted in these
historical books, in addition to the early Israelite
corpora, consists principally of the Book of the Covenant.[2] This contains in addition to early Israelite
matter the law practised by the pre-Israelite inhabitants of Palestine. Its chief tendency is to take
over and permeate with the religion of Yahweh the
pre-Israelite law which had been adopted.[3] It is an
essential point here that no conscious distinction is yet
made between law and morality.[4] Again, these precepts
acquire their validity only owing to the fact that they
are established by God, not because of their inherent
goodness or usefulness. It is true that God demands

[1] A. Schlatter, *Einleitung in die Bibel* ([4]1923), p. 15.

[2] The Book of the Covenant (Exod. xxi-xxiii) probably dates
from the Palestinian period before the monarchy, but was no
doubt for a long time after that still the basis of the law. Cf.
Procksch pp. 231 f.; A. Jepsen, *Untersuchungen zum Bundesbuch*
(1927), pp. 96 ff.; Alt pp. 18, 25 ff.

[3] Eichrodt I, pp. 28 ff. (ET pp. 75 ff.); Jepsen pp. 100 ff.

[4] To consider this, as e.g. Jepsen pp. 102 ff. does, to be a misfortune, is to take a modern view. Whether this judgement corresponds to the facts is open to question. The principle of placing
law and morality side by side is derived from the whole OT
conception of God.

the good, but it is to be performed because God demands it.

Another kind of laws consists of the divine ordinances which regulate the cult. They are understood to be the ones by which Yahweh himself determines the worship to be offered to him (Exod. xx.24b).[1] This means too that no worship originated with men, nor is it offered freely as their own achievement, but that the only 'lawful' worship of God is that which is brought into being by the fact that God has revealed himself to the nation and which consists in the recognition of that fact. However fragmentary and primitive the cult-law may be of which these narrators tell us, yet this, their basic understanding of the cult, is perfectly clear, that it is the gracious directive of God telling the people how it may worship the holy God, indeed how it must do so. This involves the fact that the cult and the practice of the law cannot be separated if the law in J and E is to be understood.

Consistent with this is the early usage of priestly legislation in the narrower sense and the understanding of the law expressed in it. The main contents of the special priestly instructions for the cult is the rule concerning clean and unclean. Here the essential point is that this whole instruction concerning the question of clean and unclean is imparted by order of Yahweh and as his commandment. The question is not: what will have the most influence with the deity? but: what does Yahweh appoint as the worship due to him from his people? But the task of the priest is not only to give directions about clean and unclean. He has also to declare at the national assemblies the law as handed down, and to preserve it at the shrine. Furthermore

---

[1] Kautzsch, *Die heilige Schrift des AT* ([4]1922), I p. 127 f. translates: *In every place in which I cause you to honour my name.* Admittedly the meaning is not quite clear.

he is concerned with the divine judgement in those
difficult cases in which the community approaches the
shrine for a legal decision.[1] This does not mean that
the priest actually exercises a judicial function. The
relationship between priest and law makes it proper
to look for the formation of the Book of the Covenant
in priestly circles.[2]

All law is the will of Yahweh; the reason for this is
the fact that Yahweh has made this nation his own by
a historical event and now wishes to see it living as
befits his property. But since the relationship of
Yahweh to his people is a matter of history, there is
nothing incompatible in this understanding of the law,
if the law itself is seen as coming into being in the course
of history. It is nevertheless to be considered the
law of God, and this is expressed by connecting all
valid law with the revelation of God at Sinai. This
connexion is therefore not so much a historical as a
theological judgement.

3. *The attitude of the prophets to the law*

The preaching of the prophets is based on a fresh
meeting with God and on the reality of this God breaking into the midst of the devout life of the nation, a life
which is in fact godless. The essence and basis of the
prophets' preaching is not a fresh idea of God, but a
fresh meeting with him.[3] This also explains the attitude
of the prophets to the law. They do not suppose that
they must first inform the people of what Yahweh
demands. Their preaching presupposes that man has
been told what is good and what the Lord expects from

---

[1] L. Köhler, *Die hebräische Rechtsgemeinde* (Züricher Rek-
toratsrede (1931)), pp. 13 ff.; ET 'Justice in the Gate' in *Hebrew
Man* (1956), p. 163.   [2] Procksch p. 230; Jepsen pp. 99 f.
[3] For the following cf. Eichrodt I pp. 185 ff. (ET pp. 345 ff.);
K. Marti, *Geschichte der israelitischen Religion* ([5]1907), pp. 184 ff.

him (Mic. vi.8). Certainly the prophets often put this
will of God into a fresh form and add new features to it,
but without being themselves conscious or making
others conscious of bringing forward for the first time
a hitherto unknown demand. Indeed the prophets'
preaching acknowledges not only the law but also its
basis: Israel is the people whom God has chosen
(Amos ii.9, iii.2; Isa. i.2; Hos. viii.13 ff.). To break
the law is apostasy from Yahweh (Isa. i.27 ff.). The
prophets throughout condemn the infringement of the
commandments (Amos v.7, 10 ff.; Hos. v.10, iv.2;
Jer. vii.9). Hos. viii.12 even expressly assumes a
written law.

But there is nevertheless comparatively seldom any
direct appeal to the precisely formulated law, such as
the Decalogue or the Book of the Covenant (Hos. iv.2;
Jer. vii.9); and where it occurs no special emphasis is
given to it. In view of what has been said, this can be
explained neither as due to ignorance nor to rejection
of what the law contains. There remain only two explanations of this situation: a definite realisation by
the prophets of the nature of the law, and the different
objective of the prophets' preaching.

As regards the first point: the prophets were met by
the fact that it was possible for men to combine an
appeal to the law and its wording with a refusal of
genuine obedience and with uncharitableness towards
one's neighbour[1] (Amos ii.6, viii.4 ff.; Jer. viii.8).
They therefore express the law in its simplest terms, as
when Amos says: *Hate evil and do good* (Amos v.15).
This is not intended to represent the overriding of a
narrow viewpoint in favour of a 'purely ethical' one,[2]

---

[1] cf. Eichrodt I pp. 198 f., ET p. 374; Marti pp. 184 ff.

[2] cf. Marti p. 169: The good in the universally human, inter-
national, purely ethical meaning, namely that which must be
regarded at all times and everywhere as good.

but the resistance to attempts at introducing disobedience through the gaps in the fence of the official
and outwardly respected law (cf. Hos. vi.6; Mic. vi.8).
When the law is thus reduced to its simplest terms, it
is at the same time deepened and unified, and so the
real meaning of the old law, e.g. the Decalogue, is
discovered. The law is not to replace complete
obedience to the God who in direct and vital challenge
meets his people and the individual; it is therefore not
quoted and used directly, although it is recognised as
an institution set up by Yahweh.

But there is the second point too: in view of the
meeting with God which had been granted them and
of their judgement of the people's situation as seen
from this experience, the prophets could no longer
expect salvation to derive from a life ordered in accordance with the law, particularly now that the will of
Yahweh had been grasped in this fundamental manner.
A fresh chance still exists for Israel only in the free
activity of God who miraculously creates new things,
for which the prophets are looking; 'It is only when
there is some vision of a new existence for the nation
beyond the annihilation of the present order, that the
divine imperatives are brought out more strongly.'[1]
After judgement and renewal, Jerusalem will be called
the city of righteousness (Isa. i.26); even the heathen too
will come to the new Zion to receive *tōrāh* (Isa. ii.3).
The prophets' attitude to the law, affirming and at the
same time criticising and abolishing it (this is seldom
expressed, but does in fact happen) is intelligible on no
other grounds than their being directly possessed by
the divine holiness.

It is only with this fundamental attitude in mind
that we can understand the position of the prophets
with regard to the divine service in the narrower sense,

[1] Eichrodt I p. 190, ET p. 359 f.

namely the cult.[1] The cult, as the prophets find it, serves to cover up disobedience, and to gain control over God. Wrongdoing and lack of love are linked with this cult, indeed they actually find their justification in it. Consequently conflict arises between the prophets and this manner of serving God (Jer. vii.11; Hos. iv.6; Zeph. iii.4b; Jer. ii.8). Some sayings of the prophets certainly go even further and completely reject the cult[2] as not being appointed by God (Amos v.25; Isa. i.12; Jer. vii.22). It seems that they did not think that the manner of worshipping God was remediable. The essential point is that the prophets' censure does not propose a manner of worshipping God without a cult, but that this censure can be understood only by discerning the incongruity between the God who calls his people to account and the activities of the public worship as known to the prophets which ostensibly serves the honour of God.

4. How Deuteronomy understands the law

Deuteronomy contains a conception, complete in itself, of the law of Yahweh, which, in the original form of the book,[3] is consistently applied in the admission and modification of mainly old legal material. The characteristic quality of this concept of the law

[1] For the following see especially Eichrodt I 193 ff., ET pp. 364 ff.; E. K. Kautzsch, *Biblische Theologie des AT* (1911), pp. 233 ff. [Cf. also, on recent literature, H. H. Rowley 'Ritual and the Hebrew Prophets' in S. H. Hooke, *Myth, Ritual and Kingship* (1958), pp. 236-60.]

[2] cf. P. Volz, 'Die radikale Ablehnung der Kultreligion durch die alttestamentlichen Propheten', ZSTh (1937) 63 ff. [But many scholars would disagree with Volz, and would interpret the prophetic sayings differently; cf. Rowley *op. cit.* in previous note, esp. pp. 241 ff.]

[3] Especially the passages in which the first person singular (or 'I') is used in the speeches. Cf. in particular G. von Rad, *Das Gottesvolk im Dt.* (1929), for this point and on this whole section.

lies firstly in the emphasis with which the law's demand is based on the action of God, by which He had made Israel to be His people, to be a *holy people*. Deuteronomy emphasises no less strongly than JE that the religious and national existence of the Israelite people rests solely upon the covenant sworn to their forefathers (iv.32 ff.; vii.9, 12 ff.; ix.5 *et passim*). It is therefore a main task of the law to guard the exclusive bond of Israel with this God. Consequently it carries on a passionate warfare against *other gods*. No doubt the struggle for one place in which to worship the one God is connected with this (xiii.7 ff.). Secondly it is part of the peculiarity of the Deuteronomic law that a serious effort is made to enable the individual member of the nation to share in the blessing of this relationship to God. In Deuteronomy the fate of the individual too is certainly closely bound up with that of the whole people, but the emphasis now lies very heavily on the proper distribution of duties and particularly of the rights of the individual members of the people of God, so that none may lack the blessing of God in this life.

This distinctive quality of the whole book provides the clue to the characteristic features of Deuteronomy considered in detail:

(*a*) Deuteronomy in its proclamation of the law is in fact also a sermon, not a colourless enumeration of legal standards, but exhortation[1] which aims at arousing a joyous performance of the law out of gratitude for what God has done, and this is evident from the whole plan of the book. The people is to be confronted not with a legal code, but with the living God himself who will not let himself be hidden behind his law. All teaching about the law is first of all teaching

[1] cf. for this especially H. Breit, *Die Predigt des Deuteronomisten* (1933), p. 228 *et passim*.

about God's activity[1]; the law gives this history actuality in the present. In line with this is the trend towards greater inwardness, which shows itself for example in the phrase found several times *with all your heart and with all your soul* (vi.5; x.12; xxvi.16 *et passim*) or in the summons to cleave closely to Yahweh (x.20; xxx.20). Thus there must not only be an outward observance of the law, but all actual behaviour must be rooted in the love of God in the heart.

(*b*) This law is to embrace every sphere of life, even if it is more interested in 'ethics' than in 'ritual'.[2] Yet in spite of this comprehensive character this law does not try casuistically to regulate all the eventualities of life. Its aim is rather to point out the general lines (cf. e.g. in the legislation concerning the cult how little interest is shown in complete correctness).

(*c*) The principal objective of Deuteronomy is to show the obligation to one's neighbour, in fact to one's fellow-countryman.[3] Its motive is not humanitarianism but the right ordering of the people of God. Therefore my neighbour stands before me not only as the object whereby I fulfil the law, but actually as my brother. Indeed the word *brother* plays a special role in Deuteronomy (xv.2 f., 7, 9, 11 f., xix.18 f. *et passim*). Now this means that the obligation to one's neighbour is one of love, not a particular commandment. Hence the law is again and again summed up in the command to love (vi.5, vii.9, x.12).

(*d*) But with all this, Deuteronomy endeavours to maintain at the same time also the distance between

---

[1] cf. O. Weber, *Bibelkunde des AT*, I (1935), p. 49.

[2] Thus e.g. von Rad (p. 36) draws attention to the fact that the ethical interest in the position of the country Levites is greater than in the means by which the cult is carried out in Jerusalem.

[3] This is the most important fresh conception in comparison with the Book of the Covenant. Cf. von Rad, pp. 14 ff.

God and man, not only in general terms because one
'partner' in the covenant is plainly the superior, but
also practically by combating the sub-moral worship
of God according to natural instincts. This is to be
achieved chiefly by the way the cult is ordered. So the
cult offering can be converted into money (xiv.24 ff.),
and it is not the act of propitiation which effects forgiveness, but the mercy of Yahweh (xxi.7 f.). The
centralisation of the cult too is not an irruption of
magical ideas, but the limitation of the cult to the
place chosen by God and hallowed by that fact alone
and not by man himself.

If thus the purpose of the law is to shape the people
to be the people of God, and to unite it to God alone,
in both cases because it has already been adopted by
God, then it is in the nature of things that the divine
blessing is promised when the law is kept. For this
blessing consists precisely in the full and untrammelled
enjoyment of that which is given to the people by its
God in its land, just as the curse for the contempt of
the law means the withdrawal of this gift.

In criticism of this, perhaps the most profound
attempt to understand God's OT covenant and to
fashion life by it, the OT attains also to the deepest
understanding of the nature of the law. In all prob-
ability this criticism is expressed in Jer. xxxi.31 ff.[1]
This exegesis assumes that Jeremiah concurred with
the Deuteronomic reform and its aims.[2] Yet Jeremiah
recognises that the weakness of this attempt lies in the
fact of sin by which the undisturbed relationship
between God and people is broken so that it cannot be
reconstituted by any law. Only the act of God in

[1] cf. von Rad, pp. 98 ff.
[2] Marti, pp. 182 f., 186 certainly explains many passages in
Jeremiah by reference to Deuteronomy in such a way as to make
it appear that he rejected it; yet this exegesis is often arbitrary.

creating the whole man anew and putting the law into his heart, and therefore only a new covenant of God, can guarantee the time of salvation. In this way Jeremiah points to something which is outside the scope of the OT revelation, but is fulfilled in the NT.

5. *The understanding of the law in the Priestly writings and related passages*

P differs characteristically from Deuteronomy in that he does not aim at influencing the reader by means of sermons for instruction, but propounds his material harshly and sternly in a tone which almost serves to discourage obedience.[1] This is probably not merely a difference of style, but is connected with a different conception of God, since in P, to an even greater extent than in Deuteronomy, the transcendent and absolute other-worldliness of God is the basis of all theological thinking. Besides, Deuteronomy's peculiar concept of the nation is not in the same way a controlling factor. In general P is not concerned with Israel alone, but takes mankind beyond Israel into consideration, even though the special position of Israel is nearest to his heart. But P regards the relationship of Yahweh to Israel not so much from the point of view of loving election, as from that of the rule of God set up to bring salvation. Now it is just here that in P the law has its theological place and its purpose. It protects the purity of the divine revelation by preserving God's otherness and ascendancy over the world. It is all the more significant that P aims at being a historical presentation, by no means for the purpose of edification but in order to demonstrate that God's action and therewith His revelation provides the justification and

[1] cf. von Rad, *Die Priesterschrift im Hexateuch* (1934), p. 187. For the following see also Eichrodt, *Theol.*, I, pp. 209 ff., ET pp. 392 ff. Also W. Eichrodt, 'Gottes ewiges Reich und seine Wirklichkeit nach alttestamentlicher Offenbarung', ThStKr 108 (1937), pp. 1-27.

obligation for the religious life of Israel, and indeed of
the world. Thus he underlines the fact that the supra-
mundane holy God is not an impersonal power, but a
personal will.

The divine order established by God through His
creative activity tells the individual and the nation
how they can and should live, without forfeiting their
existence by offending against the glory of God, the
creator. By God's new revelation to Abraham, the
people is appointed to be his possession. At Sinai the
promise, implicit when the covenant was established,
is fulfilled. In this way according to P, history shows
how the ordinances which substantiate and safeguard
the welfare of the people of God were manifested.[1]
Thus the sovereignty of the God who creates and
chooses expresses itself in the law and determines how
the life of mankind—and especially of Israel—can be
fitting for this holy God. This way of understanding
the law provides the clue to the positive law in P.

In the tent of revelation (for the Tent of Meeting is
in P characteristically the place where God appears,
not where He dwells [Exod. xxv.22; Num. xiv.10]),
Moses receives the ordinances and instructions for the
people (Exod. xxv.22; Num. vii.89). In the will of
God thus manifested, the standards of morals and of
the cult have a deeper unity,[2] for both are testimony
to God's dominion. The one regulates the relationship
to one's neighbour, the other is a token of the intimate
bond with God. This unity is expressed by the fact
that Aaron acts only through Moses on the directions
which the latter has received from God and handed on
to him (Lev. xvi; Num. xvii.11 ff.). It is true that the
cult is of great importance to P.[3] but it stands in this

---

[1] von Rad, *Priesterschrift*, p. 188.
[2] Eichrodt, *Theol.*, I, p. 228, ET p. 424.
[3] Apparently, indeed, to an increasing extent, as a comparison

whole framework of the revelation of the law to Moses. Consequently beside the cult, without any differentiation as to their value, we find the other ordinances of a legal and religious nature, which have been imposed and justified by history, as well as the moral standards in the narrower sense.

But this understanding of the law by no means excludes deep joy, humble and reverent worship, and selfless devotion. On the contrary P's description is itself evidence of this (cf. e.g. the story of the creation in Genesis i) and is thereby altogether in line with the tenor of the psalms of the law (e.g. Ps. xix, cxix). This removes P far from what is often called the religion of the law or Nomism on the basis of the NT hostility to Judaism.[1]

The Holiness Code (H) in Lev. xvii-xxvi also has an intimate relationship with P's view of the law. Here too man attains his highest worth by submitting himself to God's will. What differentiates this from P is not so much the stress laid on the moral obligation to one's neighbour (Lev. xix.15 ff., xxv.35 ff.), as the smaller extent to which the laws and institutions are justified by their history, although this latter aspect is not altogether lacking (Lev. xviii.1 ff.).

6. *Law in the post-exilic period*

The exile brought about a significant development in Israel's attitude to the law and consequently in the understanding of it. What the prophets had threatened had been fulfilled. Israel had fallen under Yahweh's judgement because it had been disobedient to him. So now after the return it becomes the predominant concern to carry out God's will. Israel must obey God's

of the two strands of the P tradition, demonstrated by von Rad *op. cit.* p. 163, enables us to see.

[1] cf. von Rad, *Priesterschrift*, p. 187, n. 34.

law in order to live. The exile had made this clear to the people.

To begin with this did not involve a change in the theoretical position of the law. The duty of keeping the law was still, indeed in a renewed sense, the result, not the basis, of their election. This applies to the presentation of history by the Chronicler and even to Ezra. His activity stands or falls by the certainty that God who is beyond the world has nevertheless chosen just this people for himself (Ezra ix.5 ff.).[1]

To fulfil the law does not create the relationship to God, but keeps unimpaired the existing one (cf. e.g. II Chron. xxxiii.8). Yet in fact the emphasis and passion are directed more and more to the second proposition that everything depends on the people's fulfilling the law. The transition to the later conception of the law according to which the relationship to God is first created by it is often not hard and fast. The law acquires an ever increasing independent importance, acquires a primary significance for the relationship to God. Besides the praise of what God did for their forefathers, the praise of the law for itself gains ever greater prominence (cf. too the two parts of Ps. xix) as being the God-given means for the nation by which it maintains itself in his favour.

(a) An important stage in the development of the law to its key position in the religious world of Judaism is the Deuteronomic and the Chronistic writing of history.[2] They both take for granted throughout the standard set by the law. Saul is rejected because he transgresses God's command. All the kings of Israel are judged from the point of view of the law. The throne of David is indeed guaranteed by God's promise, but yet in practice all depends on the law being kept

[1] cf. Schaeder.
[2] G. von Rad, *Das Geschichtsbild des chronistischen Werks* (1930).

(cf. e.g. II Chron. xxvii f.). The revision of the early
historical material to be found in Judges describes this
period according to the pattern: the nation sins, is
penitent, appeals to God in its distress, God gives help
by sending a deliverer, the nation sins anew (Judges
ii.11 ff.). This presentation of history is prompted by
the seriousness of the penitence which looks upon
calamity as a just punishment for the violation of the
divine will. This standpoint also leads, it is true, to
the thought of guilt becoming unbearable in the case
of periods and men in obvious enjoyment of God's
favour. Chronicles passes over in silence David's sin
and Solomon's fall. Nevertheless this writing of
history brings home to the people that its existence is
bound up with the keeping of the law. The prophets
too are commandeered on behalf of the law and turned
into its guardians and proclaimers (e.g. II Kings
xvii.13).

(b) But it is not only this kind of historical writing
which reveals the mounting importance of the law. It
is seen just as much in the growing extent to which it
is made the basis of the community's whole life.[1] This
is the real meaning and purpose of Ezra's efforts
(Ezra ix f.). Here too lies the point of departure for a
continuous development, which has momentous consequences, but does not appear fully until later. From
being a nation tied to the law Israel becomes a religious
community gathered round the law.[2] To keep the law
becomes the distinctive mark for membership of God's
people. This begins to be of decisive importance for

[1] cf. E. Würthwein, Der 'am ha'arez im AT (1936), p. 66.
[2] cf. G. Kittel, Die Religionsgeschichte und das Urchristentum
(1932), p. 69. Some of the Wisdom material clearly expresses
this point of view, although as a rule 'wisdom' denotes a parallel
movement which in the first instance has very little to do with the
law.

the problem of the proselytes, just as on the other hand this problem naturally fosters this inner development.

(c) In the cult too a reassessment is being prepared for. It is becoming supremely important that the divine service should be performed in conformity with the law,[1] so that finally it came to be understood altogether solely—or at any rate primarily—as the carrying out of the law, and this conformity with the law supplied not only the justification for the service, but its whole meaning. So Jewry could later endure the loss of the temple without a great shock to its religious system.

(d) Finally, the new position of the law shows itself in the fact that a new profession emerges to give religious guidance to the people (Ezra vii.10). Up till then the priest was intended to administer the Torah; but henceforward the study of the law becomes an independent task which can be completely detached from the priestly office.[2] The high esteem paid to the scribes expresses the desire of the community to recognise the authority of the law alone, before which all, including the priests, must bow.

All this need not mean[3] that casuistry becomes dominant, that my neighbour as an individual person disappears behind my fellow-man as the person through whom I keep the law. It need not mean that this obligation to observe the law is used for the secret evasion of obedience, or as a guarantee against God. That it need not mean this is evident from the genuine piety of many psalms of this period (Ps. xix, xxxvii, xl,

---

[1] cf. e.g. the exclusion from the cult of those priests who cannot prove their priestly descent with certainty (Ezra ii.62).

[2] cf. Eichrodt, *Theol.*, I, p. 214, ET pp. 400 f. Does II Chron. xv.3 perhaps indicate a distinction in this sense between *tōrāh* and the priests' teaching?

[3] cf. Kautzsch, pp. 352 f.; Schaeder, pp. 3 f.

cxix). But it can mean all this. With a certain inner
conformity it did come to be all this in actual fact.
And this illustrates the danger of this development,
although its undoubted value is seen in the fact that to
a large extent it really did create the will to subject
oneself unreservedly to God's judgement and law.

7. *The meaning of the word Torah*

Amongst the various words in the OT which are
used from time to time with different shades of meaning for 'law',[1] *tōrāh* is the expression which acquired
the most comprehensive meaning and became predominant. In addition, through its translation in the
LXX by νόμος, it has exerted greatest influence.

In the Hebrew text of the OT, *tōrāh* occurs about
220 times, with fairly wide differences of meaning. It
does not occur in the J strand, in the E strand it occurs
only seldom if indeed at all.[2] The earlier prophets use
it rarely, but under certain circumstances with considerable emphasis. The Deuteronomic historical
writings and Deuteronomy in its present form introduce
it frequently. Similarly it is often found in the priestly
laws, in the Chronicler's historical work, as well as in
some of the Psalms.

For the understanding of the meaning of the word,
nothing reliable can be gained from its etymology, even
if this were established.[3] The only possibility is to

[1] cf. the survey in L. Köhler, *Theologie des AT* ([3]1953), 192 ff.,
ET *Old Testament Theology* (1957), pp. 203 ff.

[2] Exod. xiii.9, xvi.4, xviii.18, 20, xxiv.12 must be considered,
but are open to question; though the doubts are perhaps least in
xviii.16, 20. On xvi.4 cf. Procksch p. 203, n. 2.

[3] The customary derivation of the word from *yrh* to *throw*, to
cast the lot of the oracle, has recently been contested by Begrich,
pp. 68 f., cf. p. 69, n. 1, where nevertheless no detailed alternative
explanation is given. [Cf. also G. Östborn, *Tōrā in the OT* (1945),
ch. I.]

throw light on what is designated by *tōrāh* from those
passages which are the earliest from the literary point
of view and to proceed from there both forwards and
backwards. Such passages testify to the administration
of the Torah as the particular duty of the priest (Hos.
iv.6; Zeph. iii.4; Mic. iii.11; also Jer. xviii.18; Ezek.
vii.26, xxii.26). Yet Jer. ii.8 seems already to know of
an administration of the law by persons other than
priests.

But the earlier prophets also use *tōrāh* for the divine
word proclaimed through them[1] (Isa. viii.16, cf. also
v. 20; Isa. xxx.9 f.; perhaps also Isa. i.10). Besides
this, certain passages in the earlier prophets use the
word *tōrāh* also for the commandment of Yahweh
which was written down: thus Hos. viii.12. Moreover
these are clearly examples not only of ritual matters,
but also of ethics.

Hence it follows that at any rate in this period *tōrāh*
had the meaning of a divine instruction, whether it
had been written down long ago as a law and was
preserved and pronounced by a priest, or whether the
priest was delivering it at that time (Lam. ii.9; Ezek.
vii.26; Mal. ii.4 ff.), or the prophet is commissioned by
God to pronounce it for a definite situation (so perhaps
Isa. xxx.9).

Thus what is objectively essential in *tōrāh* is not the
form but the divine authority. Normally it will at first
have been a matter of actual cases which were decided
by *tōroth*,[2] even though *tōrāh* can then too include a
larger whole (e.g. Isa. i.10; and later Isa. ii.3; Mic.
iv.2; Isa. xli.4, li.4, 7). At the same time, all this
establishes the fact that in the usage of the early

---

[1] Jeremiah apparently does not. Perhaps in his case *tōrāh* has
already become more definitely tied to the other type of meaning
by the Deuteronomic movement.

[2] Köhler, *Theologie*, p. 195, ET p. 205.

prophets the word *tōrāh* does not seem to convey any precise definition of its contents. Thus legal, cultic, political and other instructions can be designated as *tōrāh*, if they have divine authority. This simply corresponds to the basic understanding of the law ascertained above.

But beside this there is the fact that in some of the priestly corpora in Leviticus and Numbers *tōrāh* stands for the regulations concerning certain cultic and ritual procedures, at times attached to a small coherent section as a title or a colophon.[1] Possibly these statements are inserted so that these several instructions appear as parts out of the greater entity of the 'law',[2] but perhaps this too is only a later idea.

The meaning of *tōrāh* ascertained in the foregoing is carried on into later times in a twofold manner. Firstly *tōrāh* is still found subsequently too as the word for the cultic directions for the priest (Hag. ii.11; Mal. ii.6 ff.). At the same time, especially in Proverbs, *tōrāh* can have the general meaning of instruction.[3] Yet other parts of this collection of wisdom sayings use *tōrāh* only in the sense which became customary subsequently (Prov. xxviii.4, 7, 9, xxix.18).

The change in the meaning of *tōrāh* which became decisive for the future is brought about by the Deuteronomic writings. It is true that in the original Deuteronomy *tōrāh* seems still to be used in the old sense (Deut. xvii.11. It is often hard to distinguish, e.g. Deut. xxxii.46). Deuteronomy probably did not yet call itself 'the Torah'. But this happens already in the later

---

[1] Lev. vi.2, 7, 18, vii.1, 11, 37, xi.46; Num. v.29 f.; similarly no doubt Ezek. xliii.11 ff.

[2] There is e.g. a 'statute of the *tōrāh*' in Num. xix.2, xxxi.21; cf. Köhler, *Theologie*, pp. 195, ET, p. 206.

[3] Instruction by the mother in Prov. i.8, vi.20; or by the father in iv.2; the teaching of the sage in iii.1, vii.2. Perhaps Job xxii.22 belongs here as well.

strands and in the historical books which received the
Deuteronomic imprint (II Kings xxii.8, 11). Now the
individual instructions of the law are spoken of as *words
of the tōrāh*, whilst up till then the plural *tōrōth* had been
used.[1] Deuteronomy itself is a *book of the tōrāh* and
when the king has to have a copy made of *this law*, then
tōrāh is simply this law set down in writing (Deut.
xvii.18 f.; Joshua viii.32).

As regards the content, usually *tōrāh* means Deuteronomy which is to be written on stones (Deut. xxvii.3, 8)
and preserved with the ark (Deut. xxxi.26). According
to the context, the Decalogue in particular may perhaps be meant (Deut. iv.44), but that is not normal.
In this *tōrāh* are found not only laws. There are
for instance the curses of the covenant (Deut. xxix,
xxx). There are sicknesses and calamities which
Yahweh can send and which are not recorded in this
book of the law (Deut. xxvi.16; Joshua viii.34). This
book of the law itself contains the explanation, namely
that it inculcates the law with exhortations (Deut. i.5).
Therefore to translate by 'law' restricts it too much.
Tōrāh frequently has the general meaning of instruction, direction (cf. II Chron. xvii.9, xix.10; Neh. viii),
even divine revelation as a whole (especially too in the
Psalms: i.2, xix.8, xciv.12). Nevertheless to use νόμος
for its translation in the LXX is appropriate in so far
as this *tōrāh* is after all *a parte potiori* an authoritative
direction. This is confirmed by the fact that even
earlier *tōrāh* was reproduced in Aramaic by *dath* (*law*)
which points in the same direction.[2]

---

[1] Gen. xxvi.5; Exod. xvi.28; Lev. xxvi.46; Ezek. xl.5; Ps.
cv.45; probably also Deut. xxxiii.10 (cf. Begrich, p. 64, n. 9) and
especially Exod. xviii.16, 20. Some of these passages are later;
thus they show that in these matters there is no hard and fast rule.

[2] cf. Schaeder, p. 44; Ezra vii.12, 14, 25 f.; Esther i.8 ff.,
viii.12. *Dath* is used of a royal decree, of public law, and of divine
law in these biblical passages. Cf. below, p. 48.

In the works of the Chronicler and the later Psalms there is no further basic change in the use of *tōrāh*. But there is a change regarding its content, for now the whole of the Pentateuch is called *tōrāh*.[1] The principal names for this *tōrāh* are *tōrath Yahweh* (I Chron. xvi.40, xxii.12 *et passim*), *tōrath Moses* (II Chron. xxiii.18, xxx.16 *et passim*) or a combination of the two (II Chron. xxxiv.14; Ezra. vii.6 *et passim*), but *tōrāh* alone is now no longer ambiguous.

ADDITIONAL NOTE

νόμος *in the Septuagint*

In the LXX *tōrāh* is translated by νόμος in by far the largest number of cases (in about 200 out of 220). But compared with *tōrāh*, νόμος has been employed somewhat more (c. 240 times). A change in the meaning of the word itself has resulted from the fact that νόμος in the LXX renders *tōrāh* at a later stage of its development and imposes this later meaning on other cases also. Thus for example in Isa. viii.16 what the prophet hands on to his disciples will probably, according to the LXX, have no longer been thought of as anything but the *Torah* in its later sense, that is to say the epitome of the divine teaching and the divine law. In other respects too a greater uniformity is attained by pushing into the background the earlier meanings of *tōrāh*. This occurs particularly in the conversion of old plurals of *tōrāh* into the singular νόμος (thus e.g. in Exod. xvi.28, xviii.16, 20; Isa. xxiv.5).

---

[1] For the books of Chronicles see the full index in von Rad, *Geschichtsbild*, pp. 38 ff. Also G. von Rad, 'Die Levitische Predigt in den Büchern der Chronik' in *Festschrift für O. Procksch* (1934), pp. 113 ff. (reprinted in *Gesammelte Studien* (1957), pp. 248-61). This is not intended to indicate that in these books the Pentateuch as we have it today is always meant.

Moreover the same is seen in those cases in which *tōrāh* is not translated by νόμος. The changes can mostly be explained by the fact that the Hebrew text contains a meaning of *tōrāh* which does not agree with the main trend of the post-exilic sense of νόμος and of *tōrāh*. There are firstly again the cases of *tōrāh* in the plural (Gen. xxvi.5; Prov. iii.1; Jer. xxvi.4 (LXX xxxix.23)).[1] Here the LXX translates mostly with νόμιμα, once with προστάγματα. Secondly there are cases where *tōrāh* is an instruction given by human beings, as in Prov. i.8, vi.20 (θεσμοί),[2] xxxi.26 (a paraphrase). Lastly there are those cases where *tōrāh* means a single instruction (II Chron. xix.10; Ezek. xliii.12).[3] But it must be noted that the variations in this sense are by no means carried through consistently; the cases quoted show only the general shift in the meaning.

In addition to the rendering of *tōrāh* by νόμος in the LXX, the extension of use of the latter to cover other Hebrew terms does not produce a different picture. This use consists firstly in the absorption of the Aramaic terms *dāth* (c. 14 times) and *pithgam* (once). Next is the assimilation of some passages which have *ḥōq* (statute) (3 times) or *ḥuqqāh* (c. 12 times). The same can be said of various small inconsistencies which individually do not amount to anything of importance (c. 12 times) and

[1] It is true that in several of these passages the MT now has the singular, but this is no doubt secondary.

[2] In Greek θεσμός is a rather more solemn word than νόμος. Since in Judaism νόμος stands for *tōrāh*, there can be no more solemn word than this.

[3] In these cases we must disregard simple errors, as e.g. in Isa. xlii.21 where the LXX assumes *tōdāh* (praise, thanks) instead of *tōrāh*; similarly in Job xxii.22 (cf. the opposite in Amos iv.5). In some other cases we cannot see why the rule has not been followed; thus e.g. in Deut. xvii.19; II Kings xxi.8 *et passim*. In Deut. xvii.18; Joshua viii.32 the LXX understands the Hebrew *mišnē tōrāh* (copy of the law) in the technical sense and so gives τὸ δευτερονόμιον τοῦτο as the translation.

moreover in some cases the LXX has here a variant reading.

On the one hand, the aspect of the law prevailing in *tōrāh* in the later period won a complete victory and became predominant when *tōrāh* was replaced by νόμος. On the other hand, those elements in the meaning of *tōrāh* which reinforce the view of the law as teaching, instruction, revelation, have for their part been to a certain extent transferred to νόμος and this sometimes bursts through the limitations which this word derived from its earlier Greek usage.[1]

[1] For the relationship between νόμος and *tōrāh* cf. also C. H. Dodd, *The Bible and the Greeks* (1935), pp. 25 ff.

III. LAW IN JUDAISM

1. *Law in the Pseudepigrapha and the Apocrypha*

THERE is very little unity as regards content and language in the apocryphal and pseudepigraphical literature of Judaism. Nevertheless all these writings have a common bond in the matter of the law. In all of them the law is the foundation on which they rest.[1] Some of these writings are devoted to the law in particular; they are intended to inculcate it, to defend it, to praise it, and so forth. In the case of those dealing with other matters as well (as e.g. especially the apocalypses) the law is nevertheless of decisive importance.

(*a*) In the linguistic usage ὁ νόμος used absolutely has been widely accepted. This is not only true of the writings under Palestinian influence, as, for example, I Macc. where νόμος appears almost without exception absolutely and in the singular. It is true also in those books which are in other respects typical of Hellenistic Judaism, as for example the Letter of Aristeas (39, 122, 309). Besides this, νόμος appears as well without the article with no recognisable difference of meaning. *They turned away from the law of God* in Bar. iv.12 means simply that they have departed from God's Torah.[2] It is used in the same way in I Macc. iv.42 and especially frequently in Ecclus. (e.g. xix.20, 24, xxi.11 *et passim*).

Beside the predominant meaning of law in the sense of the imperative will of God, νόμος comes to stand

---

[1] cf. Bousset-Gressmann, pp. 119 ff.

[2] Nor is there here any question of a qualitative meaning when the word is used without the article (cf. below, p. 102, n. 3).

more and more for 'the Pentateuch', probably because the law was felt to be the essential part of it. This appears in the twofold formula *the law and the prophets* in II Macc. xv.9; Ecclus. Prol. i.8 f., 24 (cf. also Zech. vii.12 for the idea), and also in the more precise description *the book of the law* (I Esdras ix.45). It is also possible to say 'he brought the law' when the book is meant (I Esdras ix.39), 'the law is in one's hand' (Letter of Aristeas 46). At the same time νόμος is used for the book even when it is not to be understood as the actual law. So II Macc. ii.17 f. is concerned with inheritance, kingship and priesthood, and the consecration of the people *as he* (sc. God) *promised through the law*. The deeds of the Shechemites are written down in 'the law' (Jub. xxx.12).

Naturally beside the absolute use there are found the fuller expressions: *the law of the Lord* in I Esdras i.33 *et passim*; *the law of God* in III Macc. vii.10, 12, Test. Reuben iii; *the law of Moses*, I Esdras. viii.3, Tob. vi.13 (MSS BA), vii.13 (MSS BA).

Other phrases are also used which are not derived from a direct rendering of the Hebrew *tōrāh*. First of all the plural οἱ νόμοι. Probably this is used for the benefit of the Greek reader or it is an expression familiar to the authors (I Macc. x.37, xiii.3; Additions to Esther iii.13de, viii.12p; Judith xi.12; especially II Macc. iii-x; Jub. *passim*). That this expression definitely shows Greek influence is evident from other phrases which are not found in the OT, but are strongly reminiscent of Greek thought such as *to die for their laws and their country*, II Macc. viii.21, xiii.10, 14. Similarly expressions in a style alien to the OT are found such as *the law of their fathers* in III Macc. i.23 *et passim*, *the laws of their fathers* in II Macc. vi.1, where it is identical with *the laws of God*; also *the law of the Most High* (Ecclus. xlii.2, xliv.20 *et passim*); *the divine law*

(Letter of Aristeas 3). But in all these cases no material change is involved. For instance II Macc. in particular, with its strictly Pharisaic attitude, shows no sign that the Jewish point of view concerning the law has been relaxed in favour of Greek influences. Seen as a whole the expressions characteristic of the OT are found also in those writings which in other respects are open to the Hellenistic spirit. Thus the Letter of Aristeas uses mainly the singular; in 111 alone the plural stands for the Jewish law, in 279 it is used in a more general sense.

(b) It should be observed that the content of the law, like the word itself, is understood in two ways. The position reached in the post-exilic OT period was firmly held, though certainly the outline was more sharply drawn in some respects. This took place partly through the continued development of legal thought itself, partly owing to historical events. In addition, new features were brought in by spiritual and intellectual influences from outside.

(i) What is strongly maintained in all this literature is the absolutely binding, divine force of the law. This is nowhere questioned, even in the Hellenistic-Jewish writings.[1] In the specifically Palestinian material, there is no sign of a substantiating of the validity of the law nor of real apologetics aimed at the apostate, which after all might be conceivable, for example, in view of the subject-matter of I Macc. God's law is eternally

[1] When in the Letter of Aristeas more cautious phrases seem occasionally to be used, this is probably to be attributed to the situation presupposed there, and not to the liberal opinion of the author, as when we read in 31: *the law which they contain, in as much as it is of divine origin, is full of wisdom and free from all blemish.* For the author himself, the law possesses divine validity even before it has been proved to be in accordance with reason, but this is not immediately true for the Gentile whose views he is here expressing.

valid; that is assured by its divine origin (Bar. iv.1; Jub. ii.33, vi.14 *et passim*).

Moreover the superiority of the law to all other religious activities becomes clearly apparent. The prophets inculcated the law (II Macc. ii.1 ff.; I Esdras viii.79 (EVV 82) *et passim*). The sacrificial worship of the temple makes sense only if the law is observed with the utmost care (Jub. xlix.15, l.11; Ecclus. xxxv.1 ff.; I Macc. iv.42 ff.). Indeed the law is more important than the temple, the learning of the scribe than the activities of the priests.[1] In the times of the Maccabees the various religious groups of the people gathered together to fight for the law and it was the question of the law which kindled the revolt (I Macc. i.41 ff.). It is particularly characteristic that, when it was no longer only a matter of freedom to carry out the law, but of political freedom as well, a strong group withdrew very definitely from the fight.[2]

This was the Pharisaic group, determined under all circumstances and whatever might be the consequences to adhere to the law and to the law alone. In fact the layman versed in the law becomes more and more the ideal of the pious person (cf. the description of him in Ecclus. xxxviii.24-xxxix.11).[3] The fact of apostasy within and proselytism without compelled it to be recognised that the religious classification of the individual was no longer fixed merely by his belonging to the Jewish nation, but only when his attitude to the law was known.

The historical circumstances of alien government and of the diaspora resulted in special value being

[1] cf. L. Couard, *Die religiösen und sittlichen Anschauungen der alttestamentlichen Apokryphen und Pseudepigraphen* (1907), pp. 141 f.

[2] cf. W. Förster, 'Der Ursprung des Pharisäismus', ZNW 34 (1935), pp. 35 ff.

[3] cf. Schaeder, p. 59, n.1.

placed on those parts of the law which distinguish the Jew externally from other men, e.g. the Sabbath, circumcision and the food laws. It is these points which give rise to the struggle of the Maccabees. Apologetics concerns itself primarily with these matters. Historical writing establishes these laws particularly firmly (cf. especially Jubilees).[1] The separation of the Jews from the other nations is thus often regarded actually as the purpose of the law.[2]

Above all the significance of the law and of keeping the law for the condition of the individual and of the nation is seen with ever greater distinctness. God's verdict, positive or negative, depends on the observance of the law. The whole history of the people is set out even more consistently than ever before from the point of view of reward and punishment for the performance and infringement of the law (I Esdras viii.81 ff. (EW 84 ff.); Bar. iv.12; Prayer of Manasses). This is now carried into explanations of externals, as in II Macc. xii.40, where in the case of all who fell in a certain battle it was ascertained that they wore charms *which the law forbids the Jews to wear*, and then everyone realised that this was the cause of their death. It is of course a great support for this theory that the reward for keeping the law can also be attained in the beyond.[3] Resurrection will be the reward for faithful performance of the law (II Macc. vii.9). Hence the law is the hope of the pious in Syr. Bar. li.7; Test. Jud. xxvi. The pattern (performance of the law—reward, infringement of the law —judgement) controls also to a large extent the eschatological and apocalyptic expectations for the future, even when, as perhaps in Jub. i.23 ff., a complete fulfilment of the law is expected to come through

---

[1] At least two of these points are raised in the struggle over the law in the days of early Christianity as well.

[2] cf. Couard, p. 142.   [3] Volz, *Eschatologie*, §§ 37 f.

the spirit. The keeping of the law is the decisive factor in God's verdict on man (and on the nation) and thus on their fate in this world and in the hereafter.

(ii) But there are also new features concerning the way the law is understood in this literature, arising chiefly out of its contact with the Hellenistic spiritual and cultural world. It is essentially an attempt at demonstrating that the law is true wisdom and its observance true reason. That the debate with Hellenism should take place so vigorously just around this question shows once again the preponderant importance of the law in the consciousness of the Jewish community. The Jewish parts of the Sybillines (chiefly books III-V), the Letter of Aristeas, III and IV Maccabees, the Wisdom of Solomon, Ecclesiasticus, all endeavour to bring about this synthesis of law and wisdom, of observance of the law and reason whether these books have a missionary or an apologetic trend.[1] Bar. iv.1: *She* (sc. Wisdom) *is the book of the commandments of God, and the law that endures for ever.* Ecclus. xv.1: *he who holds to the law will obtain her* (i.e. Wisdom). Piety based on wisdom had indeed already earlier become familiar in Judaism, but it can be accepted only if it can be combined with the piety of the law. In the canonical book of Proverbs the way is prepared for this by identifying the wise man with the righteous, the fool with the sinner. But now it is no longer enough to assert that they are identical. After all there were in fact passages in the law which could not at once be regarded as obviously reasonable and these were actually just those to which for other reasons particular

---

[1] Kautzsch, *Apokryphen und Pseudepigraphen*, xvi f.; Couard, 143, For the whole question of Judaism and Hellenism cf. W. Knox. 'Pharisaism and Hellenism' in *Judaism and Christianity*, II (1937); *idem, St. Paul and the Church of the Gentiles* (1939).

importance had to be attached.[1] The Letter of
Aristeas (130 ff.) is especially instructive for the
apologetic treatment of these questions, probably
already at the beginning of the second century B.C.[2]

On the other hand, the identification of wisdom and
law resulted also in the idea that strictly speaking all
men equally should keep the law. This is found at any
rate as an eschatological hope and becomes actually a
favourite idea of Hellenistic Judaism.[3] God's Torah,
like wisdom, becomes a universal law. Sib. Or. III 757
(cf. 719 f.) promises that *there will be one law in the
whole world*. The law is now no longer, as in the OT,
the rule of life for those belonging to the chosen people,
which they must lead because of their election. It is
now the timeless expression of the divine will with a
validity of its own.[4] We see the same trend when the
patriarchs before Moses are described as observing the
law with ever greater strictness. The reproach of being
without the law must not fall on them. This concern
is voiced especially clearly in Jubilees. Abraham
observed God's law (Jub. xxiv.11).[5]

Finally, at this point the idea of the law's pre-

---

[1] cf. pp. 53 f.

[2] cf. Schürer, III, pp. 608 ff. (4th ed.). ET (of 2nd ed, II.3,
pp. 308 ff.)

[3] Volz, p. 172. For the whole subject see W. Knox, *op. cit.*

[4] There is the further theory that the Gentiles knew God's law,
but had then rejected or forgotten it, without any need being felt
to demonstrate how this took place, IV Ezra iii.33 ff.; Syr. Bar.
xlviii.38 ff.

[5] It is true that in Jub. an occasional mention is made of the
fact that the law was not yet perfectly revealed before Moses'
time. Only since then has it become an eternal law for all races
of men (Jub. xxxiii.16). Accordingly there is sometimes an
allusion to a first law (ii.24, vi.22). It is of interest with regard to
Rom. ii.15 to note the way this idea is expressed in Syr. Bar.
lvii.2: the patriarchs performed the works of the commandments,
the law, though unwritten, was known to them.

existence is no longer distant. It is after all actually identical with divine wisdom which derives its existence and validity from itself.[1]

Thus the law has fully reached the position of intermediary between God and man, not only in practice, but also in theory. But this is now also the assumption underlying the hopelessness and despair arising out of the law, as seen in IV Ezra and Syr. Bar. There is no attempt at undermining the divine origin and the eternal validity of the law (IV Ezra iii.19, v.27, vii.8, 81, ix.36 f.), nor even the fact that the law bestows life on him who observes it (IV Ezra vii.21, xiv.30). But it is just this which takes away every hope of escape from a man who faces and takes seriously the actual transgressing of the law. For sin prevents the law bearing its fruit. IV Ezra iii.20: *thou didst not take away from them* (i.e. the patriarchs) *their evil heart, so that thy law might bring forth fruit in them.* It is just the knowledge of the law which makes sin grievous; vii.72: *though they received the commandments they did not keep them, and though they obtained the law they dealt unfaithfully with what they received.* Hence arises the lament in vii.46: *For who among the living is there who has not sinned, or who among those born who has not transgressed thy covenant?* and in ix.36: *we who have received the law, and sin, will perish.* It is to this that the Jewish understanding of the law leads when it is taken seriously.

2. *Josephus*

(*a*) In Josephus νόμος is used normally to designate the Jewish religious law; certainly the plural οἱ νόμοι also appears even more frequently, no doubt owing to his endeavour to speak good Greek and to be understood by readers trained in Hellenistic culture. Moreover in poetic language ὁ νόμος or οἱ νόμοι often become

[1] Couard, pp. 145 f.; Bousset-Gressmann, p. 121.

the subject of actions. The laws sigh in *Bell.* 3.356. The laws command in *Ant.* 16.3. Of course there can be no question of a personification of the law. νόμος without the article for the divine law is rare.[1] In other cases νόμος in Josephus is the OT or the Pentateuch: *a soldier, finding in one village a copy of the sacred law* (τὸν ἱερὸν νόμον), *tore the book in pieces . . .* in *Bell.* 2.229. *With a copy of Moses' laws* (τοὺς Μωυσέως νόμους) *in his hands . . .* in *Vit.* 134. Yet Josephus distinguishes between νόμος as the Pentateuch and the rest of the scriptures in *Ap.* 1.39.

But Josephus, when he does not mean the Jewish law itself, uses νόμος also for laws of other nations, sometimes even in comparison with the Jewish law (*Ap.* 2.172). There are also examples of military laws, cf. *Bell.* 5.123f. In addition, νόμος can be the prevailing custom without it being necessary to think that it was being raised officially to legal status, e.g. in *Ant.* 16.277 of the νόμος to avenge the murder of a kinsman. In this sense νόμος can be the custom, the rule, even what nature commands. There must be no grief for death *since undergoing it is in accordance with the will of God and by a law of nature* (φύσεως νόμῳ) in *Ant.* 4.322 (cf. *Bell.* 3.370, 374; also 5.367, 4.382). On the other hand Josephus does not identify this rule of nature with the Mosaic law, although they are not opposed to each other (*Ant.* 1.24), and although Josephus was for example impressed by the cosmic interpretation of certain regulations in the cult (*Ant.* 3.179 ff.).

There is still less Jewish feeling about the use of νόμος for the normal standard of a thing in *Bell.* 5.20: *the laws of history* (τῷ νόμῳ τῆς (συγ)γραφῆς) *compel one to restrain even one's emotions*: that which calls for the manner appropriate to the writing of history, the relevant, customary standard . . . (similarly *Bell.* 2.90).

[1] cf. Schlatter, *Theologie des Judentums*, p. 64.

But this usage of νόμος is rare in Josephus and in any case does not determine his understanding of the law.

(*b*) Just as Josephus' usage reveals his intermediate position, so also does his understanding of the nature of the law. In all essential matters his thought is Jewish, yet he enters very fully into the requirements of a cultured, non-Jewish reading public. The law has for Josephus the predominant position in religion.[1] The Jews are people who stress *the observance of our laws and of the pious practices based thereupon, which we have inherited* (*Ap.* 1.60). He admires those who set the observance of the law above all else (*Ant.* 11.152. The law controls the whole of life: *he* (i.e. Moses) *left nothing, however insignificant, to the discretion and caprice of the individual*; but for everything he gave the law as *standard and rule* (*Ap.* 2.173 f.; *Ant.* 3.94). At the same time the 'customs' are part of the law (*Ant.* 12.324; cf. *Ant.* 20.218, 13.297). This shows that Josephus belongs to the Pharisaic movement.[2] The circumcision demanded by the law and the acceptance of the law imply incorporation into Jewry (*Ant.* 13.257 f.); this means at the same time that the relationship of a man to God is brought about through the law. Hence Josephus is certainly not a mystic.

The reason for attributing this importance and authority to the law lies in its divine origin, which Josephus considers to be certain. *Such was the code of laws which Moses . . . learnt from the mouth of God and transmitted in writing to the Hebrews* (*Ant.* 3.286). To disobey the laws means therefore to disobey God (*Ant.* 20.44). Yet occasional more guarded ways of expressing himself are not lacking (*Ap.* 2.184). In particular he lays strong emphasis on Moses' function as a lawgiver. *Ant.* 3.266: *Moses would never have issued to his own*

[1] P. Krüger, *Philo und Josephus als Apologeten des Judentums* (1906), p. 20.
[2] Schlatter, p. 63.

humiliation statutes (i.e. the laws concerning leprosy) *such as these*. Moses tried to find a form of government in which God is the highest authority, i.e. the theocracy (*Ap.* 2.165). This praise of the lawgiver as a pious and wise man is obviously a concession to Greek ways of thought, especially if we add to this the argument that the excellence of the law is proved by its age (*Ap.* 2.279) and its unalterability (*Ap.* 2.184, 221; *Ant.* 20.218). The clearest pointer in this direction is the attempt to give a rational explanation and basis for the laws. For example, *Ant.* 2.274 is typical: the reason for forbidding adultery is that Moses believes that legitimate children are useful for the city and the house. Accordingly Josephus undertakes a work in which he plans to expound the *causes* (αἰτίαι) of the laws (*Ant.* 4.198 *et passim*). Of course the laws are not conceptions of human wisdom (*Ant.* 3.223), but nevertheless Josephus considers the endeavour worthwhile, perhaps to demonstrate by a comparison of the different laws and constitutions of the nations whose laws are the best (*Ap.* 2.163 ff.). Therefore Josephus considers it important that men in all countries should recognise the law (*Ap.* 2.284).

The two currents meet also when Josephus reflects on the purpose and aim of the law. It brings about a life pleasing to God (*Ant.* 3.213); but above all, and here Josephus' Pharisaic attitude again becomes evident, the law is intended to prevent sin: *the learning of our customs and law . . . so that we may not sin* (*Ant.* 16.43; cf. *Ap.* 2.173 f. The law makes it impossible to try to excuse sin by ignorance (*Ant.* 4.210). Moreover it is prized as the rule for public life. By giving the law God has *dictated for you rules for a blissful life and an ordered government* (*Ant.* 3.84). He who observes the law attains to blessedness. Adapting himself still more closely to Greek thought, Josephus can explain the law as enjoining the virtues, especially charity: *we possess a code excellently designed to promote piety, friendly relations with each other, and humanity towards the world at large, besides justice, hardihood, and contempt of death* (*Ap.* 2.146: cf. *Ap.* 2.291; *Ant.* 16.42).[1]

In his consideration of the motives for keeping the law Josephus follows on the whole the customary lines. Fear of punishment and hope of rewards play their part (*Ant.* 3.321, 4.210, 6.93 *et passim*). But he emphasises above all the fact that the Jews have the law impressed upon them at an early age (*Ap.* 2.178; cf. *Ant.* 4.211; *Bell.* 7.343). For him the importance attached to the Jews' practical training in the law is a main reason why it is superior to the laws of other nations (*Ap.* 2.172, 20.44). But with his eye upon apologetics he once again emphasises the fact that in Judaism it is a matter of observing the law joyfully and willingly. What is most clearly seen is *our voluntary obedience to our laws* (*Ap.* 2.220). Indeed it is his conscience which drives the Jew to fulfil the law (*Ant.* 3.319).

Thus Josephus' understanding of the law is seen on the one hand to be based in its essential content on Jewish, and indeed on Pharisaic, thought; but on the other hand a considerable adjustment has also been made, probably with apologetics primarily in view, to the rationalistic and moralistic world of Hellenistic thought.

3. *Philo of Alexandria*

(*a*) In his linguistic usage of νόμος, Philo does **not** differ essentially from Josephus. ὁ νόμος and νόμος are normally the Torah of the Palestinians. The *humanity*

---

[1] It is true that Josephus stresses the fact that these virtues are all rooted in piety: *for he* (i.e. Moses) *did not make piety a department of virtue, but the various virtues . . . departments of piety* (*Ap.* 2.170 f.).

of the law (Spec. Leg. 2.138), for example, is the love for
one's fellowmen enjoined by the OT law. There are
exhortations to piety διὰ τῶν νόμων (*Deus Imm.* 69). But
the law of a state can equally well be called οἱ νόμοι.
Now in a democracy, physicians are represented by laws, in
Jos. 63, is of quite general application. Gentiles too
have a *law against adultery (Vit. Mos.* 1.300). Yet ὁ νόμος
is also the Pentateuch. The law says that the quantity
of corn amassed by Joseph could not be counted
(*Poster. C.* 96). In *Abr.* 1 he writes that the sacred laws
are written down in five books. Indeed a single saying
from the Scriptures can apparently be called νόμος
even if it is not in the nature of a command: *in the
laws* . . . (*laws, that is, in the proper sense of the word*)
. . . *there are two leading statements, one that 'God is not a
man'* (Num. xxiii.19); *the other that 'He is as a man'*
(Deut. i.31) (*Deus Imm.* 53).

Philo gives a far wider range of meaning than
Josephus to νόμος as an ordinance and law of nature
(ὁ τῆς φυσέως νόμος, *Abr.* 135), and moreover in a
twofold meaning (though these two can often hardly
be distinguished): (i) as a law of nature: it is *nature's
incontrovertible law* that what has come into being ranks
below the producer of it (*Plant.* 132); (ii) as an ordinance: Laban does not observe *the true laws of nature*
(*Ebr.* 47). Indeed something can be written *on the
tables of nature* (*Spec. Leg.* 1.31), just as something else is
written *on the most holy tables of the law* (*Op. Mund.* 128).

Philo also uses νόμος for the standard assigned to and
appropriate for a particular sphere or subject, as in *the
laws of perfect music (Op. Mund.* 70.54; *Omn. Prob. Lib.*
51); *according to the laws of allegory* (*Abr.* 68).

Finally in a figurative sense a person can be an
embodiment of the law. In *Vit. Mos.* 1.162, we read
that before Moses became a lawgiver he was *the
reasonable and living impersonation of law.* The life of

Abraham was not only a *life obedient to the law* (νόμιμος),[1] but *himself a law and an unwritten statute* (*Abr.* 276; cf. *Abr.* 8).

(*b*) It will hardly be possible to give an objective and consistent account of Philo's statements about the law and the way he understood it; for the real centre of his religious thought is not the law nor the necessary religious feeling with regard to the law. His fundamental religious and philosophical attitude is that of a mystical ecstatic; the highest level of religion for him is contemplative oneness with the deity, to dwell in solitude in the otherworldly realm of wisdom (*Spec. Leg.* 3.1).[2] From this central position he can have only an indefinite outlook upon the law of the OT; indeed he probably ought really to renounce it. But this he cannot do, and more particularly this he does not wish to do. On the contrary he desires to cling to the sole authority of the divine law, for he is and remains a Jew.[3]

This dichotomy between the presuppositions which he cannot give up and the actual theological and philosophical mainspring of his existence, explains also what he says about the law.

In Philo's treatment of the law, his crucial concern is to prove the congruity between the OT law and the ordering of the world as a whole by reason and nature. For him this is an extremely personal question, and he is no doubt influenced by an interest which is not simply apologetic.

Moses gave the law, *holding that the laws were the most faithful picture of the world-polity* (*Vit. Mos.* 2.51). *What else are laws and statutes but the sacred words of nature?*

---

[1] cf. also below, p. 143.

[2] Krüger, p. 57; Bousset-Gressmann, pp. 443 f., 449 f.

[3] Schürer, III, p. 700. ET II.3, pp. 36 f, 364 f. Another reason for the lack of consistency in Philo is the variety of his sources.

(*Spec. Leg.* 2.13).[1] He sees the strongest evidence for the harmony between law and reason, world-order and nature, in the oneness of God; in this, creation and revelation are one. In *Vit. Mos.* 2.48 Moses shows *that the Father and Maker of the world was in the truest sense also its Lawgiver.* The order of events in the Pentateuch, which records the creation of the world before the giving of the law, offers him the proof of this.

Moreover Philo uses Israel's patriarchs to demonstrate this harmony. For without knowing the revealed law, they live nevertheless in complete harmony with it.[2] Indeed they are its embodiment, they are the unwritten law (*Abr. passim*). They practice the law by nature; therefore natural reason and the revealed law are in harmony.

This does not mean that Philo wishes to deny the supernatural origin of the law. In *Decal.* 15 he says that *the laws were not the inventions of a man but quite clearly the oracles of God.* God himself made the Decalogue known in a miraculous way without human agency (*Decal.* 10). On the contrary all this merely corresponds with the other proposition that man can after all never raise himself by his own strength into the world of the deity.[3]

In order to demonstrate that this basic concern of both theology and philosophy has a concrete and consistent application, and that nature and revelation, philosophy and the law, are in agreement, the allegorical interpretation of the law is required.[4] Philo

---

[1] In contrast to this, the laws of the other nations are not in the same way the authentic expression of the natural order, but are additions to it (Philo, *Jos.* 31).

[2] This is a self-evident axiom which requires no further proof, cf. p. 56.   [3] Schürer, III, p. 714. ET II.3, p. 379.

[4] E. Stein, *Die allegorische Exegese des Philo aus Alexandrien*, BZAW 51 (1929); idem, *Philo und der Midrasch*, BZAW 57 (1931).

certainly allows the literal meaning also to have its rightful place, but a further step is necessary *to allegorical interpretations (Conf. Ling.* 190). *Let us rather in obedience to the suggestions of right reason expound in full the inward interpretation (Sobr.* 33).

It is true that Philo defends himself against those who neglect to keep the commands because of such an allegorical exegesis, and he maintains on the contrary that they impose an obligation even in their literal sense (*Migr. Abr.* 89). But this reasoning, which objectively is very weak, merely reveals that this opinion does not arise as the logical consequence of his premise, but is an inconsistency to be attributed to his Jewish way of thinking.

Beside the allegorical treatment of the law, there is in Philo a scientific one. This differs in its method from the former, but in the last resort it proceeds from the same need. It takes the form firstly of unifying and systematising the legal material, and then giving the laws a reasoned explanation, especially those laws which make a distinction between Jew and Gentile.[1] In both cases Philo succeeds in placing in the background or removing what is offensive when brought forward for judgement before the standards of speculative reason and of universal ethics.[2] Here it is likely that there is operative a more definite intention to introduce apologetics. In consequence we cannot fail to recognise a striking agreement with Josephus or even with the Letter of Aristeas. But here too Philo shows sufficient characteristics of his own. The whole law can be traced back to one simple requirement: *But among the vast number of particular truths and principles . . . there stand out . . . two main heads: one of duty to God*

[1] cf. pp. 53 f.
[2] This tendency is especially marked when Philo calls the law the preacher and teacher of virtuous behaviour (*Virt.* 119).

as shewn by piety and holiness, one of duty to men as shewn by humanity and justice, each of them splitting up into multiform branches, all highly laudable (*Spec. Leg.* 2.63; cf. *Spec. Leg.* 1.300). The Decalogue in particular is the summary of the whole legislation, the foundation for everything else. The purpose of systematising and harmonising is to enable the legislation to be grasped by reason, a typically Hellenistic concern.[1] The rational basis given for the individual commandments follows the same lines; for example circumcision is presented in *Spec. Leg.* 1.3 ff. by means of a number of hygienic and theological and allegorical considerations as the only correct course of action.

Finally as regards the manner in which the law achieves its object, Philo emphasises in particular its liberal nature. It encourages more than it commands. In *Vit. Mos.* 2.51 he says: *In his commands and prohibitions he* (i.e. Moses) *suggests and admonishes rather than commands, and the very numerous and necessary instructions which he essays to give are accompanied by forewords and afterwords, in order to exhort rather than to enforce.* It is certainly important to inculcate the law by reading it and meditating on it daily (*Spec. Leg.* 4.161). But basically the perfect man does not need to be admonished by the law. In *Leg. All.* 1.93 f. he says: To the perfect man the law is not something outside himself, alien to him; it is natural for him to act in accordance with divine reason and wisdom, and the law is simply the expression of these. Therefore it is not really an arduous matter to observe the law.

All this shows that Philo bears witness to the veiled, though actually unmistakable, disintegration of the law in favour of Hellenistic speculation and ethics, a disintegration brought about by allegorical exegesis, scientific

---

[1] Similar features amongst the rabbis and in the NT have a different motive (cf. below).

reasoning and the reconciliation of moral principles, as well as by the preservation of the practice of the law.[1]

4. Law in Rabbinic Judaism

The expression used to designate the whole of what the rabbis understood as the law is *tōrāh*. The rabbinic *tōrāh* is at the same time in most cases the equivalent of the NT νόμος.

(a) The usage of *tōrāh* in rabbinic writings is at the start the same as at the end of the OT period. Nevertheless it had been subjected in the interval to characteristic developments.

Torah is primarily the whole of the Mosaic law regarded as law (the following section contains references). This is the foundation of all the other meanings of the word *tōrāh* in the rabbinic literature. Thus *tōrāh* can certainly be used in particular for the Decalogue, but the Decalogue is never by itself the Torah. 'The ten commandments ought really to be recited daily; and why are they not recited? Because there is no wish to provide a basis for the assertions of heretics, so that they cannot say that these alone were given at Sinai (are divine)' (j Ber. 3c 32 f.).[2]

Beside the meaning of Torah as the Mosaic law, Torah stands just as often for that part of the OT canon which contains this law, i.e. the Pentateuch.[3] In most

[1] However arresting may be the resemblance of Philo's attitude to the law to that of the OT, yet in essentials the gulf is very great, for they each start from a completely different point. Consequently the fact that in the Early Church Christian criticism accepted and understood the law in Philo's way (cf. Epistle of Barnabas) had important consequences.

[2] J. Wohlgemuth, 'Das jüdische Religionsgesetz in jüdischer Beleuchtung', *Beilage zum Jahresbericht des Rabbinerseminars in Berlin* [1921], p. 21.

[3] For the following cf. the discussion of Canonical and Apocryphal works in TWNT III, pp. 979 ff..

cases it is difficult to discriminate between Torah as 'Law' and Torah as the Pentateuch. Yet the Pentateuch is called Torah in those cases also where there is no question of the legal nature of its contents. (References from the Torah = Pentateuch: S Deut. 1 on i.1; 47 on xi.21; TBM 11.23; b Taan. 9a). This normal usage of Torah can then also be extended to indicate all the writings of the OT, because these other writings are in harmony with the Torah, and derive their whole authority simply from their agreement with the Torah. In S Deut. 54 on xi.26, Ps. xxxiv.14, Prov. xvi.4 are introduced by the set phrase *the tōrāh states*. In M Ex. 15.8 references for the proposition of the school of Ismael: 'There is no earlier or later in the Torah' are given in passages from Isaiah, Jeremiah, Hosea.[1] The juxtaposition of Torah in its wider and narrower senses is illustrated particularly well in Tanch. 10 (ed. Horeb 123b): 'the Torah (i.e. the OT) contains Torah (i.e. Pentateuch), Prophets and Writings'.[2]

Moreover in a particular context, Torah can have the still more extended meaning of authoritative teaching in general. Tradition as distinct from the Scripture is called *tōrāh which is upon the mouth*.[3] In this most extended sense of Torah it is often not appropriate to translate it by 'law'. It has here rather the more general meaning of *authoritative teaching, revelation*, although the person's action which this Torah regulates is always the first consideration. Therefore there can be only one Torah. Thus the plural *tōrōth* occurs

---

[1] W. Bacher, *Die exegetische Terminologie der jüdischen Traditionsliteratur*, I (1884, ²1903), II (1890): I, pp. 167 ff.

[2] W. Bacher, *Die Agada der Tannaiten*, I (²1903), p. 476.

[3] *tōrah šebᵉᶜal pe*. W. Bacher, *Tradition und Tradenten in den Schulen Palästinas und Babyloniens* (1914), pp. 22 ff. gives passages and basic material.

merely so to say *per negationem*; as for example when it
is said that the difference between two schools is so
great that one might suppose the Torah had broken
into two Toroth (b Sanh. 80b).

Finally, Torah can have the special sense of 'Study
of the Torah', particularly when contrasted with
miṣwah (commandment) meaning 'fulfilment of the law'.
Thus according to Ex r 31 on xxii.26 the study of the
Torah[1] is inseparable from the fulfilment of the law
and vice versa. b Sota. 21a[2]: 'A transgression nullifies
[the merit of] a commandment but not of [study of]
Torah.' Indeed the study of the Torah is occasionally
placed above obedience to the commandments.

(*b*) As regards its subject-matter, the way rabbinic
Judaism understood the law can be summed up in two
propositions which are in fundamental accord with
each other: (1) God revealed himself once for all in the
Torah and in the Torah alone; (2) man's relationship
to God exists only through his relationship to the
Torah. Thereby the basic starting point of the OT
which can be summarised in the propositions: God revealed himself to Israel as its God, therefore Israel
owes obedience to this God, is characteristically and
decisively altered and invalidated. In theory, it is
true, both these propositions remain in force, but in

---

[1] Wohlgemuth, p. 77, n. 1.

[2] Shab. 30a is a particularly interesting passage: 'As soon as a
man has died he is released from the Torah and the commandments.' This sentence appears at first sight to be a parallel to
Rom. vii.1. But it is preceded by: 'Let a man be always occupied
with the Torah and the commandments before he dies; for when
he has died the Torah and the commandments will have ceased
for him, and the Holy One, blessed be He, will no longer be
praised by him.' This makes it evident that here 'Torah' must
mean the study of the law, and 'commandments' obedience to the
commandments. Thus the parallel to Rom. vii.1 falls to the
ground.

fact the Torah forces itself right into the foreground
and indeed primarily as the law laying claim to men's
will.

(i) The central and dominating position of the Torah
as the law contained in the Pentateuch is seen already
in the dependent relationship in which all the other
sections, authoritative in some measure, stand with
regard to the Torah. This is of course the implicit
assumption in the extension of the concept of the Torah
just described. The rest of the OT writings contain
basically nothing different from the Pentateuch; at
the very least everything must be anticipated in it. At
any rate they only possess authority if this agreement is
present. For instance the only reason why Koheleth
(Ecclesiastes) was not withdrawn from use was because
'it begins with the words of the Torah and ends with
the words of the Torah' (b Shab. 30b).[1] This view is
expressed characteristically in the name *qabbālāh*
(*tradition*) given to the writings of the OT not included
in the Pentateuch.[2] These writings too are valid because they are 'Sinaitic' (cf. (ii) below), though they
were only fixed later. This part of the OT explains
and inculcates the law, but is not in itself absolutely
necessary. 'If Israel had not sinned, he would have
been given only the five parts of the Torah and the
book of Joshua' (b Ned. 22b). On principle there is
the same relationship also between the written and
the oral Torah. In the case of the latter it is at first a
tacit assumption that it agrees with the Torah. But
after about the time of Johanan ben Zakkai,[3] the

[1] Moore, I, pp. 246 f. For a more detailed discussion cf.
TWNT III, p. 985.

[2] Bacher, *op. cit* (p. 68, n. 3) pp. 2 f.

[3] N. Glatzer, *Untersuchungen zur Geschichtslehre der Tannaiten*
(1933), p. 5. See also R. Herford, 'The Law and Pharisaism', in
Judaism and Christianity, Vol. III, edited by E. Rosenthal (London
1938).

practice of establishing the exegesis of traditional material firmly on the Torah was carried through in accordance with definite exegetical methods. What could not be fitted in was considered to be *halākāh* given to Moses at Sinai.[1] Actually the theory that the traditional material originated in the exegesis of the Torah is of course artificial. It has dogmatic, not historical, validity. But the theory demonstrates how forcibly this concept of the law has taken control of all the other parts of authoritative doctrine, since they maintain their authority only in so far as they can be understood as exegesis or elaboration or even reconstruction[2] of the Torah.

(ii) The authoritative nature of the law is preserved by adhering strictly to the direct divine origin of the Pentateuch.[3] So b Sanh. 99a: 'If a man says that the whole Torah came from heaven with the exception of this verse which was said not by God, but by Moses out of his own mouth, then it is true to say of him: he has despised the word of Yahweh'. Here too is the right place for the peculiar assertion that all valid doctrine, every recognised rabbinic tenet, every accepted conclusion of exegesis was revealed to Moses on Sinai.[4] This theory undoubtedly springs from the desire to show that revelation at Sinai took place once for all and was a unity because of its all-embracing divine nature. Thus it is a judgement of faith, not a historical theory, and so it is naturally not maintained in many non-essential cases. In b Pes. 54a it is stated that the Torah is one of the seven things which were created before the world came

---

[1] Bacher, *op. cit.* (p. 68, n. 3), pp. 21 f., 33 ff. S. Kaatz, *Die mündliche Lehre und ihr Dogma* I (1922), II (1923), II, pp. 1 ff.

[2] Kaatz, II, p. 5.

[3] Pesikt. r 22; 111a, Strack-Billerbeck, IV.438. For the age of this view cf. Philo (see p. 64).

[4] Kaatz, I, pp. 130 ff.

into being.[1] Because the Torah is more precious than anything else, it was created before all else (referring to Prov. viii.22) : S Deut. 37 on xi.10.[2] Hence the Torah is handed to Moses in a finished form. He himself plays a completely passive role. He is an agent; the Torah is given to him in writing or dictated to his pen or even taught him by word of mouth,[3] but he is never regarded as its spiritual originator.[4] Moses' sin, on account of which he is punished, is written down 'so that it cannot be said that it seems that Moses made false statements in the Torah, or that he said something which he was not ordered to say' (to which his punishment might otherwise be ascribed) (S Deut. 26 on iii.23). Therefore when the Torah is copied, it is as if a world were to be destroyed if one letter more or less is written down (b Sota 20a). Moreover the sacredness of the Torah finds expression in the tenet that the sacred writings defile the hands (i.e. make it necessary to wash them before a profane occupation), Yad, 3.5 *et passim*. This sacredness gives to the study of the Torah its pre-eminent dignity. God says to David: 'I prefer one day during which you sit and concern yourself with the Torah rather than 1000 burnt sacrifices which your son Solomon will one day offer me upon the altar' (b Shab. 30e).

(iii) This divine authority of the law is also the basis of the reticence shown by the rabbis—apparently to

[1] Not eternal pre-existence, against F. Weber, *Jüdische Theologie* (²1897), p. 15. The Torah too was created, though first of all. This must be affirmed all the more strongly in consideration of the fact that the pre-existence of the Torah probably arose because the same value was placed in Hellenistic Judaism on the Torah as on the principles of world-order.

[2] For further passages and details cf. Strack-Billerbeck, II, pp. 353 ff.   [3] Strack-Billerbeck IV, p. 439.

[4] The wisdom of the law is never attributed to the wisdom of Moses, as it is for example in Philo and Josephus.

an increasing extent—towards the questions concerning the *ṭaʿᵃmē hattōrāh*, the *reasons* (the αἰτίαι cf. Jos.) for the Torah. Johanan ben Zakkai says: 'By your life, the dead man does not defile nor does water cleanse, but it is an ordinance of the All Holy, the reasons for which must not be sought out' (Pesikt. 40a). Thus for example they refuse to derive from God's compassion the prohibition to slaughter the female animal and her young on the same day (j Ber. 9c 20 ff.). No doubt this again is only the basic theoretical attitude intended to meet the danger of superficiality.[1] For in practice finding reasons for the commandments is a favourite device for showing acumen and it is employed for edifying purposes.[2] But there is no real concern behind this, particularly no apologetic concern. There is no intention of bringing out the real meaning of the law by means of a standard lying outside the law itself. Argument is consciously avoided in the case of just those laws for which reasons are often given in the apologetics of Hellenistic Judaism and in discussions with Gentiles.[3]

(iv) The precise and consistent working out of the authoritative nature of the Torah is carried so far that God himself is conceived as tied to the Torah, studying it and observing it, b AZ 3b: 'During the first three hours of the day God sits and occupies himself with the Torah'. Of course this must not be taken in a dogmatic sense, but as a more or less poetical expression. Yet it is a characteristic indication of the position of the Torah towering above everything else, to which God has committed himself wholly and completely.[4] The

[1] Strack-Billerbeck, III, p. 398.
[2] Wohlgemuth (pp. 39 ff.) produces a large number of examples; for the principle involved, *ib.* pp. 30 ff.
[3] Examples in Wohlgemuth, pp. 71 f.
[4] Wohlgemuth, pp. 80 ff.; Weber, pp. 17 ff., 159 f.

Torah is therefore eternally valid; R. Johanan (c. 250) can say 'Prophets and scriptures will come to an end, but not the five books of the Torah' (j Meg. 70d, 60).

Even the Messiah does not, it seems, bring a new Torah. On the contrary he will himself study and observe it, possibly he will also teach the reasons for it.[1] He will bring apostates back into submission to the Torah[2] and will impart at least a part of the law to the Gentiles.[3] He receives the promises due to him because he occupies himself with the Torah (Midr. Ps. ii.9).

All this establishes the Torah as the one and only mediator between God and man, indeed between God and the world. 'When two are sitting together and they occupy themselves with the words of the Torah, then the Shekinah dwells amongst them' (Ab. 3.2). 'Usually when a man buys something valuable in the market, is it possible for him to acquire its owner at the same time? But God has given the Torah to Israel and has said to them: "It is as though you are receiving Me" ' Ex. r 33, 7 on xxv.2 (towards the end).

(v) All other relationships between God on the one hand and man, Israel, or the world on the other, are subordinated to the Torah. 'It is the instrument with which man was created' (Ab. 3.14; S Deut. 48 on xi.22). When creating the world God took counsel with the Torah; it is the overseer for every act of creation.[4] Indeed the world, man and Israel are brought into being for the sake of the Torah alone (Gn. r on i.1 (towards the beginning); Ab. 3.14; M Ex. xiv.29). History too is fitted with complete consistency into the

[1] e.g. Tg. Cant. viii ff.; Strack-Billerbeck III, pp. 570 f.

[2] e.g. Tg. Is. liii.11b, 12; Strack-Billerbeck I, pp. 482 f.

[3] e.g. Midr. Ps. xxi.8 (89a).

[4] Thus the relationship assigned to creation and revelation by the rabbis and indirectly expressed here is completely subjected to the supremacy of revelation (unlike Philo, for example).

pattern of the law, its violation or its observance. Thus the Torah holds the key position in the whole religious life of rabbinic Judaism.

(vi) The Torah has therefore the power to sort men out into their order among themselves. Israel and the Gentiles are distinguished essentially according to whether or not they possess the law. It has indeed been given to all nations in seventy languages (b Shab. 88b) or at least it has been offered to them,[1] but they have not accepted it or at any rate they do not carry it out (S Deut. 343 on xxxiii.2). R. Meir (c. 150) said, though without the approval of the majority, that even a Gentile who occupies himself with the Torah should receive the same esteem (or respect) as the high-priest. He finds evidence for this in Lev. xviii.5, by emphasising: 'by doing this a man shall live' (b Sanh. 59a). In the same way individuals belonging to Israel are differentiated according to their knowledge of the Torah and their attitude towards it. This is the origin of the important position held in the community by the man learned in the law. If a man learns both the Scripture and the Mishnah, but has not served under a wise man (as a pupil) he is considered to be *'am hā'āreṣ*.[2] He who has learned merely the Scriptures without the Mishnah is considered a *bōr* (uneducated person). But of him who has learned neither the Scripture nor the Mishnah, such words as those in Prov. xxiv.20 may be used (b Sota 22a).

(vii) Now it is the purpose of the law to show a man what he should do, or leave undone, as the case may be.[3] By this means, because he obeys the law, he

---

[1] For further details, including ideas concerning the manner in which this was done, see Strack-Billerbeck, III, pp. 38 ff.

[2] [Literally 'people of the land', but employed in this technical sense.]

[3] The negative side, not to transgress a command, carries

possesses God's approbation, righteousness and so life itself, and a share in God's future world. 'Why has God given us commandments? Is it not that we may perform them and receive a reward?' (S Nu. 115 on xv.41). R Hananiah ben Akashya (c. A.D. 150) said: 'God wished to let Israel earn many merits; therefore he gave much Torah and many commandments, as it is written: "It pleased Yahweh, in order to bestow merit on him (Israel) to make the Torah great and mighty" ' (thus Isa. lxii.21 according to the Midrash).[1] The Torah therefore signifies life. As food maintains the life of the fleeting hour, so the future life is contained in the Torah (M Ex. xiii.3). R. Simeon (c. A.D. 150) said: 'God speaks thus to man: "My Torah is in thy hand and thy soul is in my hand; if thou keepest what is mine, I will keep what is thine; if thou destroyest what is mine, I will destroy what is thine" ' (Dt. r 4.4 on xi.26). For one the Torah is the spice of life, for another the speice of death (b Yoma 72b). Transgression of the Torah does not destroy the Torah itself, but its transgressor (Lev. r 19 on xv.25).

Now of course the obligation to observe the Torah can also be regarded from the point of view that it involves man in danger of death and condemnation. Just as the Torah became disastrous to the Gentiles, because they could and indeed should have learned it, but did not learn it (b Sota 35b), so there are also voices speaking for Israel among the Rabbis who are dismayed at the difficulty of keeping the law completely. 'As R. Gamaliel (II) read this verse (Ezek.

greater weight with the rabbis than the fulfilment of the positive commands. In discussion what is forbidden is usually laid down much more precisely than what is commanded. The righteous man is praised for his avoidance of sin even more than for his knowledge of the law (b Shab. 31b).

[1] Strack-Billerbeck, IV, p. 6; Bacher, *Tannaiten*, II, p. 376.

xviii.9) he wept and said: "He who performs all this, is righteous; but alas, not he who performs only one of these".' It is true that Akiba referring to Lev. xviii.24a then says to him that on the contrary even one is sufficient (b Sanh. 81a).[1] On the whole the view that it is possible on principle to fulfil the law is firmly maintained; that is in fact an inner necessity. At least it is asserted that certain individuals were completely sinless. 'We find that Abraham, our father, kept the whole Torah before it had been given' (Kid. 4.14).[2]

(viii) The fact that life depends on fulfilling the Torah makes it a very important concern that the law should be developed in the direction of case-law. The law and its development and practice support the religious existence of the Jew. Yet this is not to say that only the casuistical obedience to the individual commandments and prohibitions was regarded as a proper fulfilment of the law, however predominant this obedience may be.[3] There are other statements which name sincere piety and fear of God as the

[1] cf. for this whole question M. Löwy, 'Die paulinische Lehre vom Gesetz', MGWJ NF 11 (1903), pp. 322 ff., 417 ff., 534 ff.

[2] cf. further Strack-Billerbeck, III, pp. 186, 204 f. This idea is old, cf. p. 56. Philo's interest in it cannot be seen amongst the rabbis.

[3] The rabbis do indeed take note occasionally of a summary of the law in one or several main commandments. But this summary, as too the distinction between superficial and serious commands (cf. Wohlgemuth, pp. 13 f.), has no fundamental importance. In b Shab. 31a the story is told of a Gentile who asked Hillel if he could tell him the Torah whilst standing on one foot. So Hillel answered: 'Do not do to your neighbour what you do not like for yourself. That is the whole law; everything else only explains it. Go and learn it.' David reduced it to 11 (commandments), . . . Isaiah to 6, . . . Micah to 3, . . . Amos to 1 (Amos v.4), Habakkuk to 1 (Hab. ii.4) (Mak. 23b/24a). Yet basically one law is worth as much as any other, and statements like this are playful and edifying rather than a matter of serious interest.

essential prerequisite of study (b Yoma 72b). 'All
that you do, do only from love' in S Deut. 41 on xi.3.
Rabba b R. Hona said: 'A man who knows the law
but does not fear God is like a treasurer to whom have
been entrusted the keys of the interior (of the house),
but not of the exterior; how can he get in?' But all
this makes no difference to the fact that man secures
for himself righteousness and life by his study and his
fulfilment of the Torah.

IV. LAW IN THE NEW TESTAMENT

A. *Jesus and the law according to the Synoptists*

1. *The occurrence of the word*

The significance of what is denoted positively and negatively by the word νόμος in the Synoptics is by no means covered by the extent to which the actual word occurs in them. In order therefore to understand what was in fact Jesus' attitude to the law according to the Synoptists, it is necessary to refer also to certain passages in which the word νόμος is lacking.[1] In Matthew νόμος is found only eight times, in Luke nine times, in Mark it is absent altogether.

In the few passages where νόμος is found, the usage is simple. ὁ νόμος is used, except in Luke ii.23. Here νόμος has no article and appears in the phrase νόμος κυρίου which is no doubt derived from *tōrath Yahweh*.[2] Normally νόμος means the Pentateuch. When in addition the whole Scripture is to be included ὁ νόμος καὶ οἱ προφῆται is found (Matt. v.17, vii.12, xi.13, xxii.40; Luke xvi.16, xxiv.44 (expanded here by ψαλμοί). The twofold meaning of νόμος and *tōrāh* to be observed in Judaism holds good also for the synoptic use of νόμος: it means the *Law* and the *Pentateuch*, the *Scripture*. In the forefront appears its character as law, as instructions for what to do and what not to do. In Matt. xxii.36 the question ποία ἐντολὴ μεγάλη ἐν τῷ νόμῳ; does not mean which commandment in the

---

[1] Furthermore, in several passages it is doubtful whether the expression was originally part of the respective saying or statement; cf. e.g. Matt. vii.12 with Luke vi.31. A. Harnack, *Beiträge zur Einleitung in das NT*, II: *Sprüche und Reden Jesu* (1907), pp. 11 f.

[2] It is true that Luke ii.39 is different: κατὰ τὸν νόμον κυρίου.

Pentateuch is the greatest, but what kind of commandment is important within the whole range of the law.[1]
But here it is plain also how far from clear-cut the distinction can be. For although the Pentateuch consists
essentially of the law, the law is to be found nowhere
except in the Pentateuch. A great deal about the
relationship between the meanings of law and Pentateuch for νόμος can be learned from Matt. v.18 f.
Here Matthew places side by side: ἰῶτα ἓν ἢ μία κεραία
οὐ μὴ παρέλθῃ ἀπὸ τοῦ νόμου which suggests the notion
of Scripture, and μία τῶν ἐντολῶν τούτων τῶν ἐλαχίστων
which directs attention rather to the content expressed
in commandments.

The double expression ὁ νόμος καὶ οἱ προφῆται too
usually denotes the OT as containing commands
(Matt. v.17, vii.12, xxii.40). But in each case according
to the context it may refer to the OT with its promises
in view (Luke xxiv.44; Matt. xi.13, where, to be sure,
the inversion οἱ προφῆται καὶ ὁ νόμος is probably not
accidental). In other cases γραφή or some form of
γράφω is generally used for the OT in this sense.

It may be a matter of chance that νόμος does not
occur with its meaning extended to the whole OT,
although it is not perhaps purely fortuitous that Matt.
xii.5: οὐκ ἀνέγνωτε ἐν τῷ νομῳ; referring to Num.
xxviii.9 stands beside οὐκ ἀνέγνωτε; by itself (verse 3)
referring to I Sam. xxi.7. But νόμος is not used for the
'oral Torah', the traditional teaching, and in view of
passages like Mark vii.1 ff. this cannot be considered
an accident. The παράδοσις τῶν πρεσβυτέρων in Mark
vii.5, since it is called a παράδοσις τῶν ἀνθρώπων in Mark
vii.8 cannot be recognised as having the nature of νόμος.

2. *Jesus' negation of the law*

In Jesus' preaching according to the Synoptists, His
<hr>
[1] cf. Zahn, *Matthäus* ([4]1922), *ad loc.*

acceptance and negation of the law, censure and approval of it, stand inextricably side by side. There are no clues by which His statements may be listed according to their respective dates.[1] Hence the attempt must be made to understand these differing statements as they are found together.

Jesus rejected the essential nature and basis of the law by depriving it of its position as mediator. The relationship of man to God is no longer determined by the law and man's relationship to it. But now at the point where the nature of this relationship is determined there stands Jesus' word, in fact Jesus Himself. Man now has access to God through his relationship to Him and to the kingdom of God breaking through in Him.

Man is not finally separated from God when he transgresses the law and denies it (Matt. xxi.28 ff.). According to verse 31b the question here is not, it seems, the conflict between word and deed, but between the actual renunciation of God's law and the new experience that it is after all still possible to repent and that God's will is being done. That to transgress the law is a sin is not denied, but the point is that the hopeless situation arising out of this is brought to an end. This is the meaning of the sentence: οἱ τελῶναι καὶ αἱ πόρναι προάγουσιν ὑμᾶς εἰς τὴν βασιλείαν τοῦ θεοῦ (xxi.31b). The parables in Luke xv make this even more clear. They must be understood with xv.1 in mind. Tax collectors and sinners are with Jesus and He associated with them so far as to sit at table with them. So by this means the lost sheep and the lost coin

---

[1] cf. e.g. also Harnack, *Hat Jesus das alttestamentliche Gesetz abgeschafft?* pp. 227 ff. On the other hand H. J. Hotlzmann, *Lehrbuch der neutestamentlichen Theologie,* I (1911), pp. 202 f., attempts to establish Jesus' continuous development until He rejected legalism completely.

are found, by this means the lost son has returned home
(vv. 3 ff., 8 ff., 11 ff.). Then in verses 25 ff. the contrast
is shown: how the son who stayed at home derived no
benefit from just staying at home. The pious son does
not possess his final relationship to God, nor does the
sinner attain his, through relationship to the law,
neither by constantly keeping the commandments,
which is not called in question, nor by openly flouting
it, which is not glossed over. Only when the sinner has
been admitted into the forgiving companionship of
Jesus, has he found his way home to his father's house.
And this fact confronts the other son, whose righteousness is based on the law, with the question whether he
will rely on his obedience to the law as his hard-won
prerogative, as he indicates by his complaint at the
reception of his lost brother, or whether he will regard
the fact that he has been preserved in obedience as
permission to remain happily in his father's house. But
this means that in both cases the law has been ousted
from its place as mediator and that the relationship to
Jesus' word and deed alone decides relationship to God.

The sayings in Matt. x.32 ff. say essentially the same.
To acknowledge Jesus or to deny Him decides the
eternal fate of men. Similarly the events put together
in Mark ii are possible only if the law no longer plays
the decisive role between God and man and thus a man
is no longer justified or condemned in the sight of God
according to whether his behaviour corresponds or
does not correspond to the law.[1]

The pericopes about the blessing of the children in
Mark x.13 ff., the beatitudes in Matt. v.3 ff. or the
saying in Matt. xi.28 ff. point in the same direction.
It is just to those on whom the law weighs so heavily

[1] A. Schlatter, *Markus* (1935), *ad loc.*: 'What Jesus did was
based on the fact that He determined man's relationship to God
not by the law, but by virtue of His mission.'

that they have no ἀνάπαυσις that this rest is brought by
Jesus. The tax collector who bows himself in penitence
before God and relies on God's mercy alone, receives
the verdict: κατέβη οὗτος δεδικαιωμένος εἰς τὸν οἶκον
αὐτοῦ παρ' ἐκεῖνον (Luke xviii.14)—rather than the man
who could boast of his fulfilling of the law (cf. also
Luke xvii.7 ff.). Scribes and Pharisees shut up the
kingdom of heaven (Matt. xxiii.13) because they will
only let those enter who fulfil the law which they
control.

Moreover, this basically different position of the law
occurs also in such sentences and contexts as those
where the dawn of the new age is regarded as the
essence of the new order of things. This supplements
what has been established so far and guards it against
misunderstanding, by pointing out that there is no
question of disclosing what had always been present,
of clearing up a pernicious error, but that a new act
of God is involved, which had existed only as a promise
and had not yet been carried out.[1] Ὁ νόμος καὶ οἱ
προφῆται μέχρι Ἰωάννου· ἀπὸ τότε ἡ βασιλεία τοῦ θεοῦ
εὐαγγελίζεται (Luke xvi.16; cf. Matt. xv.13). Luke is not
likely to have imported an impossible meaning into
this sentence by placing before it the saying against
those who justify themselves before men, but of whose
hearts God knows ὅτι τὸ ἐν ἀνθρώποις ὑψηλὸν βδέλυγμα
ἐνώπιον τοῦ θεοῦ (Luke xvi.15) and by stating in the
sentence following after it that the law retains its
significance and does not lose its validity by being

[1] B. Weiss, *Lehrbuch der biblischen Theologie des NT* (⁷1903),
p. 82, probably means something similar when he distinguishes
Jesus' new understanding of the law from older thought by
saying that in it 'the standard of God's perfect will . . . had not
yet everywhere found adequate expression corresponding to the
perfected state of the theocracy or the kingdom of God'. Jesus
interprets the meaning of the law having in mind the complete
revelation of God which has appeared in Him, *op. cit.*, p. 86.

violated (verse 17 f.). Thus, now that the dawn of God's kingdom is being announced, the criterion which God applies is no longer the law and the works of the law achieved by man by himself (cf. the similies of the old garment and of the wineskins in Mark ii.21 f.).[1]

But this changed situation and age are wholly tied to the word and person of Him who brings the change about. Mark ii.21 demonstrates this by using as the occasion for these sayings the antithesis between Jesus' disciples and those of John. Because the disciples belong to Jesus, they belong to the new age. This means that the Synoptists interpret this freedom from the law with Jesus as fundamentally messianic, christological (cf. Luke ii.41 ff.). So Matt. xvii.24 ff.: as the son Jesus is free from the law, even though He nevertheless observes it.

Jesus bases man's relationship to God on his relationship to Himself and to the kingdom of God which He is bringing in. Thus as the dispenser of forgiveness He addresses a call in particular to sinners. By these acts He definitely negates the law which stands as a mediator between God and man, and thereby rejects the righteousness derived from the law. It is by means of the person of Jesus Himself that the law has been expelled from its key position.

3. *Jesus' acceptance of the law*

This new position and the rejection of the law arising out of it alone make it possible to understand correctly Jesus' acceptance of the law. For it is obvious that by ousting the law from its place as mediator, there is no intention of rejecting it altogether.

(*a*) Jesus recognises the law by behaving as the dispenser of forgiveness when for example He calls the

---

[1] Rengstorf, *Lucas* (NT Deutsch) *ad loc.*; Wellhausen, *Markus*, *ad loc.*

tax collectors and sinners to join His company (Luke xv). On these occasions the opinion is quite openly expressed that He is dealing with the sick (Mark ii.17), with the lost, with those about to die (Luke xv.3 ff., 24, 32). Thus by the verdict to which His forgiveness is attached, Jesus gives the law particular prominence.

The law is right in demanding obedience, since to refuse it means death. Therefore a doctrine which enlightens the merely alleged sinner cannot create a new situation. This can be done only by the eschatological act of forgiveness, i.e. an act which bears witness to God's kingdom. Consequently it is not a new doctrine about God and His will, a new religion, which fashions the new relationship to God. It is the dawn of the age of salvation, and therefore the act of forgiveness. Hence not only is the law driven out from its position as mediator, but the verdict of the law and thus its claim are at the same time recognised as just, and indeed it is presupposed as necessary.[1]

(b) Moreover, all the pericopes cited show that Jesus does not wish to eliminate obedience, even though He does not base the relationship to God upon it (cf. Matt. xxi.28 ff.). When the lost son decides to go back home, it means that he is ready to return to his obedience (Luke xv.19; cf. also Luke xix.1 ff.). When Jesus delivers a man from the weight of the law's yoke, He calls him to take up His yoke (Matt. xi.29). The righteousness of the disciples must exceed that of the scribes and Pharisees, not in the subtlety of their legal casuistry, but in their whole-hearted devotion to the will of God (Matt. v.20). By bringing in the βασιλεία τοῦ θεοῦ, Jesus proclaims and produces true obedience and thereby recognises the law in such a manner as to

[1] A. Schlatter, *Geschichte des Christus* ([2]1923), p. 174, says that Jesus' 'ethical propositions are not meditations on problems of ethics, but parts of His call to repentance'.

lead to its fulfilment. The good tree bears good fruit
(Matt. vii.16 ff.). This simile does not represent the
relationship between deed and intention, but that
between these two on the one hand and on the other
the status of child of God reached through Jesus. If
this makes the tree good, then the good fruit must
come.

(c) So it is not surprising that according to the
account of the Synoptists Jesus Himself keeps the law.
For instance He wears as a matter of course the gar-
ments prescribed by the law (Matt. ix.20 f., xiv.36).[1]
In Luke's story of the childhood, he takes a serious
interest in the fact that Jesus was placed under the law;
and indeed He receives the prophetic witness just
because He is being placed under the law (Luke
ii.24-25, 27-28).[2] But there is something more: the
goal of the messianic activity will not be reached *until
all is accomplished* (Matt. v.18)[3] The coming of Jesus is
just what is meant by the fulfilment[4] of the law, and
the cross is understood as the union of the consummated obedience to the will of God declared in the
scriptures with love towards the brethren in the act of
self-offering. It is true that the Synoptists did not
explicitly state that in this they saw Jesus fulfilling the
law, but their presentation suggests it (cf. also Matt.
iii.15).[5]

(d) As, according to this, Jesus acknowledges that
the law represents God's good purpose for Himself, so

---

[1] Branscomb, pp. 115 f.   [2] Zahn, *Lucas* ([3],[4]1920), *ad loc.*

[3] Schlatter, *Matthäus, ad loc.*

[4] According to verse 19 πληροῦν is not to be understood as
'making perfect' in regard to its content, but in the sense of
'putting it into effect'. Contrary to A. Harnack, 'Geschichte eines
programmatischen Wortes Jesu (Matt. v.17) in der ältesten
Kirche', *Sitzungsbericht der Preussischen (Deutschen) Akademie . . . zu
Berlin* (phil.-hist. Klasse) (1913), pp. 184 ff.

[5] cf. Schlatter, *Matthäus* on v.18.

it does also for others. When questioned about right action Jesus replies: τὰς ἐντολὰς οἶδας (Mark x.19). He recognises that no other purpose is good than that of God revealed in the law.[1] Beyond this there is no other goodness represented by Him (Mark x.18, similarly Luke x.25 ff.).

Jesus accepts the law because it requires obedience in action and is not content with a disposition which cannot be checked. He rejects those who confess Him as Lord whilst at the same time doing ἀνομία[2] (Matt. vii.23). The law is concerned with doing; it is not enough merely to know God's good purpose (Luke x.28).

In concrete terms the law demands self-denying love of God and of one's neighbour[3] (Mark xii.28 and parallels); the addition in Matt. xxii.40 is to the point. This unvarying summing up in the law of love is expressed in other passages also. Thus for example in Matt. vii.12 or Matt. xxiv.12: διὰ τὸ πληθυνθῆναι τὴν ἀνομίαν ψυγήσεται ἡ ἀγάπη τῶν πολλῶν. Lawlessness and lovelessness correspond to one another (cf. also Matt. v.43 ff.).

Thus there exists also a direct positive connexion between the law and Jesus as the Christ, in so far as genuine obedience to the law is fulfilled by following Christ. The rich man would bring his fulfilment of the law to completion by the utter surrender of himself in following Jesus (Mark x.17 ff.). When in Mark xii.34 the questioner acknowledges the law's radical demand for love, he is not far from the kingdom of God, but he does not yet belong to it, in so far as he still expects his observance of the law to be his own achievement.[4]

---

[1] P. Feine, *Theologie des NT* (⁴1922), pp. 24 ff.
[2] cf. on this word, below, pp. 135ff.
[3] cf. also Harnack, p. 229.
[4] cf. Schniewind, *Markus* (NT Deutsch, 1952), *ad loc.*

(e) Side by side with this definite affirmation of the law there stands Jesus' censure of it. But it is a censure which actually serves to affirm and support it, not to bring it to an end. Jesus criticises the law *firstly* in so far as it protects man's disobedience against God's demands. He does not accept as perfect obedience a man's observance of the law's individual precepts, if he is not also ready for complete surrender (Mark x.21 and parallels). Even the fourth commandment is set aside by Jesus if it is brought forward as a hindrance to hearing Jesus' call to follow Him (Matt. viii.21 f.; cf. also Luke xii.52 f.). Similarly if the law is observed primarily for the sake of being recognised by men, Jesus did not recognise this observance at all (Matt. xxiii.5 ff., vi.1 ff.). Thus Jesus did not, for example, reject only the appeal to the 'tradition of the elders' in face of the plain duty of the law (ἀφέντες τὴν ἐντολὴν τοῦ θεοῦ κρατεῖτε τὴν παράδοσιν τῶν ἀνθρώπων Mark vii.8 ff.), but also the appeal to what is demanded by the letter of the law in face of the absolute claim of God, as well as of the claim of one's neighbour.

This is the meaning, for example, of the pericope concerning the sabbath in Mark iii.1 ff. When the question concerning good and evil is raised, i.e. in this case the question concerning the will of God as revealed in that actual moment by the neighbour's need for help, then the question of what is permitted or prohibited by the commandment about the sabbath is solved as well. Certainly God's will appears in the law, but it is not tied to the law to such an extent that by an appeal to it God's will concerning the obligation to one's neighbour can thereby be evaded.

Thus it is not a case of reducing the law to a system of morality, but of exposing its basic principles by raising the question concerning actual obedience in loving one's neighbour.

This removal of all limits to the duty of obedience is assisted by tracing the law back to the love of God and of one's neighbour. As contrasted with similar examples in Judaism, this summary does not spring from a concern for a systematic clarification of the multifarious precepts of the law, nor does it derive from a kind of playful edifying tendency, nor does it aim at relaxing the law and making God's will innocuous. On the contrary, its purpose is to expose the law's basic principle,[1] to admit nothing as fulfilling the law which is not at its heart obedience to God and service to one's neighbour. Above all its object is to prevent obedience and service being refused by appealing to the observance of the commandments. At the same time the rabbinic distinction between a legal obligation and a voluntary act of love disappears (cf. Matt. iii.15; Luke x.28 ff.; Mark x.17 ff.).[2]

The censure on the law implicit in thus unifying it, is therefore an affirmation of it in a fundamental sense, and means bringing it back to its original OT meaning, namely that God has a claim on man and uses this claim to direct his attention to his neighbour. Thus, in the manner in which the prophets understood the law, a way is made through the law to reach God Himself and His will is to be recognised both within the actual law and outside it. There is this difference between Jesus and the prophets, that they only promise the act of God which produces this obedience, whilst Jesus himself offers and in fact is this act.

Therefore when Jesus rejects casuistry, it is not to be thought that He wishes to make the OT commandments more humane, or rational or moral,[3] nor to

[1] R. Bultmann, 'Jesus und Paulus', in: *Jesus Christus im Zeugnis der heiligen Schrift und der Kirche* (1936), pp. 74 ff.

[2] Bultmann, *Die Bedeutung* . . ., pp. 193 f.

[3] Certanly Jesus makes the position of men before the law clear

release them from the nationalistic restrictions into a broad universalism.[1] But Jesus' first desire is to attach serious importance to God's holiness which claims the whole man, as contrasted with the protection which man seeks in the law from the sheer absoluteness of this claim. This is made particularly clear in Matt. xxiii.23 where Jesus is not objecting in any way to keeping the small precepts of the law, but condemns severely the idea that one can thereby feel free to neglect the observance of the βαρύτερα τοῦ νόμου.

Secondly, this is closely connected with the fact that Jesus criticises the law in so far as it does not lay bare the root of sin, since, although it condemns the deed, it does not condemn the condition of the heart and mind which causes the deed.

Thirdly and lastly, this is the place to speak of the censure of the law which arises from the fact that the law as it is assumes the sin of man to be an accepted, unalterable state of affairs. Mark x.5: πρὸς τὴν σκληροκαρδίαν ὑμῶν ἔγραψεν (sc. Moses) ὑμῖν τὴν ἐντολὴν ταύτην. Belonging to Jesus and to the βασιλεία τοῦ θεοῦ marks the restoring of order in accordance with creation, an order which does not presuppose sin as an accepted unalterable state of affairs.[2] This is part

especially by means of ethical precepts, not by cultic or ritual ones. But in any case the essential point which He wishes to make with regard to the law does not consist in placing the former on principle above the latter, even if there can be any question of such a thing. Even in Mark vii the alternatives are not primarily concerned with an 'ethical' or a 'ritual' understanding of the law, but with real obedience or the concealing of disobedience by an appeal to the law. Cf. also F. Büchsel, *Theol. des NT* (1935), pp. 22 f. For another view cf., for example, H. Weinel, *Biblische Theologie des NT* (1928), pp. 82 ff.

[1] Weinel, pp. 85 ff. lays stress on this and so does Herkenrath p. 132.

[2] The treatment of this particular question shows how freedom is not excluded by a direct referring of the commandments to

of the meaning in the antitheses in Matt. v.21 ff., particularly clear perhaps in verse 38 ff. The law curbs the unrestrained thirst for vengeance; Jesus frees His own completely from it. In so far as the law presupposes the sin of man, it is annulled by Jesus, because He creates the obedience of love which gives up all claims to itself and its rights, and relies on God alone.

In this way the law is established all the more firmly. But at the same time it is completely clear that the law in Jesus' new conception of it is no longer understood as something to be fulfilled by man with the idea that thereby he wins for himself God's verdict vindicating him. On the contrary, the fulfilling of the claim presupposes his status of a child of God,[1] a status which comes into existence through companionship with Jesus and has its being in the forgiveness thus bestowed.

4. The relationship between the negation and the acceptance of the law

It is thus evident that the recognition of the law by affirming and censuring it has two main aspects. It is a call for total repentance to which the demands of the law give depth and reality, and it shows the nature of genuine obedience, of the new righteousness. Neither of these can be dissociated from the fact that Jesus does not base the relationship between man and God on the observance of the law, but establishes it on God's new creative act of forgiveness. On the one hand a way has been opened up through the law to God's direct claim and it is recognised that its quite new interpretation involves condemnation; on the other hand man has been set free from the mediation of the law

God. Because marriage is divinely ordained, it is completely binding for those who are bound to God. But for this very reason there may be release from this order for the sake of the kingdom of God.   [1] cf. Büchsel, p. 26.

and its observance. These two sets of circumstances
challenge and condition each other.[1] It is only when
a man renounces his own achievements and accepts
forgiveness that he becomes capable of really facing the
judgement of the law and of offering the obedience of
love. But at the same time the thorough establishment
of its claim and of its verdict raises the question concerning God's new act for man and for the world.

B.   *The conflict concerning the law*

1. *The primitive community*

The sources provide no reliable picture as to how
the primitive community understood the law during
the earliest period. It is no doubt true that the community did in fact observe the law. But in what sense
it did so cannot be gathered unequivocally from the
account in the Acts of the Apostles, since we must note
its tendency to obliterate differences in this matter.[2]
Theological reflexion was likely in its beginnings to
have been concerned much less with the law than with
understanding Jesus as the Messiah promised by the
scripture.[3] The problem of the law made its appearance as a subject requiring attention only when the
community began to spread to former Gentiles or into
Gentile spheres generally.[4] The first place where we
can get a clear indication of the points of view regarding

[1] The contrary holds good in Judaism. The position of the law
as mediator is maintained and the attempt is made to be vindi-
cated in God's sight by one's own efforts, and this attitude cannot
be dissociated from the secret refusal of obedience with the help
of the law and from renouncing complete penitence.

[2] O. Weizsäcker, *Das apostolische Zeitalter der christlichen Kirche*
(1902), pp. 169 ff., ET of 2nd ed. 2 vols, (1894/5), I pp. 200 ff.

[3] cf. P. Wernle, *Die Anfänge unserer Religion* (²1904), p. 108.

[4] The problem of winning the Samaritans (Acts viii) was not
quite so difficult, yet similar in some respects.

this problem occurs at the 'Apostolic Council'. Acts
xv and Galatians ii agree to a large extent in their
account of it.[1] The basic understanding of the law by
the primitive community can be most readily deduced
from the decisions taken on that occasion.

(a) The situation at the Apostolic Council, according
in the main to Galatians, is as follows: firstly, the
agreement of the gospel preached by Paul with that
of the primitive community was confirmed. Such
agreement was not brought about for the first time
on this occasion. (Cf. Gal. ii.2: ἀνεθέμην αὐτοῖς
τὸ εὐαγγέλιον ὃ κησύσσω ἐν τοῖς ἔθνεσιν, and verse 6:
ἐμοὶ οἱ δοκοῦντες οὐδὲν προσανέθεντο).

Since from the outset the problem at issue concerned
the law, it is impossible to assume that this agreement
did not apply also to the basic problem of the attitude
to the law. If it did so, then the agreement on the
separation of the εὐαγγέλιον τῆς ἀκροβυστίας and the
εὐαγγέλιον τῆς περιτομῆς (Gal. ii.7) does not mean that
Paul recognised a ἕτερον εὐαγγέλιον (Gal. i.6). This is
corroborated by Gal. ii.16: εἰδότες δὲ οὐ δικαιοῦται
ἄνθρωπος ἐξ ἔργων νόμου . . . , καὶ ἡμεῖς εἰς Χριστὸν
Ἰησοῦν ἐπιστεύσαμεν, ἵνα δικαιωθῶμεν ἐκ πίστεως
Χριστοῦ καὶ οὐκ ἐξ ἔργων νόμου.[2] Whether or not the
verses in Gal. ii.15 ff. are to be considered as addressed
to Peter makes no difference to the fact that Paul
takes Peter's assent to this statement for granted and
assumes it to be well known. The dispute concerns
the practical conclusions to be drawn from this common basic point of view. Acts xv for its part confirms
this formulation of the problem and this agreed
answer. Those who came from Judaea to Antioch
taught the brethren ὅτι ἐὰν μὴ περιτμηθῆτε τῷ ἔθει τῷ

---

[1] There are too many objections to the thesis of Weizsäcker
that Acts xv was written with Galatians ii in mind.

[2] cf. Weizsäcker, p. 160, ET I, pp. 190 f.

Μωυσέως, οὐ δύνασθε σωθῆναι (Acts xv.1; cf. xv. 5). And Acts xv.11 gives the reply: ἀλλὰ δία τῆς χάριτος τοῦ κυρίου Ἰησοῦ πιστεύομεν σωθῆναι καθ' ὃν τρόπον κἀκεῖνοι. Although it is obviously most improbable that this report contains Peter's own words, yet it is equally obvious that a definite conclusion follows from Acts xv in its agreement with Gal. ii, namely that there was unanimity in a negative sense as regards the question whether the law was necessary for salvation, since for both parties the σωτηρία, the δικαιοῦσθαι, was through faith in the Lord Jesus alone.

Secondly, it is just as certain that the practical problems extending beyond this fundamental unanimity had however not been settled so far as to render impossible the dispute in Antioch described by Paul in Gal. ii.1 ff.

In order to understand this passage it must be noted that Paul has no word of blame, either directly or indirectly, for those coming on behalf of James (cf. the distinction made in Gal. ii.4: παρείσαπτοι ψευδάδελφοι).[1] The practical question is, whether and how far Jews by birth may live together in one community with Gentile Christians who do not keep the law, and in particular may have fellowship with them at table and at the celebration of the Lord's supper,[2] since in that case they would have to sacrifice essential parts of the strict observance of the law. So a clear position was reached for purely Gentile-Christian and for purely Jewish-Christian communities to the extent that the former with the assent of the primitive community were free from the law and the latter with Paul's assent kept the law.[3]

[1] cf. Kittel, pp. 145 ff., 152.

[2] According to Kittel, p. 149, n. 1, it is not certain that fellowship at the celebration of the Lord's supper was in dispute.

[3] Schlatter, *Geschichte der ersten Christenheit*, pp. 70, 150 ff.,

The outcome of the Apostolic Council is thus as follows: The law is not to be kept with the idea that its observance procures justification. Salvation is secured for Gentiles and for Jews by faith in Jesus; but nevertheless the law remains obligatory for Jews. For this reason it seems to have been recognised as necessary and appropriate by Paul and the primitive community alike that the preaching of the gospel to the Gentiles and to the Jews should be kept separate (Gal. ii.7).

(b) Now this raises the question as to the reason for which the obligation on Jewish Christians to keep the law was maintained. This matter can be judged by considering whether Paul could give his consent to the argument. The circumstances of the conflict made it necessary that the reasons should be considered at this point. Up till then the situation had been taken for granted without there being any need to think out particular grounds for it.

The main reason is a concern for the possibility of a mission to the Jews. For to preach Jesus as the Christ of the scripture was no longer acceptable for Jews if his adherents abandoned God's law. In that case this community would in their eyes have been condemned from the outset.[1] I Cor. ix.20 f. proves quite clearly that Paul could agree to this point of view. He himself behaved τοῖς ὑπὸ νόμον ὡς ὑπὸ νόμον, μὴ ὢν αὐτὸς ὑπὸ νόμον in order that he might win those under the law. He neither demands nor demonstrates his freedom from the law by transgressing the law.

Naturally the practical questions in the mixed com-

J. Weiss, *Das Urchristentum* (1917), p. 205; Weizsäcker, pp. 164 ff.. ET I, pp. 196 ff. A different view in Meyer, *Ursprung*, III, pp. 424 ff.

[1] cf. J. Weiss, p. 198; Schlatter, *Geschichte der ersten Christenheit*, 14.

munities were bound to become difficult. If we are to understand these matters, we must see the decisive part played by the Apostolic Decree (Acts xv.23 ff., xxi.25), which is certainly not an invention of Acts.[1] On the contrary the only question which arises is whether it is part of the Apostolic Council or is the outcome of the subsequent incident in Antioch. In no case is the decree to be understood as the lowest ethical standard, as an extract from the law by way of a compromise to make at least its fundamental basis compulsory in place of the whole law.[2] That is ruled out by the choice of the conditions as well as by the general Jewish understanding of the law; it would also have made Paul's assent impossible. Nor does the chief object in view seem to be to guard against 'libertine' Gnostic ideas; for in that case the third and fourth points would remain unintelligible, and moreover it is hardly possible to think that no reason for such action should have been given. On the contrary there are no general grounds at all for distrusting the motive given in Acts xv.21 : Μωυσῆς γὰρ ἐκ γενεῶν ἀρχαίων κατὰ πόλιν τοὺς κηρύσσοντας αὐτὸν ἔχει ἐν ταῖς συναγωγαῖς κατὰ πᾶν σάββατον ἀναγινωσκόμενος. Now since in the Jewish synagogues of the Diaspora fellowship at the divine service with the uncircumcised took place, such a fellowship between Gentiles and Jews in the Christian community could be justified to Jewry, if the rules laid down in the decree were accepted by Gentile Christians. This did not mean that the obligation to keep the law was restricted to these matters for Jewish Christians. But they could enter into fellowship with those Gentiles who accepted these rules, without offending the Jews.[3]

(c) From the way the primitive community made its

---

[1] Weizsäcker, pp. 175 ff., ET, I, pp. 208 ff.

[2] cf. Schlatter, *Geschichte der ersten Christenheit*, pp. 158 f.

[3] cf. J. Weiss, p. 237; Weizsäcker, p. 180, ET I p. 214.

decisions in these cases on principle and in practice, it is possible to deduce its view of the law even during the earlier period. The fact that it was bound by the law was not legalism in the sense that observance of the law was a prerequisite for membership of the Messianic kingdom. But it considered this obligation as the obedience demanded of it practically as a result of its membership, an obedience also to be rendered by it in the service of the gospel for the sake of love. But what held the community together and kept it apart from the rest was not a particular understanding of the law, but faith in Jesus as Lord and Christ.

Now whence comes this peculiar attitude to the law, being at the same time both free from it and bound by it? The presentation in the Synoptic gospels tells us that this attitude to the law is derived from Jesus.[1] And indeed the agreement between Jesus' attitude to the law as portrayed by the Synoptists and that of the primitive community is in fact so striking that there must be a direct connexion between them. The only question to be asked is whether that picture of Jesus' attitude to the law does not owe its existence to the understanding of the law in the primitive community.

But in this last case only two sources of this attitude call for consideration. Either it was deduced from the confession of Jesus as Lord by reasoning and was demanded by the historical events; the primitive community would then have had to understand it as revelation and guidance from their Lord present with them in the Holy Spirit. Or on the other hand there were amongst them influences from Hellenistic Jewry which toned down in various ways the strictly Jewish point of view towards the law. The story of Cornelius (Acts x f., cf. Acts xv.7 ff.!), for example, seems to be an argument for the first possibility; for the second the

[1] cf. Weizsäcker, pp. 625 f., ET, II pp. 341 ff.

events concerning Stephen (Acts vi f.). But on closer examination this latter possibility drops out. For in that case Stephen with his conception of the law could not have met with opposition from the Hellenistic-Jewish synagogue in particular (Acts vi.9 ff.). Moreover in essentials, in attitude and motive, none of the Hellenistic-Jewish conceptions of the law approximated in the least to the primitive Christian one. It is perhaps going too far to expect from this direction even a greater readiness and openness towards that aspect of Jesus' message which proclaimed freedom from the law.[1] Stephen was condemned for his Christian, not his Hellenistic, attitude to the law.

As regards the first of the possibilities mentioned, it must at any rate be observed that the Jewish theology of the Messiah and the ideas attached to it concerning the relationship of the Messiah to the law, would not have assisted the primitive Christian attitude to develop out of the confession of Jesus as Lord, but on the contrary would have hindered it.[2] Besides in view of the nature of the tradition almost insuperable difficulties would arise on just this question, if the synoptic presentation were derived from the primitive Christian attitude.

Thus it is most likely, speaking historically, that the Synoptists' accounts concerning Jesus' attitude to the law are on the whole true to history, and that therefore the primitive community owed its attitude to the law fundamentally to that of Jesus.[3]

[1] For this question cf. J. Weiss, pp. 121 ff., 198; M. Meyer, *Ursprung*, III, pp. 271 ff.; Weizsäcker, pp. 52 ff., ET, I pp. 63 ff.; M. Maurenbrecher, *Von Jerusalem nach Rom* (1910), pp. 113, 114 f., 115.   [2] cf. p. 74.

[3] This does not make such a story as that about Cornelius unnecessary, since it was not left to the community to decide when freedom from the law became for it actually necessary and right.

(d) The struggles, motives and decisions which emerged into daylight at the Apostolic Council and from the resultant events enable the further development within the primitive community to be understood as well. The extreme party, customarily called Judaisers, maintains in spite of the Apostolic Council that circumcision and the law must be imposed on Gentile Christians too, since otherwise they could not attain to salvation, to the community of Christ.[1] They disseminate this idea zealously, especially in the Pauline communities. Nevertheless it remains an open question whether the circumstances presupposed in Romans are likewise to be explained by Judaistic propaganda.[2]

Their motives are, according to Galatians, fear of persecution for the sake of the cross, coupled with lust for personal power (Gal. vi.12 f.). Behind this there might be the change in the missionary attitude of the primitive community which desired to avoid all unpleasantness from Jewry, even to the extent of renouncing the gospel of justification by faith in Jesus alone.[3] It must be assumed that there were also morally less unworthy motives for the attitude of the Judaisers. For to some of those who had grown up in the law the idea that through faith in Jesus the law could, or indeed must, be renounced, would have seemed quite simply impossible.

The considerations advanced by the Judaisers in support of their teaching were apparently firstly a reference to the commands of the scriptures, as the polemic in Galatians iii f. shows, next a reference to the practice of the primitive community, even no doubt

[1] Weizsäcker, pp. 216 ff., ET, I pp. 257 ff.; Schlatter, *Geschichte der ersten Christenheit*, p. 152.

[2] cf. Weizsäcker, pp. 424 ff., ET, II pp. 99 ff.

[3] There may have been associated with this the idea that only in this way could the advantages be preserved for Christendom which the protection of the Roman Empire involved for Jewry.

to that of Jesus Himself. This was combined with dis-
crediting Paul's apostolate, as may be seen for example
in II Cor. xi; I Cor. i.12; Gal. i. A reference to the
ethical results, believed necessarily to follow from the
Pauline doctrine of the law, will have contributed in
part, and indeed no doubt particularly in the more
important cases. This may even have been the chief
motive. Yet this seems to be presupposed in Romans
more than in Galatians.[1] In these matters it is in itself
not probable that there was behind this activity a
homogeneous theological reasoning, likely to be the
same everywhere, since the first consideration for these
people seems to have been not the reasoning, but
interest in the law itself.

A later continuation of this trend which was bound
to lose ground in the course of time with the historical
changes which took place, is found in the group of the
Ebionites who then separated from the church. They
upheld the binding force of the law on all Christians.[2]
Perhaps they are to be distinguished from the Nazar-
enes[3] who only clung to the law for themselves, but
released the Gentile Christians from it and recognised
Paul.

(e) The attitude of James and Peter and of the
community who followed their lead must be kept
separate from this Judaising trend. They seem in the
main to have kept to the line adopted by the Apostolic
Council. At any rate this corresponds to the picture
of James given in Acts xxi.18 ff. and is confirmed in
Josephus' account of James' death.[4] As regards Peter,
it is easiest to assume that he returned to the line taken
by the Apostolic Council and by James after he had for
a time in Antioch conformed to Paul's point of view.

[1] Weizsäcker, p. 428, ET, II p. 104.
[2] J. Weiss, p. 572.   [3] J. Weiss, p. 523.
[4] Jos. *Ant.* 20.200. On this J. Weiss, p. 552, n. 2; Kittel, p. 146.

At any rate the attempt to make Peter the champion of the Judaisers[1] is not sufficiently substantiated in the extant sources. Besides, it is in itself improbable.

Thus the authoritative circles of primitive Christianity understood the law as follows: they regarded it as the standard for the obedience owed by Jewish Christians, and furthermore knew that they were committed to it with a view to winning Jewry for the gospel. But they did not regard the observance of it as the means whereby man is justified in the sight of God. In consequence they held brotherly intercourse with Gentile Christians, even if the latter did not keep the law. In mixed communities, the Gentile Christians were expected to observe such rules as made intercourse with them on the part of Jewish Christians appear defensible to the Jewish community.

2. *Pauline usage*

The Pauline usage of νόμος is not quite uniform, since Paul uses νόμος also in some cases in which he is not denoting the OT law. But nevertheless the starting point is not a general meaning of νόμος, at times to be used chiefly for the Mosaic law.[2] It is in fact the traditional use of the word for the Israelite law in particular. Hence also what νόμος signifies is assumed to be self-evident and so usually no more precise designation is added.[3]

---

[1] Especially Meyer, *Ursprung und Anfänge des Christentums*, III, pp. 434 ff. For Romans, cf. H. Lietzmann, *Sitzungsbericht der preussischen (deutschen) Akademie . . . Berlin* (1930), and E. Hirsch, ZNW 29 (1930), pp. 63 ff., for a criticism of this.

[2] Cremer *Biblisch-Theologisch.Wörterbuch*, ed. Kögel ([11]1923), (ET of ed. 2, 2 vols. 1878-86) endeavours to distinguish between the term νόμος in general and its definite application to Israel's divine law. Yet he says himself that in the case of Paul too the use of the term is qualified by what he says about the Israelite law.

[3] I Cor. ix.9: ὁ Μωυσέως νόμος; Rom. vii.22, 25, viii.7: ὁ νόμος τοῦ θεοῦ (the context makes it necessary to add τοῦ θεοῦ for emphasis).

In accordance with rabbinic usage, that which νόμος is intended to convey can be exemplified by the Decalogue, which is thus, as it were, specifically 'the law' (Rom. xiii.8 ff., ii.20 ff., vii.7). Yet Paul makes no distinction on principle between the Decalogue and the rest of the legal material. With an appropriate noun in the genitive νόμος can also be employed for a particular individual law, thus Rom. vii.2: νόμος τοῦ ἀνδρός, meaning no doubt in the first place the law in force in respect of the husband,[1] signifying here the law binding the wife to the husband, not something like the law issuing from the husband.

νόμος is regarded by Paul chiefly as that which demands action by man, namely as a definite purpose. Hence the law is 'kept' (Rom. ii.25; cf. Gal. v.3, vi.13). Hence there are ἔργα νόμου required by the law, works to be performed in conformity with the law (Rom. iii.28 et passim). This alone makes sense, for example, of the question in Rom. vii.7: ὁ νόμος ἁμαρτία; which means: is the purpose of the law sinful? The positive aspect of this is in Rom. vii.12: ὁ νόμος ἅγιος. The purpose of the law, the requirement, of the law, is holy.[2]

But even if the emphasis in νόμος thus lies on its nature as God's demand, it is just in the Mosaic law of the OT that this can be grasped.[3] The shift of

[1] cf. for example Lev. vi.18 (EVV 25) = the law in force in respect of the sin offering.

[2] Schlatter, *Gottes Gerechtigkeit. Ein Kommentar zum Römerbrief* (³1959), on Rom. vii.7.

[3] cf. A. W. Slaten, 'The Qualitative Use of νόμος in the Pauline Epistles', *American Journal of Theology*, 23 (1919), pp. 213 ff. Even if Paul often uses νόμος qualitatively, 'that is with especial emphasis upon the essential law-quality of law, its "lawness", so to speak' (214), its specific relationship to the OT law is not thereby disclaimed (217 n. 1). But ὁ νόμος with the article, as in Rom. iv.15, has this qualitative meaning no less than νόμος without the article in Rom. iv.14.

emphasis, the value set by Paul on the nature of the
law as being the living purpose of God, as contrasted
with the value set by the rabbis on the declaration of
this purpose once for all, is not accidental, although
their usage agrees on the whole. Yet we must not
confuse with this the question whether or not a difference does exist between the use of νόμος with or without
the article.[1] At any rate we do not find that νόμος
means 'a' law whilst ὁ νόμος means 'the' law.

This fact should be noted in the exegesis for example
of Rom. ii.12 ff. Ὅσοι ἐν νόμῳ ἥμαρτον are not such
people who have sinned owing to the existence of some
law or other, but, as contrasted with those who ἀνόμως
ἥμαρτον (verse 12a), they are those who knew the one
divine law and yet sinned. The Gentiles in Rom. ii.14:
νόμον μὴ ἔχοντες do not know the particular OT law.
Within Paul's range of thought there was probably no
nation which had no law of some sort, and even a law
with religious sanction. If these Gentiles do by nature,
i.e. without knowing the revealed law, the things that
it commands, this makes them ἑαυτοῖς νόμος, not 'a'
law, but 'the' law to themselves.[2] If νόμος without the
article implied here a generalisation of the concept of
law, the train of thought would be broken.

Not every nation's moral or political and social code
is considered by Paul to have the nature of the νόμος.[3]

---

[1] cf. for this E. Grafe, *Die Paulinische Lehre vom Gesetz* ([2]1893),
pp. 3 ff.; there the earlier literature on the question is also to be
found. P. Feine, *Die Theologie des NT* ([4]1922), p. 218. Blass-
Debrunner, *Grammatik* (ed. 6) § 258, 2. (An English translation
of the Blass-Debrunner *Greek Grammar of the New Testament and
other early Christian Literature* is shortly to be published by the
Cambridge University Press and the University of Chicago Press).

[2] Schlatter, *op. cit.* (p. 102, n. 2), *ad loc.*

[3] Rom. v.14 is typical. Here the term νόμος is not used in the
case of Adam, although since he had transgressed a definite
command it was a matter of παράβασις of the same kind as took

Hence he does not use νόμος in the plural, not even in the manner of Hellenistic Judaism where οἱ νόμοι are used for the OT law; still less does he place similar laws of other nations beside the OT law.[1] The law is one, the revealed purpose of the one God.

Its central meaning as God's demand is also expressed by the fact that νόμος is referred to as if it were a personal power. In Rom. iii.19 the law speaks; in Rom. iv.15 it produces; in Rom. vii.1 it is binding; in I Cor. ix.8 it says. Occasionally νόμος might actually be rendered as God, in so far as He reveals Himself in the law. But this does not in any way suggest that the law is being made into some kind of hypostasis, for beside these expressions there always stand corresponding ones of an impersonal nature (Rom. iii.20, iv.15, vii.2; I Cor. ix.9.

In addition to this principal use of νόμος, the other important meaning of the rabbinic tōrāh also occurs, namely νόμος = Pentateuch, without regard to its nature as demand.[2] In Gal. iv.21 νόμος is obviously used intentionally in a twofold sense: λέγετέ μοι οἱ ὑπὸ νόμον θέλοντες εἶναι, τὸν νόμον οὐκ ἀκούετε; The second time νόμος means simply the narrative in the Pentateuch. Hence in Rom. iii.21 beside this νόμος are placed the prophets; together they mean the whole scripture. In his proofs from scripture, Paul likes to put a passage from the Torah beside one from the prophets.[3] But this does not prevent him from using

place later under the law. So here too it is not a question of an extension of νόμος in the direction of a general concept of law.

[1] cf. Brandt, pp. 8 f.; Lohmeyer, p. 14.

[2] It is true that in such cases occasionally a saying from scripture itself, containing no command, and the moral to be drawn from it, are used to inculcate again right action; yet law is here not understood directly as demand (e.g. I Cor. xiv.21).

[3] e.g. Rom. ix.12, x.6 ff., 13, 19 ff., vi.10 ff.; II Cor. vi.16 ff.; Gal. iv.27, 30. Cf. the list in Michel pp. 12 f., 53. For the rabbinic

νόμος for the whole of the OT as well. In I Cor. xiv.21 a passage from the prophets is cited with the words ἐν τῷ νόμῳ γέγραπται.[1] Similarly Rom. iii.19 sums up passages from all the parts of scripture in the phrase ὅσα ὁ νόμος λέγει.

Finally Paul employs νόμος also in a figurative sense. Usually it appears in that case with an appropriate noun in the genitive or some other word of explanation. In Rom. iii.17 νόμος πίστεως is contrasted with νόμος ἔργων. Thus νόμος has here the wider meaning of a divine ordinance which describes faith, not works, as the right behaviour of men; hence any boasting before God becomes impossible. Just as νόμος ἔργων can be understood as the law which results in works, so can νόμος πίστεως as God's ordinance demanding faith. In Rom. vii.21 the best meaning will be obtained by taking νόμος in a figurative sense.[2] The meaning of νόμος would then be the fact that evil is close at hand when I want to do right. This rule would then be called 'law' because there is no escape from its validity. In addition, νόμος is used occasionally for the claim or purpose which controls a man's action, arising from something external, defined more precisely by the *genitivus auctoris*. ὁ νόμος τῆς ἁμαρτίας = the evil purpose forced upon me by sin (Rom. vii.25, viii.2)[3]; on the other hand ὁ νόμος τοῦ πνεύματος τῆς ζωῆς (Rom. viii.2) and ὁ νόμος τοῦ Χριστοῦ (Gal. vi.2) are employed in both cases as types in contrast to the OT law. Rom.

view which lies behind this, cf. Lev. r 16, 4 on Simeon ben Azzai who 'sat and expounded and strung the words of the Torah on to the words of the prophets and the words of the prophets on to those of the writings. Fire flamed up round about him and the words of the Torah rejoiced as on the day when they were given at Sinai'; cf. Glatzer, *op. cit* (p. 70, n. 3), p. 38.

[1] Deut. xxviii.49 admittedly is added.

[2] Schlatter, *op. cit*, (p. 102, n. 2), *ad loc.* takes a different view.

[3] cf. also similarly Rom. vii.23.

xiii.8 is also of interest; here ὁ ἕτερος νόμος seems to allude to the summary of the law in the twofold commandment of love. For this reason ἐντολή, normally used elsewhere for a single command, has probably been avoided.

3. What Paul understands the law to mean[1]

(a) It is the cross of Jesus which determines for Paul his understanding of the content of the law. The whole of Paul's thought revolves round the proposition that the crucified Jesus is the Christ. In the same way it determines his attitude to the law. This alone provides an intelligible, inherently necessary, connexion between his affirmation and negation of the law. Otherwise only two dissimilar series of ideas could be worked out, a conservative-affirmative one and a negative-radical one.[2] For Paul the negation of the law follows from the cross: Gal. ii.21: εἰ γὰρ διὰ νόμου δικαιοσύνη, ἄρα Χριστὸς δωρεὰν ἀπέθανεν (cf Rom. vii.1 ff., viii.1 ff.)[3] It is owing to the particular nature and to the operation of the law that this proved the only way in which freedom from the law could be achieved.

(b) The nature of the law is summed up in the statement: the law is the good purpose of God. Not to be subject to the law is therefore enmity towards God (Rom. viii.7).

Paul does not make any fundamental distinction as regards content between for example the cultic and the ethical commands, or between the Decalogue and the rest of the law. Nevertheless he develops his position

---

[1] cf. P. Bläser, *Das Gesetz bei Paulus = Nt.liche Abhandlungen*, 19 (1941); Ch. Maurer, *Die Gesetzeslehre des Paulus nach ihrem Ursprung und in ihrer Entfaltung dargelegt* (1941).

[2] Michel, pp. 190 f.; cf. also A. Schweitzer, *Die Mystik des Apostel Paulus* (1930), pp. 184 f.

[3] cf. O. Pfleiderer, *Der Paulinismus* ([2]1890), pp. 6 f., 93.

especially in relation to the ethical commands, in particular to the commandments of the Decalogue which are applicable to all mankind.[1] This is characteristic just because it is not done on principle.

Because the law is the proclamation of God's purpose, it is directed towards what man does. When citing the sentence in Lev. xviii.5: ὁ ποιήσας αὐτὰ ζήσεται ἐν αὐτοῖς in Gal. iii.12, Rom. x.5, Paul feels the emphasis to be on ποιεῖν.

The strictures on the Jew in Rom. ii.17 ff. make the same assumption. The Jew certainly knows the law, indeed his whole make-up and attitude is that of one who possesses truth and knowledge through the law (Rom. ii.20),[2] but he does not practise it. Yet the aim of the law was that man should render obedience. This is not done simply by knowing and recognising the law. So when Paul is describing existence under the law, he does not take as an example the man who rejects the law, but the one who wants to keep it, who assents to it, but yet, because he does not fulfil it, is condemned by it.

In the case of the law it is a matter of ἔργα in contrast to πίστις with which ἀκοή is associated (Gal. iii.2 ff.). In the life under the law it is only action according to the law which makes a man to be religious. To live in the law means to base one's life on keeping the law, Gal. iii.10: εἶναι ἐξ ἔργων νόμου, and Rom. ii.23: ἐν νόμῳ καυχᾶσθαι means to have one's reputation in the sight of God from the law and from fulfilling the

[1] Paul regards the fulfilment of the law through the Spirit in the believer as the real purpose of the law, and this view governs his understanding of the law when judging the position of the sinner before the law. The purpose of the law is obedience to God and love of one's neighbour. But Paul calls the Jews to repentance on the basis of the law as it actually is, and not of theoretical considerations.

[2] cf. Schlatter, *op. cit.* (p. 102, n. 2), *ad loc.*

law. Thus to be bound to the law is regarded by Paul as the really characteristic mark of the Jew.[1]

When Paul nevertheless says of the law that it cannot give life (Gal. iii.21), it is because no one carries it out, not by any means because perhaps Paul considers the works of the law to be sin.[2] When works of the law are done amongst the Gentiles by nature, Paul recognises them as good works (Rom. ii.14).

Hence Paul considers the law, not in the first place as revelation, God's giving of Himself, although it is the chief prerogative of the Jew that the λόγια τοῦ θεοῦ have been entrusted to him (Rom. iii.2; cf. Rom. ix.4 f.). The fact that a man knows the law still does not mean for him participation with God. Only when he carries it out, is he justified before God (Rom. ii.13).[3] Within the sphere of the law, God governs his behaviour to man by that of man towards the law.[4] So it is just from here that the new message starts, and not by criticising the law for its regulations.[5]

Paul considers that what the law demands and 'the good' are the same. This does not mean that the law derives its authority only from the fact that it is obviously good, but that a man's wrongdoing is equivalent to the Jew's transgressing of the law. In the same way knowledge of what is good is equivalent to acquaintance with the law.

---

[1] Ἰουδαῖος is synonymous with ὑπὸ νόμου εἶναι in I Cor. ix.20 ff.; cf. Lohmeyer, pp. 22 f.; cf. also TWNT III, pp. 382 ff., on Paul's use of the term Ἰουδαῖος.

[2] cf. Schlatter, *Theologie der Apostel* (²1922), p. 281.

[3] Contrary to G. Kuhlmann, *Theologia naturalis bei Philon und bei Paulus* (1930), pp. 114 ff.; K. Barth, *Der Römerbrief* (⁶1929), on Rom. ii.

[4] cf. H. Asmussen, *Theologische-kirchliche Erwägungen zum Galaterbrief* (1935): no. 188 on iii, 10 ff.; Schlatter, *op. cit.* (p. 102, n. 2), on x.5. Lohmeyer, pp. 31, 49.

[5] cf. Schlatter, *Theologie der Apostel*, 289 ff.

This becomes particularly clear when Rom. ii.6 is placed beside Rom. ii.12 ff. The ἔργον ἀγαθόν in verse 7 and the κατεργάζεσθαι τὸ κακόν in verse 9 are judged by the same yardstick as the 'being a ποιητὴς νόμου' or the ἐν νόμῳ ἁμαρτάνειν in verses 12 f. Hence this does not mean that the Jew may neglect the actual law in favour of something good which he possesses and must do,[1] but that the Gentile cannot be excused, although he is not acquainted with the law. Alternatively it is a matter of giving reasons for the statement: οὐ γάρ ἐστιν προσωπολημψία παρὰ τῷ θεῷ in Rom. ii.11. God gives his verdict on the sin of Gentiles also according to what is right. It is significant that Paul does not bring forward in support of this the rabbinic theory that the law was once delivered to all nations. He appeals instead to the assent of men to the verdict of καθῆκον (Rom. i.28). He appeals also to their awareness that the μὴ καθήκοντα named in Rom. i.29 f. are worthy of death (Rom. i.32) and to their knowledge of what it is good to do which shows itself both in the phenomenon of the conscience[2] which judges an action, and in the phenomenon of the ethical discussion[3] (Rom. ii.15).

Nevertheless men alien from the faith in Christ are differentiated in the main by the possession of the law.[4] Hence different arguments are used in Rom. ii, in verses 12 ff. for those who do not possess the law and in verses 17 ff. for those who do (cf. also Rom. iii.1 ff.,

[1] Lohmeyer, p. 32. The demands of the law and the 'good' are also equated in Rom. vii.19, 22.

[2] The conscience is not brought forward in Rom. ii.11 as a source of advice on ethics, but as a court of justice for judging actions. Cf. W. Gutbrod, Die paulinische Anthropologie (1934), pp. 55 f.; Schlatter, op. cit. (p. 102, n. 2), on ii.15.

[3] That is the point of the sentence: μεταξὺ ἀλλήλων τῶν λογισμῶν κατηγορούντων ἢ καὶ ἀπολογουμένων.

[4] cf. Brandt, p. 26.

ix.4 f.; Gal. ii.15). But just at the point which is
decisive for Paul, Jews and Gentiles now after all draw
closer together, for neither can be justified by their
keeping of the law or by some other form of goodness,
because they have all sinned (Rom. iii.23). So both
alike are dependent on faith in Christ alone, and in this
are bound together in unity (Gal. iii.28 *et passim*).
For one God stands over both parts of mankind (Rom.
iii.29 f.).

(*c*) Now this understanding of the law explains also
its effect when it comes into contact with sinful man.

(i) The relationship of the law to sin is firstly quite
simply that it forbids. The law's prohibition of sin
expresses negatively the fact that the law is the good
purpose of God. It says for example in Rom. vii.7:
οὐκ ἐπιθυμήσεις. The question in Rom. vi.15 probably
cannot be understood completely if it is not taken for
granted that the law is a defence against sin; in that
case the question is whether sin is not unavoidable if
the law is abolished.[1] Thus Paul adhered on the whole
to the firmly negative nature of the law, as well as to
the negative form of the Decalogue. The law is God's
word addressed to sin. Admittedly the law is summarised positively in the statement: ἀγαπήσεις τὸν
πλησίον σου ὡς σεαυτόν (Rom. xiii.9; Gal. v.14). But
this does not alter the fact that to start with the law
forbids τῷ πλησίον κακὸν ἐργάζεσθαι (Rom. xiii.10) as
a sin.

(ii) The law by forbidding sin at the same time reveals it. Sin is revealed in its sinfulness and its nature
as rebellion against God is made clear by the law. Sin
is indeed already there before man comes in touch
with the law (Rom. v.13, vii.9), but through the law
it springs to life: ἐλθούσης δὲ τῆς ἐντολῆς ἡ ἁμαρτία

[1] cf. Schlatter, *op. cit.* (p. 102, n. 2), *ad loc.*; on this also Schlatter,
ib. on xiii.8 f.

ἀνέζησεν (Rom. vii.9). Through the command, sin
produces lust (Rom. vii.8). Thus Rom. vii.7 can mean
that through the law sin first became a reality for me
and does not simply become known to me.[1] Perhaps
too the sentence in Rom. iv.15: οὗ δὲ οὐκ ἔστιν νόμος
οὐδὲ παράβασις is to be understood in the same sense,
namely that it is the law which really turns sin into
rebellion.[2] Rom. v.20 is quite unequivocal: νόμος δὲ
παρεισῆλθεν ἵνα πλεονάσῃ τὸ παράπτωμα (cf. Gal. iii.19);
or . . . ἵνα γένηται καθ' ὑπερβολὴν ἁμαρτωλὸς ἡ ἁμαρτία
δία τῆς ἐντολῆς (Rom. vii.13). Paul can actually call
this effect of the law its purpose (Rom. v.20; Gal.
iii.19), because no effect of the law can come about
apart from the divine purpose. It is true that thereby
the statement that the law procures life for him who
keeps it has an air of unreality; so there must always
be added to it in thought an emphatic 'only'.[3]

(iii) When it is said that by the law sin is forbidden
and intensified to actual rebellion against God, the
condemnation of sin is pronounced at the same time.
ἁμαρτία δὲ οὐκ ἐλλογεῖται μὴ ὄντος νόμου (Rom. v.13).
The fact of transgressing the law, of rebelling against
God places man under the κατάκριμα (Rom. viii.1). In
fact the law does not only signify the condemnation of
sin in practice, but also as scripture declares this condemnation and demands submission to this verdict. In
Rom. iii.19 the law speaks in the manner described in
Rom. iii.10 ff.: ἵνα πᾶν στόμα φραγῇ καὶ ὑπόδικος γένηται
πᾶς ὁ κόσμος τῷ θεῷ. Rom. ii.12 reads: ὅσοι ἐν νόμῳ
ἥμαρτον, διὰ νόμου κριθήσονται. Thus the law turns sin

[1] cf. W. G. Kümmel, *Röm. vii und die Bekehrung des Paulus*
(1929), pp. 44 ff.
[2] Unless this sentence is to be explained with Schlatter, *op. cit.*
(p. 102, n. 2), *ad loc.*, as meaning the abolition of the law brought
about in Christ and therewith the abolition of guilt.
[3] The fact that the purpose of the law is to intensify sin, can be
understood and endured only when the end of the law is in sight.

into a deadly power (I Cor. xv.56; Rom. vii.9 f.), for it produces wrath (Rom. iv.15). By this means the law leads him who listens to it aright to the knowledge of sin (Rom. iii.20)[1] (perhaps Rom. vii.7 is also to be understood in this sense). Paul is, it is true, not really concerned with this in the sense that by the knowledge made possible for him by sin man receives a subjective insight into his need for salvation, but in the sense that there is no appeal to the law before God, since it is just this which unmasks man as a sinner.

This is also why it is intelligible that Paul finds no room for the attempt to make amends for deeds transgressing the law by means of deeds fulfilling the law. By transgression, rebellion against God takes place and God's judgement is provoked. This unifies the concept of sin; sin is no longer the adding together of separate offences, just as obedience can only be one whole, not the adding together of separate good deeds. By attempting to reckon up the good deeds against the bad ones man half absolves himself from God's demands and by this endeavour transforms the nature of obedience into its opposite.

(iv) As a result of all this, the real effect of the law is to keep a man subject to his sin. As the prison holds the prisoner captive, as the παιδαγωγός keeps the boy under his authority, so man is locked up by the law under sin—and this happens according to the verdict of the law, which means according to the purpose of God (Gal. iii.22 ff.). Thus the law, rightly understood, simply prevents man's every effort to obtain righteousness in the sight of God in any other way than by faith in Christ Jesus, through the forgiving grace of God. This is different from the way promised to Abraham,

[1] This passage takes no account of the question whether in fact the law can or must lead man to this knowledge even without faith in Christ.

precisely because it holds a man to be responsible for his sin. According to Paul this is the actual connexion between the law and Christ. For the law is not primarily that which leads to Christ by creating the awareness of the need for redemption.

The law has this effect only because it constrains a man by the authority of God. Every challenge can give rise to awareness of human imperfection. But only God's good purpose creates the position of a man lawfully condemned before Him, whether man rejects this purpose or acknowledges it and desires to carry it out (Rom. vii.7).

(v) This describes what Paul calls the weakness of the law. It lies essentially in the fact that it cannot deal with sin otherwise than by prohibition and condemnation. The law is weak $\delta\iota\grave{a}$ $\tau\hat{\eta}s$ $\sigma\alpha\rho\kappa\acute{o}s$ (Rom. viii.3) owing to the fact of sin which the law cannot overcome. Thus the weakness of the law can also be expressed by saying that it is not capable of making alive (Gal. iii.21). Indeed on the contrary through sin it produces death (Rom. vii.9 f.; I Cor. xv.56). Moreover this is also intended when the law as the letter which kills is contrasted with the spirit which gives life (II Cor. iii.6 ff.). It is a splendid duty to serve the law written on tables of stone, for it is the revealed purpose of God. But its effect is condemnation and death, because it approaches man from the outside and does not stir him from the centre of his being. It lets him go on living as the sinner that he is; indeed it holds him fast to this sin, without its being possible to remove this sin from him. Thus II Cor. iii.6 contains substantially the same idea as for instance Rom. vii or Gal. iii, and does not convey the contrast between the religion of the letter and the religion of conviction which has been a favourite interpretation of this verse.

The fact that Paul perceived the effect of the law in

this way is perhaps expressed most clearly by his inclusion of it amongst the στοιχεῖα τοῦ κόσμου (Gal. iv.3, 9; Col. ii.8, 20). The meaning of this term is brought out most clearly in Col. ii. 20: He who dies with Christ to the στοιχεῖα τοῦ κόσμου should not submit to orders as though he were still ἐν κόσμῳ. In Gal. iv.3, 9 too the emphasis no doubt rests on κόσμος. The law is something which belongs to the characteristic permanent substance of this world[1] and therefore cannot lead beyond this condition and give release from bondage to sin. Yet this weakness of the law exists not in spite of, but on account of its holiness as a revelation of the purpose of God with which it confronts men (cf. Rom. vii.14).

(d) This radical understanding of the law by Paul is intelligible only with his spiritual point of departure in mind, namely that the act of forgiveness and justification is accomplished by the cross of Christ and by this means man's relationship to God is established anew by him, apart from man's achievement and hence apart from the law. Paul's negation of the law springs from his affirmation of what has taken place in Jesus Christ, and not from a judgement based on reason nor from missionary tactics. Righteousness before God was bestowed on man through the cross not on account of what man did, but because he was taken up in mercy into this death, that is to say, through faith. For this reason the negation is necessary (Rom. iii.21 ff.). Hence it is Paul's aim to be found in Christ: μὴ ἔχων ἐμὴν δικαιοσύνην τὴν ἐν νόμου, ἀλλὰ τὴν διὰ πίστεως Χριστοῦ, τὴν ἐκ θεοῦ δικαιοσύνην (Phil. iii.9). οὐδὲν ἄρα νῦν κατάκριμα τοῖς ἐν Χριστῷ Ἰησοῦ (Rom. viii.1).

But apart from the death of Christ and from death in

[1] cf. M. Dibelius, *Die Geisterwelt im Glauben des Paulus* (1909), p. 84.

Christ, man is still ἐν κόσμῳ and hence handed over to
the law (Col. ii.20). So the sentence in Rom. x.4:
τέλος γὰρ νόμου Χριστὸς εἰς δικαιοσύνην παντὶ τῷ πιστεύοντι,
does not simply mean that the period of the law is over
with the coming of Christ, that the law and Christ
succeed each other in temporal history, nor even in
religious history, but in 'salvation-history'. Only when
a man lets himself appropriate the righteousness of
God in Christ, is the law abolished for him. Paul
expresses this by saying that removal from the sphere
of the law takes place only by dying (Rom. vii.1 ff.;
Gal. ii.19; Col. ii.20). Now this dying is nothing other
than having a share in Christ's death: ἐθανατώθητε
τῷ νόμῳ διὰ τοῦ σώματος τοῦ Χριστοῦ (Rom. vii.4);
Χριστῷ συνεσταύρωμαι (Gal. ii.19); ἀπεθάνετε σὺν Χριστῷ
(Col. ii.20). Beside this there stands baptism into
Christ, through which we are sons of God and no
longer slaves and hence no longer subjected to the law
(Gal. iii towards the end). In Rom. vi baptism and
death with Christ are again combined.[1] Now all this
means simply that the relationship with God now rests
no longer with man himself. Thus the law as the road
to salvation is now barred; Christ has stepped into its
place. Therefore man is now forbidden to desire still
to become righteous through the law after God has
revealed himself in Jesus Christ as the one who for-
gives, who justifies the sinner and not the man who is
just by his own efforts (Rom. iv.5). Consequently
he who still expects righteousness from the fulfilment of the law has caused Christ to die in vain (Gal.
ii.21).

(e) The positive connexion between the law and
Christ is preserved by understanding the cross as an
affirmation of the law. Firstly, it affirms its verdict.
Dying to the law, being crucified together with Christ

[1] cf. Gutbrod, pp. 190 ff.

happens precisely διὰ νόμου (Gal. ii.19).[1] Gal. iii.13
makes this still clearer: Χριστὸς ἡμᾶς ἐξηγόρασεν ἐκ τῆς
κατάρας τοῦ νόμου γενόμενος ὑπερ ἡμῶν κατάρα (cf.
II Cor. v.21: *Christ was made to be sin for us*); and so the
law's sentence of condemnation on sin reached its
fulfilment in the cross of Christ (Rom. v.6 ff.). This is
not in fact worked out explicitly in this sense in Paul's
writings, but it follows from the logic of the argument
that the cross of Christ is also the fulfilment of the law
in so far as the law's cardinal purpose came to fulfilment in the cross. The cross is the consummation of
obedience to God (Phil. ii.5 ff.), and at the same time
it is love to men made perfect (Rom. viii.34). After all
just this is the real purpose of the law. Thus it is also
disobedience to the law to desire it to be different from
this, its fulfilment. To state that here the law is fulfilled and to emphasise this fact is not Paul's present
purpose, for otherwise the primacy of the law would
have lain very near; but it was very much to his
purpose to show how faith in Christ brings the law to
fulfilment in the believer.

Through faith alone a complete recognition of the
verdict implicit in the law is reached, whilst the attempt
to be justified through the works of the law necessarily
weakens the verdict or renders it ineffective. This is
why Rom. i-iii and Rom. vii were written. But the
new obedience has its roots in dying with Christ, in
whom the relationship to God has been established
apart from the law by God's act (Rom. vi.11 ff.), and
by the same process the fruit of the Spirit springs up by
faith (Gal. v.22). The law attains its fulfilment, at
any rate negatively in the first place, by its condemnation not being challenged (Gal. v.23). This is true

[1] Zahn, *Galater* (³1922), *ad loc.* interprets this διὰ νόμου thus:
because the law showed me my need for redemption and referred
me to faith.

because its demands can be summed up in the command to love (Gal. v.14; Rom. xiii.10). In fact the twofold command to love (probably referring to Jesus in Matt. xxii.36 ff.) can be called simply the νόμος so that the command to love one's neighbour is ὁ ἕτερος νόμος (Rom. xiii.8); ὁ νόμος τοῦ Χριστοῦ in Gal. vi.2 no doubt means the same thing. Thus the real purpose of the law is fulfilled in the case of the man who has been taken up into love through Christ. Rom. viii.4: ἵνα τὸ δικαίωμα τοῦ νόμου πληρωθῇ ἐν ἡμῖν τοῖς μὴ κατὰ σάρκα περιπατοῦσιν ἀλλὰ κατὰ πνεῦμα. Paul can therefore say in Rom. iii.31 not only that through the gospel of justification by faith is the law not abolished, but that it is really upheld for the first time, and as a matter of fact the law in this passage is used not in the sense of making a promise (cf. Rom. iv), nor as condemning (cf. Rom. iii.10 ff.), but in its specific sense of giving commands.

Now by the acceptance of Jesus' death in faith, the law is brought to its fulfilment in accordance with its real purpose, namely union with God in obedience and love of one's neighbour. But in addition Paul recognises as well the fulfilment of the actual OT law from love and from obedience. It is true that he takes his stand primarily against any attempt to demand this fulfilment of the OT law, and equally that of a Christian rule, with the idea that it is necessary in order to be justified before God.[1] But he was ready himself to observe the Mosaic law in order to further the gospel amongst the Jews (I Cor. ix.20 ff.). Indeed he can advise one born a Jew not to remove the marks of circumcision (I Cor. vii.18 ff.). This does not mean that Paul retreats from his doctrine of justification into a 'legal' way of thinking, but that he is thoroughly

[1] Thus in particular Gal. ii.3 ff. on the conflict about the circumcision of Titus; also Gal. ii.11 ff. in the controversy with Peter.

consistent in his teaching about justification and in his preaching about freedom in Christ, since man can now even refrain from making use of his freedom for the sake of his love towards a weaker brother, or perhaps to build up the community, or because he just happens to be in a particular position. He is in no way justified because he carries out the law and makes use of his knowledge and the freedom he has obtained by it. On the contrary, his only claim is that he is known by God (I Cor. viii.3).

Finally Paul uses the law in addition in order to find in it guidance for the actual life of the community, that is to say, in the διδαχή. In I Cor. ix.8 f.; xiv.21, 34 the law is employed to supply by allegorical exegesis an answer (or, as the case may be, a confirmation of the answer already discussed) to questions concerning the community life. But it is noteworthy here that the argument from the law is not adduced as the decisive proof, but as the confirmation of what has been already recognised as right from other considerations.[1] The OT is not understood here to be a law to be obeyed; it has not the weight attached in Judaism to an appeal to the law. Moreover on the whole this use of the law plays no great part.[2] At any rate when the community conducts itself as the law requires, this behaviour is not to be justified merely by appeal to the law. For only that is considered right and must be respected which is the outcome of obedience to Christ in faith, according to the measure of faith given to each one (Rom. xiv.1 ff., xii.3). Sin is no longer that which does not proceed from the law, but that which does not proceed from faith (Rom. xiv.23).

---

[1] This shown by the καί in I Cor. xiv.34 and I Cor. ix.8.
[2] cf. the absence of νόμος in Rom. xii ff. (except in xiii.8 ff.; but here the actual law itself is replaced by the command to love). Moreover it is absent in Thessalonians and II Corinthians.

(f) No simple answer can be given to the question as to the origin of this understanding of the law by Paul. There is no sufficient basis in exegesis for the theory that his own painful experience when faced by the demands of the law[1] and his sense of unworthiness with regard to the law led Paul to hold this view of it.[2] On the one hand this is not required by Rom. vii, and on the other it is made practically impossible by Phil. iii.6: κατὰ δικαιοσύνην τὴν ἐν νόμῳ γενόμενος ἄμεμπτος.

Yet it is a fact that for Paul the point of view from which he regards his attitude to the law is determined decisively by his faith in the divine revelation which took place on the cross of Christ. This raises the more precise question, as to how far his doctrine concerning the law really sprang from the consistent working out of his faith in the crucified as it affected the law, or how far it was only the criterion by which to accept or reject those solutions and answers regarding the problem of the law which were already championed before him and around him. This is not the place in which to supply the answer to this question.

At all events Paul had from the beginning a penetrating view of the contrast between the way of the law and that of faith.[3] Indeed he had probably already before his conversion seen in the law the line of cleavage between Judaism and Christianity. A gradual development of his understanding of the law either in the

---

[1] Thus e.g. Grafe, pp. 13 ff. In Gal. ii.16 too the εἰδότες does not suggest that this knowledge was brought about as a result of experience.

[2] This theory arose mainly through transferring the course of Luther's development to that of Paul. Cf. Lietzmann on Gal. vii; for a criticism, Lohmeyer, pp. 5 ff.

[3] cf. Schlatter, *Geschichte des ersten Christentums*, p. 127. Certainly Gal. v.11 may not be understood as a backward glance at a Christian ministry by Paul in which he required circumcision as necessary to salvation.

direction of tightening it up[1] or toning it down[2] is in
any case not probable for the crucial points.[3]

C.   *The Period after the conflict concerning the law*

1.   *The Letter to the Hebrews*

νόμος is used in Hebrews with a meaning similar to
that used elsewhere in the NT. As a rule it is the OT
law. Only in vii.16 is it open to question whether the
translation should not be more generally 'rule' or
'ordinance'[4]; but as this is the only passage in the letter,
it would be better to explain it here too as the OT law.
ἐντολῆς σαρκίνης would in that case no doubt have to be
understood as a genitive expressing the content,[5] i.e.
according to the law concerning bodily commandments.
The plural of νόμος appears indeed twice in Hebrews,
but only in quotations (viii.10, x.16). As in the case
of Paul, there is no basic difference between ὁ νόμος
and νόμος. Even vii.12, for example, is not intended to
be a generally valid rule, but applies only to the OT
law in particular. Perhaps sometimes its subject-
matter does not include the whole OT law, but in the
first instance that part of it concerned with the ministry
of the priests and the priesthood, for example ix.22:
σχεδὸν ἐν αἵματι πάντα καθαρίζεται κατὰ τὸν νόμον. But
in no case is there intended to be a fundamental distinction. Just when it is contrasted with ἐντολή as the
single commandment, νόμος does usually mean the
OT law as a whole (e.g. vii.5).

(*a*) The fact that the meaning of νόμος tends to be
the law ordering the ministry of the priests is due to

---

[1] Thus C. Clemen, *Die Chronologie der paulinischen Briefe* (1893),
especially pp. 256 ff.; but cf. ThLZ (1902)No. 8, col. 233.

[2] Thus Sieffert in: *Theologische Studien ... B. Weiss ... dargebracht*
(1897).   [3] cf. Juncker, pp. 171 ff.; Grafe, pp. 27 ff.

[4] Thus e.g. F. Bleek, *Der Brief an die Hebräer* II, 2(1840) *ad loc.*

[5] cf. Blass, *Grammatik des neutestl. Griechisch*, ed. Debrunner,
ed. 6, § 167. (Cf. above p. 103, n. 1.)

this being the chief concern of the letter. The point of view from which the law is regarded in Hebrews is essentially different from, for example, that of Jesus or Paul. By them the law is seen as the purpose of God which requires and controls a man's actions, which aims at works, and gives life to him who puts it into practice. In Hebrews on the contrary the law is treated as that which gives to the priesthood its underlying principle, its dignity and its importance. It has a share in the nature and efficacy of this priestly ministry, and so this nature and efficacy depend on the fact that it is based on the law.[1] This means of course at the same time that the theme of Hebrews is not concerned with the relationship between law and gospel, but with that between the OT ministry of the priests and the priestly ministry and priesthood of Jesus. The comparison is extended to the law only in so far as the efficacy of the OT priests' ministry is due to its being founded on the law.

How much the fact of its being anchored to the law contributes to the importance of the OT priesthood[2] is shown not only by the frequent emphatic κατὰ τὸν νόμον or κατὰ νόμον in vii.5, viii.4, x.8,[3] but especially by some passages giving technical arguments.

The glory of Christ's priesthood depends upon this very circumstance that he is not a priest κατὰ νόμον ἐντολῆς σαρκίνης but κατὰ δύναμιν ζωῆς ἀκαταλύτου (vii.16). But this cannot do away with the fact that in

---

[1] Admittedly in x.28 νόμος also occurs with the meaning usual elsewhere: *he who violates the law must die; how much more he who has spurned the Son of God!* Cf. also ii.2. But these passages simply demonstrate the fact that the problem concerning the duty of obeying the actual law has ceased to exist. On this question cf. Brandt, pp. 34 f.

[2] cf. Th. Haering, *Der Brief an die Hebräer* (1925), pp. 62 ff.

[3] κατά passes here from the sense of 'according to', 'in the manner of' to that of 'in the strength of', and almost that of 'through'.

these statements the holiness of the law is recognised.[1]

(b) Although the OT priesthood derives its strength and authority from the law, it cannot produce the τελείωσις (vii.11). Therefore the same can be said of the law as well, on which the life of the priesthood depends: οὐδὲν γὰρ ἐτελείωσεν ὁ νόμος (vii.19).

The aim of the priestly ministry should really be to bring man near to God (vii.19), the τελείωσις and its prerequisite the καθαρίζειν τὴν συνείδησιν ἀπὸ νεκρῶν ἔργων εἰς τὸ λατρεύειν θεῷ ζῶντι (ix.14), in short ἀφαιρεῖν ἁμαρτίας (x.4).[2] This aim is summed up for instance in ix.28 or x.19 ff. For it is just that crucial part of what is bestowed on the believer through the true High Priest Christ to which the law and the priesthood depending on it could not attain, or could do so only inadequately.

The reason for this weakness and uselessness (ἀσθενὲς καὶ ἀνωφελές, vii.18) on account of which it could not attain to its object, is expounded in vii.18 ff., and this is again summed up in vii.28 in the antithesis: ὁ νόμος γὰρ ἀνθρώπους καθίστησιν ἀρχιερεῖς ἔχοντας ἀσθένειαν, ὁ λόγος δὲ τῆς ὁρκωμοσίας τῆς μετὰ τὸν νόμον υἱὸν εἰς τὸν αἰῶνα τετελειωμένον. Thus the weakness of the law and consequently of the OT priesthood lies essentially in

[1] The Epistle of Barnabas affords a typical contrast to this. In it the allegorical exegesis of the OT pointing to Christ leads even to the assertion that the actual carrying out of the commandments of the OT, for instance circumcision, is to be ascribed to the seduction of an evil angel (ix.4), since the commandment was from the beginning never intended to be carried out literally. Moreover in x.2: *So then it is not a commandment of God that they should not bite with their teeth* (i.e. the animals forbidden in the law), *but Moses spoke it in the spirit* (cf. x.9). This is a continuing development of the Hellenistic disintegration of the OT law in the manner of the Letter of Aristeas and Philo. In Hebrews this is simply not there, in spite of some formal similarities.

[2] As a matter of fact, sacrifice is looked upon in Hebrews mainly as expiation (v.1). Cf. Haering, pp. 42 f.

the weakness of the men with whom the law has
to do.

This weakness is seen in the mortal nature of the
priests (vii.24 ff.) and especially in the fact that they
must always first offer a sacrifice for themselves, that
is to say, that they are themselves bound up with sin
(vii.27: v.3). Connected with this is the fact that the
OT sacrifice cleanses merely externally, not from
within; this does away neither with the consciousness
of guilt nor with the sin itself (ix.9 f.). Hence, since the
law and its priesthood has to do with sinful men, it
cannot carry out its task; it cannot procure for men
access to the Holy of Holies, to God.

We may summarise the point thus: according to
Paul the law is weak because men do *not* do it, whilst
according to Hebrews it is so because it is *men* who do
it. The two statements start from different guiding
principles, but fundamentally they both contain the
same verdict. The close connexion between them is
seen in Hebrews by the use of Jer. xxxi.31 ff. where the
frailty of the old covenant is shown up by Israel's
violation of it. It is seen too in the fact that Jesus'
priestly ministry sanctifies better than the old one
because it is based on the sacrifice of obedience which
is well pleasing to God (x.5 ff.).

(*c*) At this point we find in Hebrews too the peculiar
turn of thought found in Paul. The verdict is pronounced in the light of the fulfilment,[1] and this verdict
is that the law not only could not reach its goal, but
also ought not to do so. On the contrary the law points
to Christ just because it holds man fast in sinfulness in
order to let him find access to God by the one manner

[1] In Hebrews too the verdict on the insufficiency of the old
worship of God does not issue from a rational criticism of it,
although sentences like ix.12a at first sound very much like this,
but from the fact of Jesus' High-priesthood, viii.1 ff., 10 ff.

proclaimed through the scripture, namely through the high-priestly ministry of Jesus alone. For the sacrifice offered in accordance with the law was the ἀνάμνησις ἁμαρτιῶν κατ᾽ ἐνιαυτόν (x.3), for the law has not the εἰκὼν τῶν πραγμάτων, but only the σκιὰ τῶν μελλόντων ἀγαθῶν (x.1).[1] So it was only with the new covenant of which Christ is the mediator that there could be a blotting out of τῶν ἐπὶ τῇ πρώτῃ διαθήκῃ παραβάσεων and a receiving of the promise (ix.15). Thus the eternal High-priesthood of Christ, which existed already before the law and was from the beginning above[2] the law, was announced by the figure of Melchizedek and was declared with an oath in Ps. cx to belong to Christ. This High-priesthood means not only the μετάθεσις νόμου (vii.5), but at the same time the fulfilment, the εἰκὼν τῶν πραγμάτων instead of only the temporary σκιὰ τῶν μελλόντων ἀγαθῶν (x.1).[3]

(d) In spite of all the differences from the Pauline understanding of the law, the strong resemblance is striking, particularly in the manner in which the old and new covenants are placed in relationship to each other, and the abrogation and the fulfilment of the old one by the new one are intertwined. Whether there are indeed direct Pauline influences here cannot be decided from these considerations. At any rate when comparing them we must observe that in Hebrews there is no question, or perhaps rather no longer any question, of the attempt to find in the law a demand for good actions to justify men. This circumstance links Hebrews in regard to the problem of the law more closely with John and James than with Paul.

[1] These good things are 'to come', no doubt from the stand-point of the law.

[2] This is the meaning of the elaborate proof that Levi paid tithes to Melchizedek in Abraham (vii.5 ff.).

[3] cf. Brandt, p. 40.

2. *The Letter of James*

The decisions on the questions as to when and by whom this letter was written and the interpretation of its understanding of the law are mutually dependent.[1] Unfortunately it must be admitted that there is not enough material to be quite sure of the interpretation. Yet two facts stand out. First the question of the relationship of faith and works is posed and answered without any reference to the law (ii.14 ff.). The subject is definitely the relationship of faith and works, not, as with Paul and his opponents, that of faith and law.

It is true that these questions overlap to a considerable extent, but they are not necessarily identical. Certainly ii.14 ff. is an attack on a misunderstood Paul,[2] but not in the name of the law, nor only with reference to the law, but in the name of showing faith in practice by works, by deeds of love (ii.16).

Second, where mention is made of νόμος, a qualifying phrase is often added: νόμος τέλειος τῆς ἐλευθερίας in i.25, νόμος ἐλευθερίας in ii.12, νόμοι βασιλικός in ii.8, which is evidently intended each time (or at least in the first two cases) to contrast what is meant here with some other meaning described by νόμος alone. Both these points probably indicate a time when the discussion of the primitive community about the law is still known, but a decision has already been made against the law.[3] The real danger is seen to be no longer either keeping the law or pushing it aside, but understanding faith in a wrong way, such as might derive from the Pauline answer to that question. This is completely

---

[1] cf. Dibelius, *Der Brief des Jakobus*, ed. Greeven (⁹1957), p. 15.

[2] We can leave the question open here whether the writer himself misunderstood Paul in this way or is only attacking a misunderstanding of this kind which owed its origin to Paul.

[3] cf. J. Marty, *L'Épitre de Jacques* (1935), pp. 248, 60; Dibelius, *Jakobus* on i.25 and ii.8.

independent of whether the writer is a Jew or not. (That he is one, appears almost conclusively from his style.)[1]

This general situation must explain those passages in which the law is mentioned: i.25, ii.8 ff., iv.11 ff.

(a) In i.25 the νόμος τέλειος τῆς ἐλευθερίας is substantially the same as, or at any rate belongs to, the λόγος ἔμφυτος δυνάμενος σῶσαι τὰς ψυχάς in verse 21, and παρακύψαι εἰς νόμον is the same as δοκεῖν θρησκὸν εἶναι and as θρησκεία in verse 26. Hence here the word of God, on which the position of Christians is established, is called νόμος.[2] It is therefore defined with regard to that aspect of its nature which is concerned not merely with passive acceptance, but with determining one's life, particularly, as verse 27 indicates, in deeds of love.[3] The addition τέλειος τῆς ἐλευθερίας then guards the expression against misunderstanding, as though it meant the command of the OT law. Therefore in so far as the gospel message lays claim to a man's life with respect to his actions also, it can be called νόμος,[4] though compared with the old law it is a perfect law of liberty. But what these phrases are intended to convey more precisely, does not appear clearly from this passage.[5] But light may be thrown on it by the two other passages.

(b) In ii.8 the νόμος is in the first place evidently not

[1] The use of νόμος too with or without the article without any difference of meaning points to this.

[2] Against A. Meyer, *Das Rätsel des Jakobus* (1930), pp. 153 ff.

[3] It is therefore perhaps not completely apposite when Windisch *Jakobusbrief*, speaks of a 'reduction' of the Torah to the 'religious and moral commandments'.

[4] The phrase 'the conception of Christianity itself as a law' (Weizsäcker, p. 365, ET, II p. 27) is at the very least a misleading one.

[5] The non-Christian parallels, cf. the commentaries *ad loc.*, do not enable us to understand this phrase so clearly as to yield an explanation by themselves. So the other statements in this letter are a better guide for exegesis.

simply another expression for the word of truth, but a command in the strict sense. The only question is whether it means the whole OT law including all its commandments, or their summary in the law of love.[1] At any rate verse 10 taken by itself can be understood to mean the whole OT law, including all its commands, represented as obligatory. Not only the attitude of the rest of the letter, however, but the context of the verse too refutes this interpretation: verse 8 says: *if you really fulfil the law of love you do well.* But then verse 9 adds: *yet if* προσωπολημψία *is found among you* (as it was described in ii.1 ff.) then it is a sin, and in fact just in view of this law; for only when the whole of the law is performed[2]—verse 10 can be rendered thus—can one escape condemnation. In that case the law in verses 9 f. would mean simply the law of love which in verse 8 was called the royal law, and βασιλικός would then describe the nature of this law as contrasted with another understanding of it, and not this one commandment alongside others equal to it in principle.[3] If those who are addressed should perchance justify their behaviour by an appeal to the law of love, which after all includes the rich man, the letter says to them: yes, certainly, but in that case this law too must be taken quite seriously. But by προσωπολημψία the law of love is denied (in an essential point)[4] and consequently this action is condemned by the commandment.[5]

[1] It may not simply be concluded that νόμος in James means the Decalogue, just because in verse 11 two commandments of it are used to illustrate the principle in verse 10.

[2] ἐν ἑνί need not mean: one commandment of the OT, but probably has a more general meaning: *in one point, in one particular way.*

[3] Both interpretations of βασιλικός are in themselves possible according to the usage outside the NT, cf. the commentaries *ad loc.*

[4] Marty, *ad loc.*

[5] To condone evil by reason of the good that was intended or by citing the commandment is rejected here as elsewhere in the NT.

If the passage is understood in this way, then we have a consistent picture, in which only the use of νόμος in verse 11 seems a little incongruous. But after all verse 11 is adduced as an example to corroborate verse 10 and does not quite fit into the train of thought. In that case τῆς ἐλευθερίας is probably added again in verse 12 just because of the different use of νόμος in this passage, a usage which corresponds more closely to the usual one. The νόμος ἐλευθερίας of verse 12 is thus the same as the νόμος βασιλικός of verse 8, that is to say the law of love, which is 'the law' in its true sense. It is therefore the standard for judging speech and action.

Hence an inner connexion can be effected between the conception of the law expressed here and that in i.25. In so far as the word is directed to a man's action, it is the law of love, and just for this reason it is the perfect law and not the sum of particular laws.

(c) Perhaps iv.11 f. throws light on the meaning of the phrase that the law is a law of liberty. The comparison of this passage with Rom. ii.1 f. or Matt. vii.1 ff. breaks down just at the point peculiar to James iv.11 f. For here alongside the judgement of others is placed not that of myself but that of the law, and only after that my own. A comparison with Rom. xiv.4 is the most likely.[1] In that case νόμος would mean here the purpose of God which alone holds good for the individual. Another person has no insight into this as a matter of course, because this purpose of God will not let itself be enmeshed in precise, unambiguous forms and actions.[2] To condemn another man because

because man has to do, not with commandments, but with God.
[1] Weizsäcker, p. 368, ET, II p. 31.
[2] cf. also the author's designation of himself as θεοῦ καὶ κυρίου Ἰησοῦ Χριστοῦ δοῦλος in i.1; Schlatter, Der Brief des Jakobus ([2]1956), on i.25.

his actions do not agree with what I consider to be right means arrogating to myself a judgement concerning the commandment which that other man should observe. But in doing so one is no longer a doer of the law.[1] Understood in this way the passage shows how serious is the statement that from the Christian point of view the law is a law of liberty which does not tie the individual down to fixed commandments but to the obedience of love with which he has just been commissioned. Thus this freedom is freedom through the bond of obedience to God, and therefore, in spite of its being free from the individual commandments, it no more hampers ethical guidance and instruction than it does in Paul. In fact it is this sense that this letter intends to give them. Indeed it does not confine the freedom of obedience anywhere within a scheme in the manner of a law.

Thus the letter of James in its understanding of the law is altogether in the Christian line of thought which bases its understanding of the law on the obedience of faith, but temporally it is remote from the actual conflict concerning the recognition of the OT law.

3. *The Gospel according to John*

νόμος occurs rather more frequently in John than in Matthew (14:8 times). Nevertheless the actual

---

[1] Schlatter, *Jakobus*, *ad loc.* offers for consideration a similar exegesis. Another exegesis of the passage assumes that καταλαλεῖν and κρίνειν νόμον is simply an expression for 'transgressing', in which case νόμος would be the law of love (cf. Windisch, *Jakobus*, *ad loc*; similarly also Harnack, *Jakobus*, *ad loc.*). In view of verse 12 this is less likely, for the sentence which says that lawgiving and judgement are united in God surely means that only He who has also given him the commandment, has the right to pass a verdict on each man's deeds.

problem of the law does not occupy nearly so pivotal a position as it does there.

The meaning of the word νόμος is the usual one. It is the Torah, especially the Pentateuch, e.g. i.45: ἔγραψεν Μωυσῆς ἐν τῷ νόμῳ καὶ οἱ προφῆται. But it occurs also in the broader sense, namely the OT generally: x.34: what is γεγραμμένον ἐν τῷ νομῳ ὑμῶν is a passage from the Psalms, so are xii.34, xv.25. Besides this, νόμος naturally has also the meaning of law in the actual sense, namely a command to do a particular thing, as for example in the discussion about Jesus' breaking of the sabbath in vii.19, 23. In this sense νόμος is also a legal ordinance, e.g. vii.51: μὴ ὁ νόμος ἡμῶν κρίνει τὸν ἄνθρωπον ἔαν μὴ ἀκούσῃ πρῶτον παρ' αὐτοῦ καὶ γνῷ τὶ ποιεῖ; or in xviii.31 in the mouth of Pilate: κατὰ τὸν νόμον ὑμῶν κρίνατε αὐτόν, or in the mouth of the Jews before Pilate in xix.7a where the indefinite form is required by the meaning.

As regards its content the chief point to notice is that the law does not particularly interest John as a possibility for the guidance or the organisation of human, or indeed of Christian, action. Even in those cases where the narrative is particularly concerned with Jesus' setting the law aside, e.g. chapters v (with vii.19 ff.) and ix, the subject of interest is not really the validity of the law, but these cases and questions provide the occasion and starting point for the development in each case of the real theme.

In John's gospel the interest lies in the first place in the law as revelation, and in this sense it is set over against Jesus.

(a) Thus we have especially i.17: ὁ νόμος διὰ Μωυσέως ἐδόθη, ἡ χάρις καὶ ἡ ἀλήθεια διὰ 'Ιησοῦ Χριστοῦ ἐγένετο. This must be understood with reference to verse 18. It is only in Jesus that God is really revealed, only here in the word made flesh does God really make Himself

known, and He does so in the gift of mercy and truth[1]
(vv. 14, 17). It is in accordance with this that a series
of expressions with which Jesus designates himself, or
with which he is designated, are contrasted with corresponding statements about the Torah. Jesus, the Light
(viii.12, ix.5, xii.35), contrasted with the Torah as the
light[2]; Jesus gives the water of life (ch. iv) contrasted
with the Torah without which Israel cannot live any
more than can fish without water[3]; Jesus, the bread
of life (ch. vi); Jesus as the Way, the Truth and the
Life (xiv.6); all these are paralleled by assertions about
the Torah.[4] So too does the designation of Jesus as the
logos made flesh, together with statements about the
pre-existence and the mediating activity of this logos
in creation.

But apart from the fact that these contrasts, which
are usually implicit, by no means apply to the Torah
alone,[5] it must be observed that the parallels are not
simply due to transferring the features associated with
the Torah mechanically and point by point so as to
make christological statements. In both places, in
John and in Jewish theology, these expressions are

[1] So it is not at all a question of a criticism of the kind suggested
by W. Bauer, *Johannesevangelium* (³1933), on i.16: As contrasted
with the high esteem in which Moses was held by the Jews 'the
Christian criticism shows that not even the whole extent of the
law goes back to Moses, much less that his actions should be considered as real divine actions (vi.32). Hence trust placed in him
is vain.' vii.22 is inclined rather to attribute a higher dignity to
circumcision because it goes even as far back as to the patriarchs.
Nor is the conclusion drawn from vi.32 consistent with the text.
[2] Strack-Billerbeck I p. 237d; K. H. Rengstorf 'Zu den
Fresken in der jüdischen Katakombe der Villa Torlonia in Rom'
ZNW 31 (1932), pp. 52 ff.   [3] Strack-Billerbeck, II, pp. 435 f.
[4] Strack-Billerbeck, II, pp. 482 ff.; for the whole argument cf.
Bornhäuser, *Das Johannesevangelium eine Missionsschrift für Israel*
(1928); also TWNT IV, p. 139.
[5] cf Bauer, *Johannesevangelium, ad loc.*

determined by the central statement in each case: in the Torah the divine revelation is present, and in Jesus the revelation is present. Now to the extent that in non-rabbinic circles other corresponding basic theories are to be found and lead to expressions of this kind, these statements about Jesus form a rival theory to these too. At any rate so far as the Torah is concerned it is contrasted as a word of revelation with the Son as the perfect revelation.

(*b*) But this does not mean that the relation between them is merely that of 'either-or'. There is also a definite inner connexion between the law as the word of the scripture and the revelation of God in Jesus.[1] In the law, in scripture, Jesus is attested and promised as the Christ, i.45: ὃν ἔγραψεν Μωυσῆς ἐν τῷ νόμῳ καὶ οἱ προφῆται εὑρήκαμεν (i.e. in Jesus): similarly in v.39 f. Even though the word νόμος is lacking here, it might after all in fact be used, as is shown by the section vii.19 ff. which no doubt fits into the context of ch. v. The scriptures bear witness to Jesus. In this sense John mentions the law several times: that which the law says or even commands is fulfilled in the existence and the activity of Jesus (viii.17, x.34, xii.34, xv.25).[2]

Certainly the emphasis here is placed strongly on the critical result of this relationship: when a man

---

[1] E. Hirsch states in *Das vierte Evangelium in seiner ursprünglichen Gestalt verdeutscht und erklärt* (1936) that 'the basic idea of the gospel, dominating the whole of it, is the fact that between Christianity and Judaism, between faith in the word which sets free and has life and the Jewish obligations which mean servitude, there exists an irreconcilable conflict' (pp. 78 f.). With regard to this statement it is not only questionable whether this really is the dominating basic idea of the gospel, but also whether the gospel shows only an irreconcilable conflict. Cf. also R. Bultmann, 'Hirschs Auslegung des Johannesevangelium', in *Evangelische Theologie* (1937), pp. 115 ff. especially 128 ff.

[2] So it is not a question of somehow adding the OT and the word of Jesus, as Bornhäuser, p. 77, understands John ii.22.

rejects Jesus as the Christ, his appeal to the law is seen to be rebellion against the scripture; thus especially v. 39 ff. Genuine faith with regard to Moses and with regard to the law, genuine listening to this revelation, must lead to the acknowledgement of Jesus. So rejection of Jesus is at the same time rejection of the revelation of the law. This means that the emphatic ὁ νόμος ὁ ὑμέτερος in viii.17, and ὁ νόμος ὑμῶν in x.34 are to be understood as meaning: it is just the law to which you appeal against me, it is just its testimony, which applies to me; therefore if you do not hear me, you do not hear the scripture either[1]—hence it does not mean 'your law with which I have nothing to do'.[2]

(c) Exactly the same relationship between Jesus and the law is shown in those passages too in which the law is thought of as the organisation of human activities. Firstly again in the antithesis: Jesus is bound solely to the will of the Father, not to the commands of the law (v.19) and accordingly the disciples are bound to the commandment given in the Son, which takes the place of the law for them and expresses itself in the law of love: ἐντολὴν καινὴν δίδωμι ὑμῖν, ἵνα ἀγαπᾶτε ἀλλήλους, . . . ἀγάπην ἔχητε ἐν ἀλλήλοις (xiii.34 f.). Verse 35 in particular shows how for the disciples the obligation to the Torah, for example, is replaced by their relationship to Jesus as his disciples, and this finds its appropriate expression in the law of love. Through this relationship they are released from that of a servant (xv.15). In Christ alone are they able to perform a fruitful work (xv.5).

And again there stands beside it the close positive connexion: He who genuinely carries out the law has

---

[1] cf. Zahn, *Das Evangeliun des Johannes* ([5,6]1921), on viii.17 and x.34. Zahn no doubt rightly compares the ὑμῖν in Matt. xxii.25. There is a greater difficulty with xv.25; yet cf. xvi.2.

[2] Thus xviii.31 in Pilate's mouth.

a share in Christ. Nathaniel is called to Jesus as
ἀληθῶς Ἰσραηλίτης, ἐν ᾧ δόλος οὐκ ἔστιν (i.47 ff.). No
doubt vii.17 belongs here too: ἐάν τις θέλῃ τὸ θέλημα
αὐτοῦ (sc. of God) ποιεῖν, γνώσεται περὶ τῆς διδαχῆς,
πότερον ἐκ τοῦ θεοῦ ἐστιν ἢ ἐγὼ ἀπ' ἐμαυτοῦ λαλῶ.

Now this at the same time implies the negative,
namely that the rejection of Jesus involves also the
rejection of the purpose of the law. In vii.19 the
design to kill Jesus lays bare the οὐ ποιεῖν τὸν νόμον.
Hatred of Jesus evades the commandment of the law
(vii.50 f.). When the Jews want to serve God by perse-
cuting the disciples, they do so because they know
neither the Father nor Jesus (xvi.3).[1]

Thus in so far as Jesus as the Son and Christ takes
the place in every respect of all the other mediators
and so of the Torah too, the Torah is thereby at the
same time abolished and fulfilled. The evidence of
this is that genuine listening to the law leads to faith in
Jesus and that rejection of Jesus is at the same time
rebellion against the law.

But the law is never used in John as a rule for the
Christian behaviour of the community. This is confirmed by the Johannine letters and similarly by the
Revelation of John. It is not a matter of chance
that νόμος is never found in any of these. John does
not even once bring forward the proof that when the
law of love is carried out the genuine purpose of the
law is fulfilled.

All this puts the gospel[2] into the generation and the
period after the real conflict concerning the recognition
of the law and sets it in this respect in a line with
James and Hebrews.

---

[1] cf. also iii.10: if Nicodemus were a true teacher in Israel,
Jesus' word would not be so incomprehensible to him.

[2] Though not necessarily the author too.

APPENDIX[1]

1. ἀνομία

THE privative prefix considered together with the
content of the word νόμος gives two shades of meaning
for ἀνομία. Either (a) it is a statement of fact: *there is or
was no law in existence*, 'without a (the) law', or (b) the
word means 'contrary to a (the) law'. In the latter
case it contains at the same time a judgement, since it
assumes that there is in fact a binding law. This gives
to ἀνομία the meaning of *wrongdoing, sin.* Yet actually
the two meanings cannot usually be at all strictly
separated from each other; the emphasis alone can be
shifted.

For (a) see P. Oxy. 1121.20; ἅπαντα ὡς ἐν ἀνομία(ι)ς
ἀπεσύλησαν[2]; Philo *Leg. All.* 3, 79: Melchizedek is a
law-abiding king, not a tyrant *the one being the author of
laws, the other of lawlessness* (ἀνομία). For (b) Philo *Conf.
Ling.* 108 speaks of *mob-rule* in which *injustice and lawlessness* (ἀνομία) *are paramount.* In *Ebr.* 143 ἀνομία and
ἀπαιδευσία (*ignorance*) are placed side by side. This is
found also in classical Greek, e.g. in Demosthenes
24.152: when a decision reached by ballot dissolves
the constitution νόμῳ καινῷ, this must not be called
νόμος but ἀνομία. So even if the change were made so
to say legally, it can be called ἀνομία.

In this sense ἀνομία can denote a total condition of
lawlessness or wickedness: Philo *Spec. Leg.* I.188:
*through their new obedience they have washed away their old
lawlessness* (ἀνομία). Yet ἀνομία, especially in the plural,

---

[1] For the words here discussed, cf. also the dictionaries.
[2] Preisigke's dictionary renders this: *as though there were no legal
protection.*

can equally well indicate a particular act. Ps. Sol.
xv.10: *Their* (i.e. *the sinners'*) *iniquities* (ἀνομίαι) *shall
pursue them unto Sheol beneath* (cf. also *Papiri Florentini*
382,49).

In the LXX ἀνομία occurs frequently, yet it has no
constant Hebrew equivalent. It corresponds most
often to ʿᵃwōn (*iniquity* c. 60 times), to 'ᵃwen (*evil*
c. 25 times, especially in the Psalms), to peša' (*sin*
c. 20 times), to tō 'ēbāh (*abomination* c 25 times, especially
in Ezekiel).[1] In the LXX ἀνομία has all the meanings
stated above. It occurs frequently in the plural and in
this form describes the individual deeds (e.g. Gen. xix.15:
lest you be dismayed with the evil deeds (ἀνομίαις) *of the city*).
The state of ἀνομία is seen e.g. in Ps. xxxii.5 (LXX
xxxi.5): *I did not hide my* ἀνομία), xvii.24 *et passim.*
Generally no direct reference is made to the law, or at
any rate not to an essentially greater extent than is on
the whole usual in the case of the OT idea of sin,
which is after all naturally brought into line with the
commandments of God. So it is of course natural that
ἀνομία becomes one of the main terms for sin. Growing
standardisation and colourlessness here go together.

In the NT ἀνομία has the same range as elsewhere.
In the plural (only in quotations), it means the simple
sinful act; in this connexion no thought is given to its
association with the law as the yardstick by which the
deed in question is shown to be a sin (Rom. iv.7;
Heb. x.17; so too in a variant reading in Heb. viii.12).
In Titus ii.14 (a quotation) ἀπὸ πάσης ἀνομίας must be
understood less definitely as a general condition because
it is contrasted with ζηλωτὴς καλῶν ἔργων.

In Rom. vi.19 ἀνομία as a single act occurs beside
ἀνομία for the general condition of being alienated from
the law brought about by such acts, though this is

[1] Besides these it corresponds to about 20 other Hebrew words,
but only once to most of these.

understood not as a statement but as a judgement.
Service to sin leads to a general condition of ἀνομία.
Similarly (in an antithesis) we find in Heb. i.9 (a
quotation): ἠγάπησας δικαιοσύνην καὶ ἐμίσησας ἀνομίαν
and analogous to this in II Cor. vi.14: δικαιοσύνη and
ἀνομία are mutually exclusive, like faith and unbelief,
Christ and Belial. Since Paul is speaking here to a
Christian community which is not tied to the standard
of the OT law, it is evident that here ἀνομία does not
derive its chief meaning from the OT, but means
simply sin, unrighteousness. The same holds good for
ἄνθρωπος τῆς ἀνομίας in II Thess. ii.3. Verse 4 depicts
what are the consequences of ἀνομία. It is true that
this behaviour is also contrary to the commandment
of the OT, but the judgement expressed here is both
more explicit and more general, and ἀνομία has in fact
no meaning other than that of ἁμαρτία which is a
reading found in some texts. The same is true of
μυστήριον τῆς ἀνομίας in verse 7. The expression
ἀποστασία in verse 3 is of primary significance for the
description which follows.

In Matthew ἀνομία may allude more definitely to
the law and its violation; at least this is likely in Matt.
xxiii.28 where it is said particularly to those practising
legal piety ἔσωθεν δὲ ἐστε μεστοὶ ὑποκρίσεως καὶ ἀνομίας.
There is a less close connexion with the law in Matt.
vii.23, xiii.41 (both are quotations) and in xxiv.12.

I John iii.4: πᾶς ὁ ποιῶν τὴν ἁμαρτίαν καὶ τὴν ἀνομίαν
ποιεῖ, καὶ ἡ ἁμαρτία ἐστὶν ἡ ἀνομία is not completely clear.
The obvious explanation is no doubt: if a man does
ἁμαρτία his action is at the same time judged to be
ἀνομία. In that case the meaning of ἁμαρτία would be
more or less fixed and defined (hence the article: τήν);
the sentence would be aimed at people who perhaps
say: The ἁμαρτία if it exists is not serious. It cannot be
held against one who has made a true confession, the

spiritual man. But if ἀνομία contains thus for readers and the writer a derogatory verdict which ἁμαρτία apparently did not have for every one without qualification, then this can hardly be due in I John to a reference to the OT law inherent in the word.[1] On the contrary ἀνομία can have its own emphasis even with a more general meaning, which would amount more or less to *rebellion against, resistance to* God, *estrangement from* God, and this would be supported by verses 6b, 9 f. Then a free translation of iii.4 would be roughly: *everyone who commits sin is thereby in a state of rebellion against God, indeed sin is nothing but revolt against God.*

Yet it may be asked whether it would not also be possible to assume νόμος in the sense understood by Christians, for whom the command to love God and one's neighbour means the law of Christ and so 'the law' in its real sense. The allusion to the achievement of Jesus in verse 5 and especially in verse 11 could support this.[2]

2. ἄνομος

Concerning ἄνομος *having no law* essentially the same

---

[1] If the passage is to be understood as a clear repudiation of antinomianism (thus Windisch, *Die Katholischen Briefe* ([2]1930, [3]1951), *ad loc.*) then the sentence must be automatically inverted and understood as 'ἀνομία is ἁμαρτία', and this is not possible because of the first part of the verse.

[2] It will hardly be practicable to think of so distinguishing ἁμαρτία and ἀνομία in meaning that ἀνομία as a sin against the law would at the same time be a sin against one's neighbour, whilst ἁμαρτία would be sin against God, (or even the other way round with a corresponding alteration in the sense). In that case the sentence would be directed against a separation of the two by saying that sin against God includes also the violation of the command which directs me to my neighbour (thus e.g. also H. H. Wendt, *Die Johannesbriefe und das johanneische Christentum* (1925), pp. 60 f.

may be said as concerning ἀνομία which is derived from
it. The emphasis can be laid (a) on the objective fact
that *a or the law does not exist* (which naturally is rare,
since in general there are laws everywhere; but cf.
e.g. Plat. *Polit.* 302e); or (b), and this is the usual
meaning, on the subjective attitude, i.e. *paying no
regard to the (existing) law, behaving as if there were no
law(s)*. Since other people as a rule regard this as
wrong, this involves expressing a judgement. In this
case ἄνομος easily acquires the more general sense of
unrighteous, with no strict allusion to a particular law.

In Judaism ὁ ἄνομος or οἱ ἄνομοι often denote the
Gentiles. Here it is difficult to distinguish where this
only states that they do not have the law or where
it passes judgement on them as sinners. Usually the
latter view seems to prevail. In Ps. Sol. xvii.18: *Over
the whole earth were they scattered by lawless men* (ὑπὸ
ἀνόμων). It is said of Pompey in Ps. Sol. xvii.11: *The
lawless one* (ὁ ἄνομος) *laid waste our land*. Here ἄνομος
has the more general meaning of *evil-doer*. In the LXX
ἄνομος occurs about 30 times for *reša'* (*wicked*) and in
other places too for more than 25 Hebrew equivalents,
mostly indeed only once each. There can be no exact
Hebrew equivalent in this case any more than in that
of ἀνομία, if only for the reason that there is no privative
prefix in Hebrew.

In the New Testament ἄνομος is used occasionally
simply to state a fact. When in Rom. ii.12 ἀνόμως
ἁμαρτάνειν and ἐν νόμῳ ἁμαρτάνειν are placed side by
side, the former means simply that the sin was committed without knowledge of the law. Similarly the
ἄνομοι of I Cor. ix.21 to whom Paul accommodates
himself are distinguished from those who are ὑπὸ νόμου
by the fact that they are actually ignorant of the law
and are not aware of any obligation to it. οἱ ἄνομοι
also occurs in a weaker sense in Luke xxii.37 (quota-

tion), and also in a variant reading in Mark xv.28
and in Acts ii.23 (here for the Gentiles).

But I Cor. ix.21 in particular shows how definitely
the meaning of ἄνομος nevertheless includes a judgement. For Paul immediately takes steps to counter a
very obvious misunderstanding by saying that he was
to these ἄνομοι indeed ὡς ἄνομος but that he was not
on that account ἄνομος θεοῦ (cf. ἔννομος below).

If ἄνομος is intended to convey a judgement, it does
not always even in the New Testament refer to the law
in particular, but has a more general meaning. Thus
clearly in I Tim. i.9: δικαίῳ νόμος οὐ κεῖται, ἀνόμοις δὲ
καὶ ἀνυποτάκτοις. Ἄνομοι are simply people who behave
wickedly. It is not implied in this expression, though
it is in the whole sentence, that this is something condemned by the law.[1] Similarly in a general sense in
II Peter ii.8: the people of Sodom vex Lot ἀνόμοις ἔργοις,
by their wicked doings. II Thess. ii.8 should not be
rendered by, for example, 'transgressor of the law' but
simply by 'evil-doers' (cf. ἀνομία, p. 135ff).

3. ἔννομος

ἔννομος is the counterpart of ἄνομος, but does not
occur so frequently. First it means simply according to
the law, he who (or that which) remains within the law
P. Oxy. 1204.24: ἵνα ἐννομώτερον ἀκουσθείη concerning
the trial which should be conducted in accordance
with the law. Aeschin. Tim. 3.230 mentions a measure
according to the law (ἔννομον), contrasted with one
that is contrary to the law (παρὰ νομον). Cf. Tim. 1.8;
Philo Abr. 242; Poster. C. 176. When applied to persons
ἔννομος means just, upright, cf. Plat. Resp. IV.424e.

---

[1] Debrunner indeed considers that the sentence would have
more point if the ἄνομοι were those who do not concern themselves with the laws (or the law), just as the ἀνυπότακτοι are those
who do not wish to submit to it (so privately).

In Judaism ἔννομος usually refers to the OT law. In Ecclus. Prol. 14: the grandfather wrote his book in order that the readers *might make progress much more by living according to the law* (διὰ τῆς ἐννόμου βιώσεως); the grandson translates it for those people who are *fashioning their manners beforehand to live according to the law* (ἐννόμως) (35 f.). More generally in Prov. xxxi.25: (the virtuous housewife) *opens her mouth wisely and according to law*.

In the New Testament ἔννομος occurs in Acts xix.39: the ἔννομος ἐκκλησία is the lawful, legally incontestable, legally summoned assembly, as contrasted with the riotous popular gathering described just before. In I Cor. ix.21 Paul says of himself that, even though when dealing with Gentiles he sets the law aside, yet he himself is not an ἄνομος of God but ἔννομος Χριστοῦ. The latter is intended to determine the meaning of the former. Since he is ἔννομος Χριστοῦ he is not ἄνομος θεοῦ. The two genitives no doubt refer to the νόμος contained in ἄνομος and ἔννομος.[1]

4. νομικός

In classical Greek νομικός occurs only as an adjective (e.g. in Plat. *Leg.* 625a). The meaning is *according to, corresponding to, the law*.[2] Later νομικός became largely a technical term for a *lawyer*, especially a *notary*. Epict. *Diss.* II.13.6: 'If one does not know the laws of a city, one consults a νομικός'. In the papyri νομικός often occurs as a title after the name (cf. P. Oxy. 237.VIII.2 ff.).[3] But νομικός also continues to be used as an adjective (as an adverb in the

---

[1] cf. Schlatter, *Paulus, der Bote Jesu. Eine Deutung seiner Briefe an die Korinther* (¹1934, ²1956), ad loc.

[2] Preisigke, *Wörterbuch*, III, p. 135; Moulton-Milligan, *Vocabulary of the Greek Testament*, s.v.

[3] Examples in Preisigke, *Wörterbuch*, III, p. 135.

Letter of Aristeas 142). In Judaism the designation νομικός acquires a connexion with the OT law, cf. IV Macc. v.4: *Eleazer, a priest by birth, trained in knowledge of the law* (τὴν ἐπιστήμην νομικός).

In the New Testament νομικός is used once as an adjective, in Titus iii.9: καὶ μάχας νομικὰς περιΐστασο, *controversies, quarrels which refer to the law (or the OT in general)*. The expression leaves it open whether it is a question of the validity of the law as a rule of life for Christians, or of theories which are to be proved from the scriptures. Since Titus i.10 mentions the party of the circumcision, the first interpretation must be considered; yet in view of the false doctrines attacked in the Pastoral Epistles the latter is the more likely.

In Matthew and Luke νομικός is sometimes used for the leaders of the Jewish people. But they are given the name only in contexts dealing with the administration or the understanding of the law. In Matt. xxii.35 (parallel Luke x.25), the question about the most important commandment is put by a νομικός When Mark says γραμματεύς (xii.26), the meaning is the same, but judging according to the context νομικός is more appropriate.[1]

In Luke vii.30 too νομικός will have been chosen intentionally just because βουλὴ τοῦ θεοῦ here has John the Baptist in view, not the law. Those who wish and ought to concern themselves with the law in a special manner do not concern themselves with the purpose of God now being made known. In Luke xi.45 f., 52 νομικός is evidently intended to underline what are the burdens in question here and how the locking up is done. Luke xiv.3 is also concerned with the understanding of the law.

---

[1] Since Mark is writing for Romans, νομικός is ambiguous owing to the technical meaning of the word already mentioned. Hence the word is lacking in Mark altogether.

It is hardly possible to decide conclusively what is the meaning of νομικός in Titus iii.13; but since Zenas is not included amongst the opponents and the addition of νομικός as a title after a name is in common use elsewhere, the more probable interpretation is *lawyer* or *notary*.[1]

5. νόμιμος

νόμιμος usually means *conformable to the rule, to the regulation, to what is right*.[2] It is used in P. Oxy. 1201.18: of lots; in Chr. II.372.13 (Preisigke, *Wörterbuch*, s.v.): of a legally valid marriage, cf. Epict. III.10.8. Used as a noun τὸ νόμιμον is that which is fair and reasonable.[3]

In the LXX νόμιμος occurs only once as an adjective: II Macc. iv.11 in the sense of *lawful*; elsewhere τὸ νόμιμον or τὰ νόμιμα are the translation of *ḥōq, ḥuqqāh* (*statute*), *tōrāh*. This usage probably assumes that there are only, so far as the law is concerned, individual regulations and rules, so that τὸ νόμιμον means something like 'legal rules'.

In the New Testament νόμιμος occurs only as an adverb: I Tim. i.8; II Tim. ii.5. In the case of II Tim. ii.8 it is evident that νομίμως does not mean 'in conformity with the OT law', but using the metaphorical language of the contest either with the special meaning *according to the rules of the contest*[4], *in the appropriate manner*, or in a general sense: *well done, efficiently*.

In I Tim. i.8 νομίμως will not mean: corresponding to the OT law,[5] but simply *in the appropriate way*,[6] although owing to the context the two are completely

[1] cf. Dibelius, *Die Pastoralbriefe* (³1955), *ad loc.*
[2] The word was formed at a time when νόμος did not yet mean 'law' (Debrunner).
[3] cf. Preisigke, *Wörterbuch*, s.v.; also Philo *Decal.* 37, *Abr.* 276.
[4] cf. Wohlenberg, *Die Pastoralbriefe* (³1923), *ad loc.*
[5] cf. Wohlenberg, *Die Pastoralbriefe*, *ad loc.*
[6] Wohlenberg and Dibelius, *ad loc.*

synonymous here. At any rate the proper use of the
law is different from that made by those who pretend
to be teachers of the law.

6. νομοθέτης

νομοθέτης means *lawgiver* (cf. Aristot. *Pol.* II.12
p. 1274a 31 f., *ib.* II.6 p. 1265a 18 ff., Diod. S. 12.11.3,
Philo *Spec. Leg.* IV.120). In Judaism Moses is in a
special sense a νομοθέτης (thus in e.g. Letter of Aristeas
131, 148, 312); so is God (Philo *Sacr.* AC 131: God is
Himself the lawgiver and fountain of laws). In the LXX the
only passage with νομοθέτης, in Ps. ix.21 (EVV 20),
depends on the Kᵉthib *mōreh* (*teacher*) instead of the
Qᵉre *mōrā'* (*fear*).

In the New Testament it occurs only in James iv.12.
The meaning of the preceding sentence must govern
the meaning of the title νομοθέτης for God in this
passage and cannot itself be determined by this[1] (cf.
p. 128).

7. νομοθεσία

νομοθεσία (derived from νομοθέτης) usually no longer
suggests the act of legislation, but what has come out
of the act, hence according to the context, the *law*, the
constitution, and also the *code of laws*. Hence in a
Jewish context, parallel to νόμος, it quite simply denotes the Pentateuch (cf. Diod. S. 12.11.4: P. Oxy.
1119.18). In the LXX only in II Macc. vi.23: Eleazar
is determined to remain steadfast owing to the *holy
God-given law* (θεόκτιστος νομοθεσία). In the Letter of
Aristeas 15 the νομοθεσία of the Jews is to be translated. In Philo even the unwritten law can be described

---

[1] Barnabas xxi.4: *Be good lawgivers one to another*, is interesting
too. Verse 5 shows that this is not used in the sense of allowing
complete freedom. But this usage shows the wide range which
the word can have.

as ἄγραφος νομοθεσία (*Abr.* 5); elsewhere in his books too νομοθεσία is often the Pentateuch: *Cher.* 87: πολλαχοῦ τῆς νομοθεσίας =in many passages of the Pentateuch.

It is true that occasionally the meaning of legislation is nearer, for instance in Philo *Vit. Mos.* 2.2: one of the faculties of Moses is concerned with lawgiving (cf. also Ditt. Or. 326.26). Here the act of legislation can at any rate be in mind. Similarly also no doubt in Plat. *Leg.* III.684e.

In the only passage where νομοθεσία occurs in the New Testament, Rom. ix.4, the most natural meaning is 'law' and not legislation in particular. It is not the act of legislation which is named as one of the prerogatives of Israel, but the actual possession of the law (cf. Rom. iii.1 f.).

8. νομοθετέω

νομοθετεῖν (derived from νομοθέτης) means (*a*) *to be active as a legislator, to frame laws*; so Plat. *Polit.* 294c; Letter of Aristeas 240. The recipient of the laws is in the dative, or in the accusative, cf. Philo *Poster. C.* 143. (*b*) *to ordain a thing by law, to settle by law*: cf. Letter of Aristeas 144. Both meanings can appear in the passive, cf. Plat. *Leg.* III.701d. The passive is more frequent where *things are ordained by law*, e.g. Philo *Vit. Mos.* II.218, P. Oxy. 1119.24.

Compared with this the LXX has no special usage; it must merely be stated that when the word is used a strict reference to the Mosaic law need not always be associated with it (cf. Ps. xxvi.11, where νομοθετεῖν almost means *to instruct* (Hebrew *yārāh* in the *hiph'il*).

The two New Testament passages reflect both these main meanings. In Heb. vii.11 νομοθετεῖν is used in the passive of persons to whom the law is given. What it is intended to describe more precisely (whether it is to be rendered as 'the law' or 'law') is decided not by

the word νομοθετεῖν, but by the context, as well as by
the interpretation of ἐπ᾽ αὐτῆς. ἐπί with the genitive as
denoting the object in respect of which the law is given
does not occur elsewhere with νομοθετεῖν (yet it does
with περί in II Macc. iii.15, Philo *Vit. Mos.* II.218).
Since moreover the meaning of the interpolated
sentence would otherwise be rather thin, it is probably
a question of the whole law, and not of the law regu-
lating the cult in particular. In Heb. viii.6 the relative
clause can refer to λειτουργία or to διαθήκη; this is
immaterial as regards its meaning, yet the expression
seems to suit λειτουργία better. In any case the new
thing in question is established, ordained. The νόμος
included in νομοθετεῖν must therefore be understood
in a more general sense and not as referring to the OT.

9. παρανομία

(*a*) παρανομία denotes in classical Greek, as in later
Greek, a general condition, (which of course shows
itself in individual acts also). Ps. Sol. xvii.20: *The
king was a transgressor* (ἐν παρανομίᾳ), *and the judge was
disobedient* (ἐν ἀπαθείᾳ) *and the people sinful* (ἐν ἁμαρτίᾳ).
In the LXX παρανομία is infrequent (nine times) and
has no constant Hebrew equivalent. παράνομος occurs
more often. As in the case of ἀνομία the distinctions
made in the original language are blurred. In παρανομία
too the connexion with the standard of the law, which
underlies the word, is no longer clearly maintained.
In the passage cited from the Ps. Sol., παρανομία does
not refer to the law any more than do ἀπείθεια or
ἁμαρτία, although of course on the other hand in
Judaism the law is the norm or criterion for all such
judgements. (*b*) παρανομία also means the *single unjust
action*; thus e.g. in Philo *Vit. Mos.* 1, 295: Balaam advises
Balak *that the one way by which the Hebrews could be overthrown was disobedience* (παρανομία); cf. P. Oxy. 1119.18,

where παρανομία against the imperial orders must be punished.

In the New Testament the only passage with παρανομία is II Peter ii.16: Balaam ἔλεγξιν ἔσχεν ἰδίας παρανομίας. As regards verse 16b, either it is a concessive clause: 'although . . . restrained him'; in that case ἔλεγξις has the meaning of punishment and the παρανομία is his promise to curse Israel for gain. Or verse 16b describes what ἔλεγξιν ἔσθεν involved. ἔλεγξις would then be the conviction preceding the act, and thus a warning, and the παρανομία would consist in the intention to curse Israel. The difference has no significance at all for παρανομία. But the question influences the meaning of the whole passage. Either the sentence means that the false teachers too refuse to accept any warning, or that, if they will not accept a warning, they will be punished like Balaam who ignored the warning. In any case παρανομία is a *wrong action*, without any direct reference to the law being implied.

10. παρανομέω

παρανομέω means to *transgress a law, an ordinance that has been laid down*. Cf. Dittenberger, *Sylloge Inscriptionum Graecarum* (³1915-24), 218, 21 f.: οἱ παρανομοῦντες are people who violate a particular ordinance. In Plat. *Resp.* I.338e: Let that which is serviceable to the ruling class be the law everywhere and let those who infringe it be punished ὡς παρανομοῦντά τε καὶ ἀδικοῦντα But παρανομεῖν has often a more general meaning: *to offend*; in Ps.Sol.xvi.8: *let not the beauty of an ungodly* (παρανομούσης), *woman beguile me*. In the LXX it occurs only five times, with a different Hebrew equivalent on each occasion; e.g. in Ps. lxxiv.5 (EVV lxxv.4) it is parallel to ἁμαρτάνειν. In the passive παρανομεῖν can also be used of a person.[1]

[1] cf. P. Greci e Latini (=P. Soc.) 330.8 cf. Preisigke, *Worterbuch* s.v.

In the New Testament it occurs only in Acts xxiii.3: σὺ κάθῃ κρίνων με κατὰ τὸν νόμον, καὶ παρανομῶν κελεύεις με τύπτεσθαι. Here the contrast with κατὰ τὸν νόμον makes παρανομεῖν mean specifically the *violation of the law* and it is probably not merely a general expression for doing wrong.

INDEX OF REFERENCES

GENERAL INDEX

WRATH

WRATH

BY

H. KLEINKNECHT, J. FICHTNER,
G. STÄHLIN ET AL.

EDITOR'S PREFACE

THIS book is a translation of the article ὀργή in the *Theologisches Wörterbuch sum Neuen Testament* (TWNT), begun by G. Kittel and now edited by G. Friedrich, Vol. V, pp. 382-448. The writing of this article was originally undertaken by O. Procksch. After his death in 1947, H. Kleinknecht, O. Grether, E. Sjöberg, and G. Stählin shared the work between them. When Grether died suddenly in the summer of 1949, J. Fichtner completed the Old Testament part. The statements to which the name of O. Procksch is attached are derived from his manuscript, part of which was placed at the disposal of the authors. Apart from some fairly substantial abbreviation in Chapter I and some curtailing of footnotes, the whole text is here translated and the order follows exactly that of the German original.

Although this particular article stands under the heading of ὀργή, its authors have in fact recognised that there is a wide range of terms used in both Hebrew and Greek to cover the ideas of wrath and anger for which English also has a variety of terms, and it has been clearly recognised that no one term covers the idea of wrath whether in the Old Testament or the New. That this is termed a Bible Word Book is appropriate enough, but it differs from some others in this series in that it is primarily a study of the problem of understanding the divine nature when it is described in terms of wrath, a description which we may recognise as real even while acknowledging the inadequacy of our terms. This inadequacy of terminology has long been recognised and in Chapters III and IV in particular, attention is drawn to early paraphrases designed to avoid what was felt to be excessive anthropopathism. But the difficulty of terminology and our consciousness that whatever terms we use for the nature of God are inevitably conditioned by the background to our own thinking, does not absolve us from the need to clarify our minds in thinking about the nature of a God whose love may be appropriately described as a burning fire (Deut. iv.24) and with whom is forgiveness that He may be feared (Ps. cxxx.4).

All Hebrew words have been transliterated and, where necessary, translated. Greek words are not transliterated. Where quotations are given from elsewhere than the New Testament (or Septuagint), a translation has been given, except where the meaning is evident or where the actual Greek word used is of particular importance. In a number of cases translations have been given of crucial Greek and Latin words, but these are to be taken only as rough guides to the meaning, since, as will appear from their contents, these are words which are deserving of full and separate study. Such of them as appear in the New Testament are, of course, so treated in other volumes of TWNT.

Biblical references follow the normal chapter and verse enumeration of the Hebrew and Greek texts, with a note of deviations in the English versions. References to the Septuagint therefore in some cases require modification, particularly in the Psalter and in the book of Jeremiah.

CONTENTS

BIBLIOGRAPHY

GENERAL

H. CREMER: *Biblisch-theologisches Wörterbuch des neutestamentlichen Griechisch*, ed. J. Kögel ([11]1923).

LIDDELL and SCOTT: *Greek-English Lexicon* ([7]1940).

W. PAPE: *Griechisch-Deutsches Handwörterbuch*, ed. M. Sengebusch ([3]1880).

F. PASSOW: *Wörterbuch der griechischen Sprache* ([5]1841 ff.): new ed. W. Crönert (1913 ff.).

E. PREUSCHEN: *Griechisch-deutsches Wörterbuch . . . NT*, ed. W. Bauer ([5]1958). ET of edn. 4 (1949 ff.) by W. F. Arndt and F. W. Gingrich (1957), sv (Pr.-Bauer).

J. H. H. SCHMIDT: *Synonymik der griechischen Sprache*, III (1879), pp. 551-572.

R. C. TRENCH, *Synonyms of the New Testament* ([15]1906), pp. 123–127 (§37 θυμός, ὀργή, παροργισμός).

A. RUEGG: 'Zorn Gottes', in RE[3] 21, 719–729.

A. BERTHOLET, H. GUNKEL, W. MUNDLE: 'Zorn Gottes', in RGG, V ([2]1931), 2133-2136.

A. RITSCHL: *De Ira Dei* (1859).

—— *Die christliche Lehre von der Rechtfertigung und der Versöhnung*, II ([3]1889), pp. 119-156.

R. BARTOLOMÄI: 'Vom Zorn Gottes', in Jahrbücher für deutsche Theologie 6 (1891), pp. 256-277.

F. WEBER: *Vom Zorne Gottes* (1862).

A. DIECKMANN: 'Die christliche Lehre vom Zorne Gottes', ZwTh NF l, II (1893), pp. 321-377.

R. OTTO: *Das Heilige* ([26-28], 1947), pp. 18-20, 91f., 101, 116-118, ET, *The Idea of the Holy* (rev. edn. 1928), cf. Index, 'Wrath of God'.

—— *Gottheit und Gottheiten der Arier* (1932), pp. 50-64.

ORIGEN: *Contra Celsum*, IV, 71-73 (GCS, Orig. I, 340-343). Cf. H. Chadwick, *Contra Celsum* (1953)

LACTANTIUS: *De Ira dei* (CSEL, 27, I, 65-132), and on this cf. W. KUTSCH, *In Lactanti de ira dei librum quaestiones philologae* = Klassisch-philologische Studien, 6 (1933).

M. POHLENZ: *Vom Zorne Gottes* = FRL 12 (1909).

Chapter I

Aristotle: *Rhetoric*, II, 2, p. 1378, a, 31-1380, a, 4.

Stobaeus: *Eclogues*, III, 20 (Wachsmuth-Hense, III, pp. 539-566).

Philodemus Philosophus: *De Ira* (ed. Wilke, 1914).

Plutarch: *De Ira Cohibenda* (II, 452e-464d).

Seneca: *De Ira*.

J. Irmscher: *Götterzorn bei Homer* (1950).

W. Marg: *Der Charakter in der Sprache der frühgriechischen Dichtung*, Kieler Arbeiten zur klassischen Philologie I (1938), pp. 13 f.

R. Camerer; *Zorn und Groll in der sophokleischer Tragödie*. Diss. Freiburg (1930) especially pp. 52-64.

K. Latte: 'Schuld und Sünde in der griechischen Religion', ARW 20 (1920-21) pp. 257-260.

R. Hirzel: *Themis, Dike und verwandtes* (1907), pp. 138, 416-418.

Chapter II

C. von Orelli: 'Einige alttestamentliche Prämisse zur neutestamentlichen Versöhnungslehre', ZWL, 5 (1884), pp. 22-33.

J. Böhmer: 'Zorn', ZAW, 44 (1926), pp. 320-322.

P. Volz: *Das Dämonische in Jahwe* (1924).

Cf. also, the discussions of the theology of the Old Testament, especially E. König: (³⁴1923), pp. 173-177; W. Eichrodt, I (³1948), pp. 124-131; ET of edn. 6 (1959), (1960), pp. 258-269; E. Sellin: (1936) *passim*.

Chapter IV

Weber (cf. above): pp. 155, 161, 172, 314.

W. Bousset and H. Gressmann = W. Bousset, *Die Religion des Judentums im späthellenistischen Zeitalter*, ed. W. Gressmann (³1926), pp. 350 f.

H. L. Strack and P. Billerbeck: *Kommentar zum NT aus Talmud und Midrasch*, I-V (²1956), see III, pp. 30 f. (Str. B.).

E. Sjöberg: *Gott und die Sünder im palastinischen Judentum*, = BWANT, F, 4, H, 27 (1939), Index sv 'Zorn Gottes'.

Chapter V, 1

Strack and Billerbeck (see above): I, pp. 276-278; III, p. 645.

M. Dibelius: *Jakobusbrief* (⁷1921), pp. 104-106.

F. Hauck: *Jakobusbrief* (1926) pp. 74 f., n. 30.

Th. Rüther: *Die sittliche Förderung der Apatheia in den beiden ersten christlichen Jahrhunderten und bei Clement von Alexandrien* = Freiburger Theologische Studien, 23 (1949).

CHAPTER V, 2

E. VON DOBSCHÜTZ: *Theologie*, p. 79.

A. SCHLATTER: *Römerbrief*, pp. 46-54.

G. P. WETTER: *Der Vergeltungsgedanke bei Paulus* (1912), pp. 16-55.

F. V. FILSON: *St. Paul's conception of Recompense* (1931), pp. 39-48.

H. BRAUN: *Gerichtsgedanke und Rechtvertigungslehre bei Paulus* (1930), especially pp. 41-44.

G. BORNKAMM: 'Die Offenbarung des Zornes Gottes (Röm i-iii), ZNW 34 (1935), pp. 239-262.

G. SCHRENK: *Unser Glaube an den Zorn Gottes nach dem Römerbrief* (1944).

A. VON JÜCHEN: *Der Zorn Gottes* (1948).

Cf. also the discussions in the theologies of the New Testament, especially in H. J. HOLTZMANN, II ([2]1911), pp. 57 f. H. WEINEL ([8]1928), pp. 109, 260 f., 322 f. P. FEINE ([7]1936), pp. 206-208. R. BULTMANN (1948), pp. 76, 283 f., ETI (1952), pp. 75 f., 288.

Reference to works mentioned in this bibliography is normally by the name of the author alone.

ABBREVIATIONS

ANET	Ancient Near Eastern Texts, ed. Pritchard (1950).
AOT	*Altorientalische Texte zum AT* (²1926).
ARW	Archiv für Religionswissenschaft (1898 ff.).
ASG	Abhandlungen der Kgl. Sächsischen Gesellschaft der Wissenschaften (phil. hist. Klasse).
BH³	Biblia Hebraica (³Kittel).
BWANT	Beiträge zur Wissenschaft vom Alten und Neuen Testament.
CAF	*Comicorum Atticorum Fragmenta*, ed. Th. Koch. (1880 ff.).
CD	Cairo Damascus Covenant (= Zadokite Document).
Cr.-Kö.	H. Cremer: *Biblisch-theologisches Wörterbuch des ntlichen Griechisch*, ed. J. Kögel (¹¹1923).
CSEL	*Corpus Scriptorum Ecclesiasticorum Latinorum* (1866 ff.)
Ditt Syll	W. Dittenberger, *Sylloge Inscriptionum Graecarum*, I-IV, 1, 2 (³1915-24).
DOTT	Documents from OT Times, ed. Winton Thomas (1958).
BZAW	Beihefte der Zeitschrift für die alttestamentliche Wissenschaft.
ET	English translation.
EVV	English versions.
FRL	Forschungen zur Religion und Literatur des AT und NT.
GCS	*Die griechischen christlichen Schriftsteller* (1899 ff.).
JSS	Journal of Semitic Studies.
MT	Masoretic text.
NEB	New English Bible.
NTD	Das Neue Testament Deutsch.
Pr-Bauer	cf. Bibliography.
RE³	*Realencyclopaedie für protestantische Theologie und Kirche* (³1896 ff.).
RGG	*Religion in Geschichte und Gegenwart* (²1927 ff.).
Stob. Ecl.	Stobaeus *Eclogae*.
Str. B.	Strack-Billerbeck, cf. Bibliography.
sv	*sub voce*.
TGF	*Tragicorum Graecorum Fragmenta*, ed. A. Nauck (²1899).
TWNT	*Theologisches Wörterbuch zum Neuen Testament*, ed. G. Friedrich.
ZAW	Zeitschrift für die alttestamentliche Wissenschaft.
ZNW	Zeitschrift für die neutestamentliche Wissenschaft.
ZSTh.	Zeitschrift für systematische Theologic.
ZWL	Zeitschrift für kirchliche Wissenschaft und Kirchliches Leben.
ZwTh.	Zeitschrift für wissenschaftliche Theologic.

I. WRATH IN CLASSICAL ANTIQUITY

1. *The meaning of the word* ὀργή

ὀργή is a post-Homeric word, attested for the first time in Hesiod, *Opera* 304. From then onwards it is frequent in poetry and prose. Corresponding to its affinity with ὀργάω/ὀργάς which means the *luxuriant rising of sap and energy*, the *impelling and germinating activity in nature*, it was originally in general (*a*) the *impulsive behaviour* of man and beast, especially the *impulsive state of the human spirit* which breaks out actively in external behaviour in contrast to the more internal and quiet ἦθος (cf. Plat. *Leg.* X.908e). When ὀργή is asserted of men's character and nature, comparisons with animals and the like point expressly to the natural aspect of the concept (cf. Hesiod, *Op.* 303). In the general sense of individual character and nature ὀργή becomes important particularly in Attic tragedy and a factor in the tragic happenings. In the ὀργή the insight or judgement of a man—whether it be true or false—takes shape and drives him to the decisive act.

As contrasted with this earlier usage the content of the meaning of ὀργή became, already in tragedy, more specialised and restricted: soon ὀργή denotes only a quite definite reaction of the human soul, i.e. (*b*) *wrath* as being the manifestation, with the most violent external effect, of the vehement internal protest of the θυμός.[1] Whilst on the one hand both concepts stand side by side and complete each other, yet on the other hand ὀργή differs from θυμός because it has the characteristic of being directed to an object, namely vengeance or punishment with a significant intention. ὀργή which already in tragedy always seeks to preserve something

[1] cf. TWNT III, pp. 167 f.

that is recognised to be right, became then in the
national life of later times the characteristic and legitimate attitude of the judge who has to avenge the
wrong. In consequence there appears as a regular
formula in legal language δεινὸν καὶ ὀργῆς ἄξιον (*a
monstrous and scandalous offence* lit. *deserving of wrath*) in
Demosth. *Or.* 9.31; 19.7, etc. Here ὀργή is not intended
to refer to the verdict (Aristot. *Rhet.* I.1, p. 1354a, 16 ff.)
but only to the assessment of the punishment.[1] This
conception led to ὀργή gradually itself assuming the
meaning (*c*) *punishment* (cf. Demosth. *Or.* 21.147; Lycurgus, *Contra Leocratem* 138).

Apart from the moral anger which restrains the
wicked[2] and is sometimes described explicitly as δικάια
ὀργή (Demosth. *Or.* 16.19; Dio Cassius, 40.51.2; Ditt.
Syll. 780.22), ὀργή came to be used in Greek principally
in a negative sense.[3] As *irritability* it is already associated in tragedy with blind[4] purposes and fancies by
which man allows himself to be driven; it appears as
the regular antithesis to γνώμη (Soph. *Oed. Tyr.* 523 f.),
λόγος and λογισμός (Menander fr. 630 [CAF IV.188];
Thuc. II.11, 4 f.; Aristot. fr. 661 [ed. by Rose]), to the
σοφόν (Eur. fr. 760 [TGF 397]). It is not only itself a
useless evil (Eur. *Med.* 446 f.), but is necessarily accompanied by many other evils (Chairemon fr. 28 [TGF]).
Therefore the ethical claim of philosophy demands that
man should be the master of this emotional disturbance
which does not even stop short before the gods. Whilst
Academics and Peripatetics explain anger as natural,
indeed as necessary for great deeds and virtues, above
all for warlike bravery, and only aim at moderating and
guiding anger by reason, in the opinion of the Stoics

---

[1] cf. Hirzel, pp. 416-418; Pohlenz, p. 15, n. 3.
[2] cf. Theophr. in Sen. *De Ira* I.14: *non potest fieri, ut non vir
bonus irascitur malis.*   [3] cf. the plentiful examples in Stob. *Ecl.*
[4] cf. Chrysipp. fr. 390 (von Arnim III.94, 43 ff.).

ὀργή and its like is one of the chief passions to be stamped out as far as possible.[1] This ethical idea was then asserted by philosophy in a special manner with regard to the anger of the deity.

2. *The wrath of the gods amongst the Greeks*

Angry gods dwell so powerfully in the consciousness of mankind that some have wished to explain all worship as being the attempt to forestall the anger of the gods or to appease it. This is an accepted fact already in pre-Homeric religion.[2] Pre-Greek divinities of the earth and divinities which bring curses, like the Erinys, have anger as their nature even in their names 'the Furies'. Instinctive, merciless and terrible as nature itself, they appear in every place where its inviolable bonds—primarily of blood and the family, but then later also of the law—are being broken and demand retaliation. Then since Homer the anger of the gods in Greek mythology and poetry is 'a mighty and effective force in the interplay of the forces amongst the powers controlling fate',[3] i.e. of reality struggling to prevail. It appears in a twofold form, occurring firstly amongst the gods themselves and secondly directed against men. In both cases it is a form of self-assertion and of protest, whether it be the conflict of particular divine claims to exist which contradict each other (Hom. *Il.*8.407, 421) or the reaction against men's overstepping their bounds, as for instance presumption towards the gods (*Il.* 24. 606), neglect of sacrifices (*Il.* 5.177 f.; 9.533-538), failure to respect priests (*Il.*1.44, 75), to observe the rights of hospitality (*Od.* 2.66 f.; 14.283), to honour the dead (*Il.* 22.358; *Od.* 11.73), etc. All this provokes divine anger which is difficult to propitiate, which leads to no

---

[1] *Stoici . . . voluerant eam* (sc. *iram*) *penitus excidere.* Chrysipp. fr. 444 (von Arnim III.108.34 ff.).

[2] cf. U. von Wilamovitz, *Der Glaube der Hellenen* I (1931), p. 35.

[3] W. Schadewaldt, *Iliasstudien* (1938), p. 154, n. 1.

good (*Od*. 3.135, 145), and before which it is better to
retreat (*Il*. 5.443 f.). Here anger and wrath are not so
much anthropomorphic traits of character but rather
something to which the god has a kind of right because
his claim to existence has been slighted. In so far as this
means that the restoration of an appointed state is
demanded, and independent existence is helped to
assert itself or a decree of fate is carried out, the anger
of the gods is not blind in its rage but clear-sighted and,
in regard to men, is in a negative manner the honour
which they do to him by indicating his nature or by
confining him within the limits assigned to him in order
that in them he may be what he is.

All this is not expressed at first by ὀργή which in any
case is not a Homeric word, but by χόλος[1] and κότος
(*anger*)[2] and especially by the term μῆνις (*anger*)[3] with its
related words derived from the sacral sphere and almost
exclusively confined to it.[4] It is first in tragedy
that ὀργή appears as well to denote the anger of the
gods[5] and from Euripides onwards it is used more frequently with this meaning (cf. Adespota fr. 296 [TGF
896]).[6] Whilst in Hesiod (*Op*. 47, 53) Zeus in his anger
against Prometheus lets the punishment follow hard on

---

[1] Hom. *Il*. 15.122. Cf. Apollonius Rhodius III.337.

[2] Hom. *Od*. 11.101 ff. Cf. Aesch. *Ag*. 1211.

[3] Hom. *Il*. 5.177 f. *Il*. 21.523 describes a city which is allowed
to go up in smoke and flames; *a burning city . . . lit by the wrath*
(μῆνις) *of the gods*. Thus the anger of the gods can strike not only
an individual, but also a city and a whole nation.

[4] The etymology and the different meanings of the numerous
Homeric words for the anger of the gods are now well presented in
Irmscher, pp. 3-26; cf. *ib*., pp. 29-36 for the different ways in
which Homer describes the anger of the gods.

[5] cf. the ὀργαί of the Erinys in Aesch. *Eum*. 847, 939.

[6] Here in characteristic Greek fashion we see at the same time
the effects of the god's anger which starts with the νοῦς of men:
eadem ira deorum hanc eius satellibus iniecit amentiam (Cic. *Mil*. 86).
Cf. also Eur. *Iph. Taur*. 987; *Med*. 129 f.; *Hipp*. 438; 1417 f.

the heels of the offence, Solon already considers it a sign of power and greatness in the god that he does not punish at once. There is a distinction between human and divine anger (cf. Solon fr. 1.25 f. [Diehl]).[1] With reference to ὀργαί (which here no doubt keeps still to the wider meaning of (a) (cf. p. 1), Euripides says in *Ba.* 1348: it is not 'fitting' that gods should resemble mortals. The ethical and rational idea of 'what befits a god' discovered by Xenophanes is aimed in particular at the stories told by the poets (cf. e.g. Plut. *Pericl.* 39 [I.173d-e]).[2] The criticism of myth arises especially out of the philosophic requirement that the divine in accordance with its true nature should be free from every passion (Sextus Empiricus, *Pyrrh. Hyp.* I.162). Therefore Cicero can declare freedom from anger in particular to be the common property of the concept of god in all schools of philosophy (*Off.* III.102).

Epicurus begins the first sentence of the *Philosophical Maxims* with the assertion (fr. 139): *the happy and the incorruptible . . . is affected neither by wrath nor by favour: for all such things belong to weakness.*[3] We can read of the same antithesis between ὀργή and χάρις (cf. Demosth. *Or.* 19.92) in Plut. *Suav. Viv. Epic.* 22 (II.1102e). Thus the Stoic, although he too rejects ὀργή, differs from Epicurus in holding fast to the ideas of grace and succour, the good will of the deity (Letter of Aristeas, 254).[4]

---

[1] A Christian version of the idea is found in Lact. 20 f.

[2] cf. Cic. *Nat. Deor.* I.16(42): *qui* (sc. Poetae) *et ira inflammatus . . . induxerunt deos*; II.28(70): *et perturbatis animis inducuntur* (sc. dei); *accepimus enim deorum . . . iracundies—ut fabulae creduntur stultissime et plena sunt futilitatis summaeque levitatis.*

[3] On its continuing influence, cf. Lucretius, *De Rerum Natura* II.651; Philodemus Philosophus, *De Ira* col. 43 (ed. by Wilke, pp. 85-87); Posidonius in Cic. *Nat Deor.* I.44(124); I.17(45); Epic. fr. 363.365 f. (ed. by H. Usener, pp. 242-244).

[4] cf. Lact. 5.1: *existimantur Stoici . . . aliquanto melius de divinitate sensisse, qui aiunt gratiam in deo esse, iram non esse.* Lact. himself holds

In this matter the philosophical doctrines must not lead us astray; on the contrary it is just these which themselves indicate how widespread not only in poetry, but also in popular belief must have been the conception of the gods, whose anger claims propitiation and expresses itself in judgements. Plato speaks of unusually serious illnesses and sufferings which befell this or that family as a result of an old resentment of the gods for some reason or other and which were cured through the religious ecstasy of the appointed priests who have recourse to prayers and vows, acts of worship, expiatory rites and solemn functions.[1] Otherwise Lucretius would neither have striven so passionately for deliverance from the fear connected with it (cf. *De Rerum Natura* V.119 ff.; VI.71 f.; Cic. *Nat. Deor.* 17.45), nor would Plutarch have heeded to discuss the sceptics' question: *But for what reason should the wrath of the gods at first sink out of sight, like certain rivers, only to resurge later against others, leading in the end to the direst calamities? (Ser. Num. Pun.* 12 [II.557e]). For even when God punishes he does not do so from anger (Plut. *Ser. Num. Pun.* 20 [II.562d]). Plutarch is aiming chiefly at popular mythological tradition, but also at cultic representations, in which notwithstanding philosophical criticism

the view that anger and mercy are both necessary for the punishment of the wicked and the recompense of the good, if the reality of God and all religion is not to be destroyed. Just as the Christian Apologists (Aristid. *Apol.* i.6; Athenag. Suppl. 21) made use of philosophical ideas when criticising the pagan conceptions of God and mythology (cf. J. Geffcken, *Zwei griechische Apologeten* (1907), p. 40), so by contrast ancient philosophy for its part reproached the Christians with what they said concerning the ὀργὴ θεοῦ. Cf. Orig. *Cels.* IV.73. For the refutation undertaken by Origen who in the abstract supports the same ideal of the ἀπαθεία of God (VI.65), cf. Pohlenz, pp. 31-36.

[1] *Phaedr.* 244 d-e. Also F. Pfister, 'Der Wahnsinn des Weihepriesters' in *Festschrift Cimbria* (1926), pp. 55-62.

ὀργή and ὀργίζεσθαι occupied their firm place as the judgement of the gods.

Thus on the one hand the ὀργὴ θεοῦ proves to be essentially a mythological concept. But on the other hand it follows from its use as a synonym for the technical term μήνιμα and μῆνις in the aetiological legends or from statements such as that in Apollodo Bibliotheca II.1.3 that there are still in later Greek strong connections with the cult.

Popular belief tends to see in unusual natural phenomena such as pestilence, storm and hail, malformations and illness, the consequences of the ὀργή of the gods and demons (cf. Clement of Alexandria, *Strom*. VI.3.31.1). In Cleonai for instance magicians understand how to avert such catastrophes by sacrifices and magical song. Clement of Alexandria who reports this (*loc. cit.* 2; cf. Plut. *Ser. Num. Pun.* 12 [II.557a-e]), naturally holds to the philosophical opinion: 'the divine is not angry' (*Paed*. I.8.68.3) and censures the Greeks, amongst whom the gods *like an old shrew losing her temper*,[1] *are embittered at what is no injury, as they say* (Hom. *Il.* 9.533-538) *Artemis was wroth with the Aetolians on account of Oeneus* (*Strom*. VII.44.23.2), so that men *in their dealings with beings* (i.e. the gods) *who are so quick to wrath naturally become superstitious and think that whatever happens is a sign and cause of evil* (*Strom*. VII.4.24.1; cf. Tac. *Historiae* II.1). This latter idea indicates a religious attitude which received a particular stamp amongst the Romans from their understanding of the *ira deum*.

3. Ira Deum *amongst the Romans*

At first the Romans admitted extensively into their literature the conceptions of the wrath of the gods as they were described in Greek poetry and mythology

[1] But cf. Solon fr. 1.25 f. (Diehl). Cf. p. 5.

from Homer onwards.[1] Similarly the philosophical
criticism to which it is subjected reproduces Greek
thought and ideas.[2] Furthermore the *revealed wrath of
the heavenly beings*, which instigated the transfer of the
statue of Serapis from Sinope to Alexandria, originated according to an explicit account in Tacitus
(*Historiae* IV.84) in a Hellenistic cult legend. But independently of Greek influence the Romans still had their
own original conception of the *ira deum* which had its
roots in the peculiar nature of their ancestral *religio*.
This is expressed by the belief in evil portents (*prodigia*)
in which to Roman thought the wrath of the gods
always appears and acts[3] (cf. Livy 5.143). The *ira deum*
which is usually provoked by *neglegentia caeremon-
iarum auspiciorumque* the *neglect of ceremonials and auspices*
(Livy 22.9.1) becomes the cause of natural disasters,
famine, sickness and epidemics in town and country
(Livy 4.9.3). Livy in 40.37.2 writes of a wholesale mortality in Rome in which the *pontifex Maximus*
gave orders for rites designed to placate the *ira deum*. In
order to exorcise the calamity and to re-establish the
pax deum (Livy 27.23.4), the good relations with the
gods, *piacula irae deum*, the technical term employed, in
the shape of *preces, vota, dona, supplicationes* and the like,
must be found (Livy 22.9.1; Lucan I.683). The *ira deum*
can be recognised by the rites of propitiation as well as
by the formalised language as a conception and an
expression of the Roman cult. Accordingly although
Cicero was aware that philosophy rejected in general

---

[1] Lucretius, *De Rerum Natura* V.399 ff.; Cicero, *Tusc.* IV.29(63);
Virgil, *Aen.*7.305 from Hom. *Il.* 9.533 ff.; *Georgics* III.152 f.;
Horace, *Epodi* 10.13 f.; Tac., *Ann.* 3.61.

[2] Lucretius, *De Rerum Natura* VI.753 f.; V.1194 ff.; VI.70 ff.;
II.651; Cicero. *Nat. Deor.* I.16 f. (42.5); III.38(91); *Off.* III.102;
Sen. *De Ira* II.30.2.

[3] For the following, cf. H. Kleinknecht, 'Laokoon' in *Hermes* 79
(1944), pp. 82, 108 f.

the wrath of the gods and himself brings out this fact
(p. 5), he admitted into the draft of the laws of his
Utopia concerning the intercourse with the gods, the
regulations to be followed by the augurs and others to
meet the *ira deum* (*De Legibus* II.21); and the universal
rule shall be observed that the impious man should not
dare to placate the *ira deum* with gifts (*loc. cit.* 22),[1]
because the wrath of the deity falls in particular upon
the impious.[2] Just as the gods can be entreated in
prayer to direct their anger against the evil-doer and
the enemy,[3] so the man who swears a solemn oath calls
down upon himself the anger of father Jupiter, of Mars
Gradivus and of the other gods in the event of perjury
(Livy 2.45.15). The *ira deum* which visits him who
scorns the gods, occupies a firm place especially in
cultic legends and tales of miraculous punishment
(Livy 2.36.5, 9.29.11; Tac. *Ann.* 14.22). Piety has often
embellished such reports further, so that the historian
occasionally refrains from expressing an opinion as to
their truth (Livy 8.6.3). In fact amongst the people as
in the army *religio*, i.e. scrupulous attention to hints
from the gods, especially in times of crisis, often became
superstitio, which in its fear immediately interprets fortuitous and natural events as signs of divine wrath (Tac.
Historiae IV.26). Thus for example when the body of
the murdered Britannicus was burned, such a cloud-
burst poured down, that the ordinary people believed
it revealed the *ira deum* (Tac. *Ann.* 13.17).[4] Finally in
Minucius Felix the fact that every conceivable cult was

[1] Phrases concerning the wrath of the gods are also to be found
frequently in Cicero's speeches: *Mil.* 86; *Pro. Q. Roscio* 46; *Pro
Caelio* 42; *In Pisonem* 59.

[2] cf. Horace, *Epodi* 10.13 f.; *Carmina* I.3.38 ff.; Tac. *Ann.* I.30.

[3] cf. Livy 9.1.8; Horace, *Epodi* 5.53 f. Cf. also Seneca's censure
of this (*De Ira* II.30.2).

[4] cf. in addition Tac. *Ann.* 1.30 and for this again the philosophical criticism in Sen. *De Ira* II.27.2.

so readily accepted by the Romans in the course of their history was traced back to the fear of the wrath of the gods.[1] This reveals at the same time the evidence for their unique religious feeling, on which the conception of the *ira deum* set a decisive stamp.

But now, since according to Roman ideas the stability of state and government depends essentially on *religio*, the averting of the evil portents and therewith the propitiation of the *ira deum* was the most far-reaching object of public concern. In addition, disastrous happenings in the history of their political life, such as internal discord, class struggles, civil war or mutinies (Tac. *Ann.* 1.39; *Historiae* II.38) are brought particularly into connection with the *ira deum* or *numinum* (cf. Livy 4.9.3). The anger of the gods is seen at work especially in defeats of armies or capture of cities, and in such passages an allusion to it is appropriate to the style of Roman historical writing (Tac. *Ann.* 16.16). The wrath of the gods had a share in bringing about the destruction of Corinth and Carthage,[2] the defeats at Lake Trasimene (Livy 22.9.1) and Cannae[3] and in the Teutoburg Forest,[4] as well as the reign of terror of a Sejanus and of a Nero (Tac. *Ann.* 4.1) or the annihilation of the Capitol in the year A.D. 69 (Tac. *Historiae* IV.54).

Usually a religious offence, neglect of ceremonials and auspices, but also *temeritas (rashness)* and *inscitia (ignorance)*, rouses the wrath of the gods who when they are asked do themselves indicate ways and means of expiation,[5] in fact they order them. The loftiest of such means of expiation and at the same time the pinnacle of old Roman *religio* and *virtus* is the sacrifice of one's own life in the rite of devotion, as it was carried out

---

[1] *Octavius* 7.2 (cf. p. 3).

[2] cf. Cicero, *Nat. Deor.* III.38(91).

[3] Livy 25.6.6; cf. Valerius Maximus I.1.16.
    Dio Cassius 56.24.2.   [5] Livy 22.9.7 f.

for the first time according to the tradition, by the consul of the year 340 B.C., P. Decius Mus, in the decisive battle of the Latin war. Animal sacrifices had been ineffectual in averting the *ira deum*. Then the consul dedicates himself and the hostile army solemnly to death. His form appears to all to wear an aspect more sublime than merely human, 'as though sent from heaven as a sacrifice to propitiate all divine wrath' which therefore falls upon the foes, and overthrows and destroys them (Livy 8.9.10). By the simile here used: *as if he had been sent from heaven*, the voluntary vicarious sacrifice demanded by the angry deity is at once transformed into an act of divine mercy, which evidently itself desires the religious offence to be expiated; for at the height of the crisis a man is sent who turns towards himself all the threats and dangers sent by the gods (Livy 8.10.7)[1] in order that the *pax deum*,[2] the good understanding between gods and men may be restored.

Amongst Roman historians this cultic religious mode of thought attained a historical significance which it never possessed amongst the Greeks. The *ira deum*, always closely connected with the *fatum* becomes fraught with destiny for the whole course of Roman history. In its endless internal discord Tacitus sees the same madness of men and *deum ira* continually at work (*Historiae* II.30), and he brings up this subject again and again because it threatens the existence of Rome itself (cf. *Ann.* 16.16). It is therefore more than a merely poetic

[1] cf. G. Stübler, 'Die Religiosität des Livius,' in Tübinger Beiträge zur Altertumswissenschaft, 35 (1941), pp. 101-201. For the historical truth of the occurrence, cf. F. Altheim, 'Der Opfertod der Decier', in Forschungen und Fortschritte, 17 (1941), pp. 112 f.

[2] This expresses the real antithesis to the concept of *ira deum*; other instances are *deum benignitas* (Tac. *Ann.* 12.45; *Historiae* V.85), *indulgentia numinum* (*Ann.* 13.57), *favor erga nos reorum* (*Germania* 33).

technique of presentation, adopted from that great model, Homer, when in Virgil's *Aeneid*[1] the wrath of the gods appears as the dominant theme and as a driving force in bringing to fulfilment the fate which led Aeneas to Latium (Virgil, *Aen.* 1.2 ff.; cf. 1.130, 5.781). The introduction closes with the question: *Can resentment so fierce dwell in heavenly breasts?* (Virgil, *Aen.* 1.11). Again and again divine beings and human seers point to this wrath of the gods (Virgil, *Aen.* 3.362-366). It has sprung from the Roman world of ideas, as can be inferred from the use of cultic terminology connected with it, from its association with prodigious events and from the rite which in what follows is to implore the *pax deum* (*loc. cit.* 369 ff.). In this matter *ira deum* and *fata* are not to be separated from each other, since they are the negative and positive aspects of one and the same situation. On the one hand Athene announces to Aeneas through the mouth of her priest Nautes: *either what the mighty wrath of the gods portended or what the course of fate demanded* (Virgil, *Aen.* 5.706 f.); on the other hand the wrath of the gods strikes the enemies of the Trojans and thereby makes them understand that[2] *Aeneas is called of fate, guided by heaven's clear will* (11.232 f.). When Aeneas has reached his goal, the god of the river Tiber appears to him in a dream with the consolation and instruction: *the wrath of the gods has abated . . . duly offer prayers to Juno, and with the suppliant's vows vanquish her wrath and her threats* (8.40 f.; cf. Livy 8.33.7). The wrath of the gods, in this case that of Juno, which is appeased and comes to an end here, is none other than the metaphysical expression of the heavy reverses and the more than human opposition[3] with which fate has to contend in working itself out in its temporal, that is to say, in its historical development. Thus Virgil has

---

[1] cf. also Petronius *Satirae* 139; cf. 134.
[2] cf. Livy 36.6.   [3] cf. Virgil *Aen.* 7.315.

filled the prescribed epic form in the poetic tradition of the Greeks with the religious content of a genuinely Roman point of view, which by its avowed application to history represents a new and essential feature in the classical conception of the wrath of the gods.

II. THE WRATH OF MAN AND THE WRATH OF GOD IN THE OLD TESTAMENT

1. *The Hebrew terms*

HEBREW is very rich in expressions each of which describes a particular feature of anger:

(*a*) the most usual term is *'ap* which is to be derived from *'ānap* to *be angry*, originally no doubt to *snort*[1] and hence may have the fundamental meaning of *snorter*.[2] From this there follows the meaning *nose*, in the dual *nose, nostrils*. The OT considers the nose not so much an organ of smell (thus in Amos iv.10; Ps. cxv.6), as an 'organ of anger', when God's anger is kindled, *ḥārāh 'ap*, smoke goes up from his nostrils (Ps. xviii.9). *'Ap* and the much more rare dual form[3] are found about 210 times in the OT—about 170 times for divine and 40 times for human anger. The combination *ḥārāh 'ap* is met with in the most diverse writings of the OT, but chiefly in the earlier sources of the Pentateuch and the historical books.[4] The verb *'ānap* occurs only 14 times, 8 times in the Qal and 6 times in the Hithpaʻel; it is used only of God. Although one might wish to deduce from this a specific usage of the verb, the employment of *'ap* and its dual form also for human anger and the rare occurrence of the verb suggests the need for caution.

(*b*) The most frequent synonym for *'ap* is *ḥēmāh* which is to be derived from the root *yāḥam* to *be hot*, to *be ardent*. It denotes also the glow of wine in Hos. vii.5,

---

[1] L. Köhler, *Lexicon Veteris Testamenti libros* (1948 ff.), 70.

[2] *op. cit.* 75; or is the noun primary and the verb derived from it?

[3] It is found for anger, e.g. in Exod. xv.8 and Prov. xxx.33, but especially in the phrases *slow to anger* (*'erek 'appaim*) and *impatient* (*qᵉṣar 'appaim*).   [4] For *ḥārāh*, cf. the detailed comments below.

the agitation of the spirit in Ezek. iii.14, the poison of the serpents in Deut. xxxii.24; Ps. lviii.5, cxl.4(3), and the poisoned arrows in Job vi.4; but much the most often (115 times) the anger and fury of God (about 90 times), as well as that of man (about 25 times).

(c) The MT uses the term *ḥārōn* exclusively for the anger of God; it is found 39 times in all,[1] and in 33 of these passages in the combination *ḥᵃrōn 'ap*. On the other hand the related word *ḥᵒrī* which occurs only 6 times and always in the combination *ḥᵒrī 'ap* is used both for the anger of God (twice) and for that of man (4 times). Both nouns are to be derived from *ḥārāh* which is used in the Qal only with regard to anger (of God and man) and appears thus 80 times; in the derived forms, it has the meaning of being *eager*, to *inveigh*. Its original meaning is probably to be *kindled*, to *glow*; thus the nouns in combination with *'ap* denote the kindling of anger and more generally the heat of anger. Owing to the fact that the Qal of *ḥārāh* refers exclusively to anger,[2] *ḥārōn* must be interpreted as anger also in the few passages where it is found without *'ap*.

(d) *'ebrāh* meaning *anger* is not to be derived from the frequently used root *'ābar* I to *flow over*, to *cross over*, to *step over* which begins in Arabic with 'ayin,[3] but from *'ābar* II the less common root, which is *ǵabira* in Arabic. Its meaning must be assumed to be to *bear ill-will*, to *be angry*. *'ebrāh*, anger, is used in 24 passages with reference to God, in 6 passages referring to man; the verb *'ābar* II occurs in the OT only in the Hithpaʻel and then

---

[1] Ps. viii.10 and Jer. xxv.38 are not counted in this, since the text is uncertain.

[2] *ḥārāh* is found 50 times with *'ap*, 26 times with a dative of the person, and in some other combinations (cf. Gen. xxxi.35, xlv.5).

[3] From this root is to be derived *'ebrāh* I *arrogance, excess* (Is. xvi.6; Jer. xlviii.30(29); Prov. xxi.24).

with the meaning to *lose one's temper*, to *be angry* (said of God and man, altogether 7 times).

(*e*) The verb *qāṣap* (occurring 28 times in the Qal[1]), from which is derived *qeṣep*, has perhaps the original meaning of to *break out*, from which to *let fly*, to *be angry* is easily explained.[2] Whilst the verb is used both for God and men being angry, the noun is used quite preponderantly of God's anger (26 times) and only twice (Eccl. v.16 and Est. i.18, hence in very late writings) of the anger, or vexation of a man.[3]

(*f*) From the verb *zāʿam* (12 times in the OT) which means to *let fly at*, to *scold*, to *be angry with*, but also to *cast a spell on*, to *curse*, was formed the noun *zaʿam* which no doubt originally in accordance with this means *anger* with its expression by invective in view.[4] So in Isa. xxx.27 it can be said of the lips of Yahweh.

In 5 of the 6 passages which use it with regard to God,[5] the verb clearly means his *anger* and even in the 6th this sense is quite likely (Num. xxiii.8) even though here the meaning to *curse* is not excluded; in the 5 passages where it is used with regard to a man the meaning to be angry seems to me nowhere to be required.[6] In Mic. vi.10 the passive participle of the Qal is used of a thing, the accursed scanty ephah. Thus the verb with the meaning to be angry is only used for divine anger. The employment of the noun *zaʿam*

[1] Hiphʿil (5 times) to *provoke to anger*.

[2] Hos. x.7 uses *qeṣep* in the concrete sense (*wood shaving* or *foam*); does this perhaps come from another root (cf. Gesenius-Buhl)?

[3] It is in any case (unlike the verb) found almost exclusively in late writings, especially in P and in the Chronicler (but cf. II Kings iii.27); for its absolute use, cf. below, p. 24.

[4] Köhler's (cf. p. 14 n. 1) rendering by to *cast a spell on, scold* (262) is too restricted; the same applies to his translation of *zaʿam* merely by *curse*; cf. Isa. x.5 where *zaʿam* occurs as a parallel to *'ap*.

[5] Isa. lxvi.14; Zech. i.12; Mal. i.4; Ps. vii.12(11); Prov. xxii.14.

[6] Num. xxiii. 7 parallel to *'ārar*; Num. xxiii.8; Prov. xxiv.24 parallel to *qābab*; Prov. xxv.23; Dan. xi.30.

agrees with this, for in the 22 passages in which it occurs it denotes without exception the anger of God.[1] Moreover verb and noun are met with only in poetic texts and in fact principally in those of later times. A special usage of za‘am is to be found in the apocalyptic writings where perhaps it can denote the *time of anger*; cf. Isa. xxvi.20; Dan. viii.19, xi.36 (cf. p. 44).

(g) The root zā‘ap, related to za‘am, is represented considerably less often. In the four passages in which the verb zā‘ap occurs (original meaning *rage, storm?*), it is used of persons and things and only in Prov. xix.3; II Chron. xxvi.19 does it mean to *be angry*; the verbal adjective zā‘ēp *sullen, angry* is found in I Kings xx.43, xxi.4. The noun za‘ap is used with reference to God twice, to men 4 times and figuratively of the raging of the sea in Jon. i.15; like the verb zā‘ap (except for Gen. xl.6) it is used only in post-exilic passages.

(h) kā‘as in the Qal (6 times) means to *be annoyed*, to *be resentful*, to *be angry*; in the Pi‘el (twice) and the Hiph‘il (nearly 50 times) it has the causative meaning of to *offend*, to *vex*, to *provoke to anger*, where it is almost always God who is the object of the provocation. The Hiph‘il is used principally in Deuteronomy, in the historical books which have undergone Deuteronomic revision (Judges and Kings) and in passages of Jeremiah handed down with this same revision, when it is a question of Israel arousing God's anger by apostasy and the worship of idols. The noun ka‘as—in the book of Job always in the form ka‘aś (cf. Job v.2, vi.2, x.17,

---

[1] This applies also to Jer. xv.17 (cf. vi.11). In Hos. vii.16 there is no doubt a textual error (cf. LXX); according to T. H. Robinson, *Die Zwölf kleinen Propheten* (1938), p. 30, za‘am here means perhaps as much as *insolence*. za‘am *Yahweh* is not found anywhere but za‘am with the pronominal suffix as applied to Yahweh occurs 11 times; elswhere it is used absolutely (with or without the article) e.g. Isa. xxvi.20; Dan. viii.19; but also in Ezek. xxii.24; Ps. lxxviii.49), most characteristically in the later period.

xvii.7)—is used 8 times of God, 17 times of man and means *vexation, displeasure (anger?)*.[1]

(*i*) Since the verb *rāgaz* means to *become excited, disturbed*—in the Hiph'il also once (Job xii.6) to *provoke to anger*—the far more rare noun is likely to denote *rage, agitation*, even *anger*; this shows a restriction of meaning, as compared with the verb which can also be used in the sense of *being happily excited* (Jer. xxxiii.9). *rōgez* occurs only 7 times, and then with a figurative meaning for the agitations of life and the raging of man against God; only in Hab. iii.2 is it to be understood of the anger of God. The verb occurs about 40 times in writings of all the OT periods, the noun only in late passages.

(*k*) *rūaḥ*[2] can hardly be called a proper term for anger, although the word approaches the sphere of anger in the shade of meaning of to *snort*; cf. *qᵉṣar rūaḥ* paralleled by *'erek 'appaim*[3] in Prov. xiv.29.[4] In Job iv.9 *rūaḥ* is found in association with *'ap*.

2. *The wrath of man in the Old Testament*

Although the same terms are used in the main for divine and human wrath, there are considerable material differences between the two conceptions. We will treat first the presentation of human wrath in the OT. Usually those who display it are individuals—Israelites[5] and non-Israelites[6]—occasionally also groups

[1] Eccl. ii.23, v.16, vii.3, xi.10 *vexation*.

[2] cf. *Spirit of God* (1960) in this series, pp. 1-7.

[3] cf. above, p. 14 n. 3.

[4] cf. Isa. xxx.28 (God's snorting with rage), xxv.4; Prov.xvi.32, xxix.11 (of men).

[5] e.g. Moses in Exod. xxxii.19; Samuel in I Sam. xv.11; David in II Sam. vi.8; Uzziah in II Chron. xxvi.19.

[6] Potiphar in Gen. xxxix.19; Pharaoh in Gen. xl.2; Naaman in II Kings v.12; Sanballat in Neh. iv.1; Haman in Est. iii.5.

of people and nations,[1] and also their rulers.[2] In the case of the nations it is their extreme wrath in war, their furious rage, against the people of God[3] which is threatening (Amos i.11; Isa. li.13; Ezek. xxxv.11), though it is declared to be ineffectual against the protection of Yahweh (Isa. vii.4; Ps. cxxix.3).

i. *Against other men.* The wrath of man is directed mainly against other men.[4] Human wrath is just and godly whenever it is aroused not merely in order to preserve individual rights.[5] Thus the wrath of David— to whom Nathan appealed as the highest judge—is kindled against the rich man in the story (II Sam. xii.5), or that of Nehemiah against the abused in Jerusalem (Neh. v.6); cf. also Saul's wrath against the Ammonites, which is attributed directly to the 'spirit of Yahweh' (I Sam. xi.6). The position is similar in the case of Shechem's assault on Dinah, which arouses the wrath of her brothers who take a cruel revenge (Gen. xxxiv.7),[6] and again in that of David's wrath against Amnon when he had violated Tamar (II Sam. xiii.21), although in these last two passages the disinterested motive of the wrath is not so clearly evident, for here the honour and existence of the clan are at stake. On

[1] Commanders of the Philistines in I Sam. xxix.7; the enemies of the righteous in Ps. vii.7; Edom in Amos i.11; Babylon in Isa. li.13.

[2] Nebuchadnezzar in Dan. iii.13; Ahasuerus in Est. i.12.

[3] Or against other nations in Isa. xiv.6; Dan. xi.44.

[4] Once only is there any note of wrath or resentment against an animal (Balaam's ass) in Num. xxii.27.

[5] The passage in the psalms (Ps. iv.5(4) cited in Eph. iv.26) ὀργίζεσθε καὶ μὴ ἁμαρτάνετε can hardly belong here; it does not have in view the possibility of a just wrath, but utters a warning lest the rising resentment become a sin (of word or deed).

[6] It is interesting to note that in Jacob's blessing the wrath of these brothers of Dinah is condemned (Gen. xlix.3-7); perhaps in fact because it was uncontrolled (H. Gunkel, *Genesis* ([5]1922) *ad loc.*).

the other hand special mention must be made of that
just and godly wrath which has to do with the defence
of Yahweh's cause directly in face of the infringement
of his claim to sovereignty, of lack of reverence for his
holiness. Thus Moses becomes wrathful with the
Israelites' want of faith in God (Exod. xvi.20), with
their apostasy at the mountain of God (Exod. xxxii.19,
23), with their sparing the Midianite women which had
been forbidden (Num. xxxi.14), and concerning a cultic
offence (Lev. x.16). There is a similar reason for the
wrath of Elisha (II Kings xiii.19)[1] and of Elihu (Job
xxxii.2, 3, 5). But above all the prophets must be
mentioned here as those who proclaim God's wrath and
amongst them in particular Jeremiah and Ezekiel.[2]
Jeremiah is obliged to say of himself: 'Therefore I am
full of the wrath of the Lord' (vi.11; cf. xv.17) and this
wrath of God is heard in many of his words as well in
those of the other prophets against the people of God
and against foreign nations.[3]

There seem to be merely selfish grounds for the
wrath of the man who feels himself to be injured in his
real or supposedly justifiable claim.[4] Thus, for example,
Cain is angry with Abel in Gen. iv.5; Esau with Jacob
in Gen. xxvii.44 f.; Balak with Balaam in Num. xxiv.10;
Saul with Jonathan in I Sam. xx.30; the tribes of Israel

[1] cf. also Elijah's action against the prophets of Baal (without
the technical term for wrath) in I Kings xviii.40.

[2] cf. p. 28 n. 2, 3.

[3] It is true that at times the blaze of wrath seems here to be
fanned by human and national passion which is in danger of
identifying its own nation's cause with that of God (particularly in
post-exilic prophecy).

[4] Here the dividing line between wrath and ill-will is often fluid;
in particular passages it is not a question of the natural violent
outburst of wrath, but of the expression of sullen ill-will against
an unexpected and unwelcome happening (as in Gen. xxx.2,
xxxi.35 f., xliv.18; I Sam. xxix.4; I Kings xxi.4; II Kings v.12).

with Judah in II Sam. xix.43; Pharaoh with his servants in Gen. xl.1 f.; Potiphar with Joseph in Gen. xxxix.19 and Ahasuerus with the queen Vashti in Est. i.12. Again when a man of God utters demands or threats, the wrath of the man concerned is kindled[1]; cf. Ahab when threatened by Elijah in I Kings xx.43; Asa when reproached by the seer in II Chron. xvi.10; Uzziah when forbidden by the priests in II Chron. xxvi.19.

ii. *Against God.* Man's wrath or ill-will can be directed against God himself if his dealings appear to him enigmatic and incomprehensible and he cannot reconcile them with God's justice; e.g. Samuel when Saul is rejected in I Sam. xv.11, David when Uzzah is killed in II Sam. vi.8, Job in view of his undeservedly hard fate in Job x.2 f.; xviii.4 and Jonah with regard to God's mercy to Nineveh in Jon. iv.1, 4, 9.[2] Basically the wrath of the 'righteous' because of the good fortune of the 'ungodly' is directed also against God and his authority (Ps. xxxvii.1, 7 f.; Prov. iii.31 f.).[3]

iii. *Critical assessment.* The Wisdom literature alone criticises human anger.[4] The wise men in Proverbs measure it in part by utilitarian standards in accordance with the general attitude of Wisdom thought. Wrath is dangerous because it produces trouble and has bad consequences (Prov. vi.34, xv.1, xvi.14, xix.19, xxvii.4); therefore it is to be avoided and calmed down (Prov. xv.18, xxii.24, xxix.8, 11). A warning is also given against the intelligible wrath about the good fortune of the ungodly who will receive their punishment

[1] It is in fact directed against God himself, by whom these men know that they are sent.

[2] The LXX renders *ḥārāh* in these passages with ἀθυμεῖν in I and II Sam. and with λυπεῖσθαι in Jon. iv.

[3] In Prov. iii.31b note *his ways*; and for *choose* read *be angry at* (Hithpaʿel of *ḥārāh*). Cf. LXX and Kittel BH.

[4] Lev. xix.18 forbids vindictiveness or resentment.

later (Prov. xxix.19 f.; Ps. xxxvii.7-9). Hence he who is slow to anger is praised as being truly wise (Prov. xiv.29, xv.18, xvi.32; Eccles. vii.8), whilst the hot-tempered man[1] is condemned as a fool (Prov. iv.17, 29).

The wise of course know too that the anger of men leads to wrong doing (Prov. xiv.17, xxix.22); the letter of James which is closely connected with the Wisdom literature takes up this theme in i.20: ὀργὴ γὰρ ἀνδρὸς δικαιοσύνην θεοῦ οὐκ ἐργάζεται (cf. p. 80). The contrast appearing in Proverbs 'the angry man—the wise man' is rooted not in Greek philosophy, but rather in Egyptian wisdom,[2] where the fool can be called simply the hot-head.[3] Job's anger against God is most severely condemned by his friends because by it he not only harms himself (xviii.4), but is 'doing away with the fear of God' (xv.4) and calling God's justice in question (viii.2 f., xi.2 f. et passim). God's speeches acknowledge formally that this view is right, but substantiate it on a much deeper level in Job xxxviii ff. and Job repents that he spoke to God irreverently in anger and humbles himself (xlii.6).

3. The wrath of God in the Old Testament

i. Discussion of the terms

In the OT the terms for wrath denote divine wrath considerably more often than human wrath.[4] Some of them are used in the OT literature exclusively for the wrath of God, such as ḥārōn or ḥᵃrōn 'ap, zaʿam and the

[1] Similarly Prov. xxii.24 and Prov. xxix.22.

[2] cf. J. Fichtner, Die altorientalische Weisheit in ihrer israelitischen Ausprägung (1933), pp. 20 f.

[3] For example in Amenemope: ' Do not consort with the hot-head.' ANET, p. 423, DOTT, p. 180; cf. Hempel, Althebräische Literatur (1930), p. 51.

[4] Nouns for wrath are used about 375 times for divine, about 80 times for human wrath.

verb *'ānap*, others predominantly, namely *qeṣep*[1] and *'ebrāh*, whilst *'ap* and *ḥēmāh* and the less frequent *za'ap* (and *rōgez*) are employed for human and divine wrath. Possibly *ḥārōn* or *ḥᵃrōn 'ap*[2] and *za'am*[3] were in fact reserved to reference to divine wrath in the current usage of the spoken language, though the precise evidence of usage is too scanty for a reliable verdict on this. It is significant that combinations of the terms for wrath are used only to denote divine wrath.[4] Apart from compound phrases *ḥᵃrōn 'ap* (33 times),[5] *za'ap 'ap* (Isa. xxx.30), *za'am 'ap* (Lam. ii.6) and *'ebrōt 'ap* (Job xl.11), syndetic combinations of two or even three of the terms are found: *'ap* and *ḥēmāh* (about 15 times), other combinations in Isa. xiii.9, Ps. cii.11(10), Deut. xxix.27 (similarly in Jer. xxi.5, xxxii.37) and Ps. lxxviii.49; cf. also Deut. ix.19; Ezek. v.15, xiii.13. The piling up of words, amongst which except in Ps. cii.11(10) the chief term is always *'ap* or *ḥᵃrōn 'ap*, brings out the difference in quality between human and divine wrath by giving an impressive and vivid picture of the mighty pressure of God's holy wrath, which no one can resist (Ps. lxxvi.8; Neh. i.6). The combinations of a word for wrath with the designations for God contain almost exclusively the divine name Yahweh. *'ap*, *ḥēmāh*, *'ebrāh* and *qeṣep* are combined more than 50 times with Yahweh.[6] *'ap 'ᵉlōhīm* is found only twice, namely in Ps. lxxviii.31—in the Elohist psalter (Ps. xlii-lxxxix) where Elohim is substituted for Yahweh[7]—and in Num. xxii.22

[1] The verb *qāṣap* is used for divine and human wrath.

[2] Perhaps to make a conscious distinction from *ḥᵃrē 'ap*.

[3] Similarly also the verb *zā'am*.

[4] The occurrence of synonyms in the parallel members of verses are not included in this (40 times, of which only 3 times of human wrath).

[5] Is found 4 times for human wrath.

[6] About 40 of these are *'ap Yahweh*.

[7] The basic passage in Num. xi.33 has *'ap Yahweh*.

where there is textual evidence for the reading *Yahweh*[1];
in Ezra x.14 we have the phrase *our God*, practically
identical with *Yahweh* combined with *ḥᵃrōn 'aṗ* and
finally in Job xxi.20 *ḥᵃmat šaddai* which is not surprising
in the dialogue in Job where the name Yahweh is
avoided. The consistent combination of the nouns of
wrath with Yahweh, the God of the covenant, is of
considerable theological importance; it shows that the
idea of wrath is to a large extent connected with the
faith of the covenant.[2]

In later times there is an evident effort to weaken or
even to break too close a connection of God with wrath.
This is brought out in the usage by the absolute use of
the word wrath, which we find especially in the case of
qeṣep occasionally in the post-exilic period, amongst the
Priestly writers in particular. In P *qeṣep Yahweh* never
occurs; once we read *wrath (qeṣep) has gone forth from
Yahweh* (Num. xvi.46 [Heb. xvii.11]), otherwise only
qeṣep (Num. i.53, xviii.5; Josh. ix.20, xxii.20, probably
also xxii.18[3] and Lev. x.6)[4]. The Chronicler indeed has
qeṣep Yahweh twice (II Chron. xxix.9, xxxii.26), but
beside it a *qeṣep* by itself (I Chron. xxvii.24; II Chron.
xix.2,[5] xix.10, xxiv.18, xxxii.25). He replaces the
wrath of Yahweh which, according to II Sam. xxiv.1,
incites David to number the people, by Satan in I
Chron. xxi.1. It is true that in both authors we also find
'aṗ Yahweh, but in the Chronicler chiefly in the material
taken from older sources. What is peculiar to them
is the absolute usage of the term for wrath and

[1] 1 MS. of the MT, the Samaritan, LXX (F and N), (Targ. Onkelos).

[2] Moreover there is no term for the wrath of God in Genesis.

[3] Following LXX, Syr. Targ. (cf. verse 20); M. Noth, *Das Buch Josua* (1938) *ad loc.* disagrees with this; he now considers Josh. xxii.9-34 to be a 'very late isolated addition to the book of Joshua' (*Überlieferungsgeschichtliche Studien* (1943), p. 232.)

[4] cf. LXX.   [5] In this passage with *from Yahweh*.

consequently this must be noted. Quite seldom, and also in later times only, we find other expressions for wrath used without direct reference to Yahweh[1]; cf. Ezek. vii.12: *wrath (ḥārōn) is upon all their multitude*[2]; II Chron. xxviii.13: *fierce wrath (ḥᵃrōn 'ap) is upon Israel* and Neh. xiii.18: *you bring more wrath (ḥārōn) upon Israel*.[3] Again in Isa. lxiii.5 the wrath of Yahweh appears strangely dissociated from Yahweh: *my wrath (ḥēmāh) upheld me*, but as the following verse shows, these words do not go further than a poetical personification.[4]

ii. *The objects of divine wrath*

The conception of God's wrath in the OT receives its particular stamp from the fact that basically Israel has to do with only one God[5] and thus the outlet into the pantheon and the world of demons[6] is barred. There is the further fact that the approach to this God involves a particular relationship established by his holy righteousness and electing love. Thus for the godly men of the old covenant the source of the wrath is not an unknown

[1] J. Böhmer, 'Zorn', ZAW, NF. 3 (1926), pp. 320-322, mentions a profusion of other examples of the independent usage of terms for wrath which do not concern us here.

[2] The words are missing in LXX(B); they occur (with *my wrath*) also in verse 14.

[3] J. Boehmer's thesis (cf. previous note), p. 321 that an original belief in 'demons which had not yet been subdued and absorbed by the supreme deity' shimmers through the absolute usage of the terms for wrath is already refuted by the late appearance of this employment of the terms for wrath.

[4] For za'am used absolutely, cf. p. 17, n. 1.

[5] cf. on the other hand, e.g. M. Jastrow, *Die Religion Babyloniens und Assyriens* I (1905), pp. 362, 477-479; S. H. Hooke, *Babylonian and Assyrian Religion* (1953, 1962), pp. 12-38; in the OT only in II Kings iii.27 is a direct mention made of the wrath of another god, Chemosh of the Moabites.

[6] TWNT II, pp. 10 ff.; cf. F. Baumgärtel, *Die Eigenart der alttestamentlichen Frömmigkeit* (1932), p. 63.

deity or even a feeling of the power of fate, but an 'unmistakable definite divine person'.[1] This does not mean that thereby the irrational would be banished from faith in God—this will become clear when we examine the conception of divine wrath more closely—but that the men of the OT, as they became aware of their faith and came to terms with life, found themselves, through their survey of their past history, through their attitude to the present and as they looked into the future, directed along one path alone and met there, not a dark problematic force, but the will of Yahweh like that of a person, with whom it is important to come to terms. The personal quality of the OT conception of God conditions particularly the 'anthropopathic' manner of speaking about wrath, but it gives it also its impressive vitality.[2] The danger of obliterating the dividing line between God and man by excessive anthropopathism is averted because the godly man in the OT had a strong sense of distance with regard to his God[3] and a deep insight into the nature of the divine wrath. This is what differentiates it from human wrath which is rooted predominantly in the tyrannical ego of man.[4]

To proclaim God's wrath is in the OT not the same as to describe the divine act of judgement[5]; this denotes not only an action but a vital process in God himself, 'an emotional disturbance' of God.[6] Now of course in so far as this disturbance does not affect the being of

[1] G. Quell, in *Lord* in this series, p. 44.

[2] cf. W. Eichrodt, *Theologie* I, pp. 98-100 (E.T. (1960), pp. 210 ff.)

[3] cf. J. Hempel, *Gott und Mensch im AT* (1936), 198, pp. 267 f.

[4] For the 'godly, just wrath' of man, cf. above p. 19.

[5] It is true that Yahweh's wrath in action acquires a visible form when he judges; cf. wrath and judgement in Ezek. v.15; Mic. vii.9; Ps. vii.7; wrath and vengeance: Ezek. xxiv.8; Nah. i.2.

[6] F. Weber, p. 11.

God himself,[1] but enters into relationship with the being established by him outside himself, with the world and its powers, those passages of the OT which speak of God's wrath, rightly raise the question at what targets it is directed.

(a) In the first place it is Israel itself at which the wrath of Yahweh is aimed. Already when the covenant is being made, he threatens each one who might approach Yahweh's holiness too closely (Exod. xix. JE), and in the history of the period in the wilderness it plays a significant role both with the Yahwist and the Elohist[2] as well as in Deuteronomy and the Priestly writings.[3] Similarly he intervenes repeatedly in the history of the people from the conquest (cf. Josh. vii. JE(?), xxii.20P) down to the exile (I Sam. vi.19, xv, xxviii.18; II Sam. vi.7, xxiv.1). The Deuteronomic survey of history has presented this period entirely from the point of view of divine wrath ever aroused afresh (cf. pp. 38 f.), and the Chronicler's historical work too has something to say about it (I Chron. xiii.10, xxvii.24; II Chron. xix.2, xxiv.18, xxix.8), as do also the historical psalms (e.g. lxxviii.31, cvi.32).[4] These passages display—especially in the earlier period—the collective involvement of the individual within the totality of God's people. God's wrath is directed against the individual in his particular function amongst the people of God, e.g. (against Moses (Exod. iv.14; Deut. i.37), Aaron (Deut. ix.20); Miriam

[1] Such a possibility is completely alien to the OT way of thinking.

[2] Exod. xxxii; Num. xi.1, 10, 33, xii.9, xiii.25, xiv.38, xxv.3, 4.

[3] Deut. i.34, 37, ix.8, 19 f. Num. xvii. 11,xviii.5, xxv.7-13, xxxii. 10-14, Lev. x.6.

[4] cf. also the exhortations of Deut. (vi.15, vii.4, xi.17, xxix.19 ff.) or the corresponding sections from the Priestly tradition (Lev. xxvi.28; Num. i.53; Josh. xxii.18; II Chron. xix.10). It is very significant that in the legal corpora of the Pentateuch there are only sporadic cases of the threatening wrath of God being made the motive for obedience (Exod. xxii.23; Lev. xxvi.20).

(Num. xii.9), Nadab and Abihu (Lev. x.6) and against kings and prophets (I Sam. xv; II Kings xxiii.26; II Chron. xxix.8; Jer. xxi.1-7). On the other hand in his wrath his judgement strikes the whole people on account of the sin of individuals (Josh. vii, Achan's theft, II Sam. xxiv, David's census). In the later period this collective bond is relaxed (cf. Ps. vi.2(1), xxvii.9, xxxviii.2(1)).

Amongst the prophets, it was especially those active before the exile who made the onset of Yahweh's wrath against his people the central subject of their message, even if they—as, e.g. Amos—do not all employ for it the term wrath.[1] Their conflict is with the false security of the people founded on their consciousness of being chosen and felt to be protected from wrathful condemnation (Amos iii.2, v.18; Hos. xiii.9-11; Isa. v.18 f., xxviii.14-22; Mic. iii.11; Zeph. ii.2; Jer. vii.4, xxviii. 1-17; Ezek. v.13, xvi.38). Amongst them Jeremiah[2] and Ezekiel[3] can actually be described as prophets of Yahweh's wrath against his people. The prophets during and after the exile do indeed see this as the consequence of Yahweh's wrath[4] and no longer like their predecessors proclaim the annihilating onslaught of his wrath on the people of God; but yet they are aware—particularly after the return—that Yahweh's wrath still rests on the people (Hag. i. 5-11; Zech. i.3, 12) or threatens it anew (Joel, Isa. liv.8); we hear the same in the laments of this period Ps. lxxiv.1-8, lxxxv.4, 6).

[1] It may be stated as a matter of principle that we make use in the first place of passages which employ the technical terms for wrath, but occasionally refer also to passages in which the concept of wrath appears without the corresponding technical terms.

[2] Jer. iv.4, 8, 26, vii.20, 29, xvii.4, xxxii.31, xxxvi.7 *et passim*.

[3] Ezek. v.15, vi.12, vii.8, viii.15, xiv.19, xvi.38, xx.8 *et passim*. cf. A. Ruegg, RE³ 21, 720.

[4] Isa. xlii.25, xlvii.6, li.17, lx.10; Zech. i.2, 13.

(b) The nations and their rulers are objects of God's wrath as well as Israel. The prophetic threats are directed against them in the so-called 'oracles of the nations' in the books of Amos, Isaiah, Jeremiah and Ezekiel and in the prophecies of Zephaniah, Obadiah, Nahum, Habakkuk and Joel and also in the book of Jonah.[1] The prophets of the exilic and post-exilic period in particular announce the wrath of God against the nations (Isa. xiii.3, 5, 9, 13, xxx.27, lix.18, lx.3, 6, lxvi.14; Jer. l.13, 15, li.45; Ezek. xxv.4, xxx.15; Jonah iii.9 *et passim*.[2] The Psalms too which speak of the final victory of Yahweh and his Anointed threaten the peoples with God's wrath (Ps. ii.5, 12, cx.5). When he breaks forth in the days to come, all the earth (cf. Deut. xxxii.22), all mankind will be affected by it (Jer. x.10; Isa. xiii.9, 11; Zeph. iii.8), just as in the days of old his condemnation struck all men (Gen. iii, vi-viii, xi).

iii. *Divine wrath in action*

The description of the divine wrath in action, of its effects and instruments, must take account of very varied material in the OT tradition.[3] One thing is common to the diverse ways in which God's wrath is shown at work; where it threatens or takes action, the very existence of him who is struck is at stake; in other words, when the existence of a man of the old covenant is threatened, he becomes aware of the wrath of his God.

The annihilating might of God's wrath and his irresistible power are displayed in the metaphors and pictorial phrases used for what that wrath brings about.

[1] cf. H. Gressmann, *Der Messias* (1929), pp. 97-148.

[2] Sometimes the names of particular nations are specified, sometimes only 'the nations' in general are spoken of.

[3] cf. II Sam. vi.7, xxiv.1 with Jeremiah's sermon on wrath or Num. i.53, xvii.11 with the experience of the divine wrath in the book of Job.

Here a distinction must be made between metaphors
which are taken from a field remote from the sphere of
wrath and illustrate a typical feature of the occurrence
of wrath, and those descriptions used not only as metaphors but in addition representing the way in which the
divine wrath at work actually makes its appearance.
This applies to the commonest metaphor of God's
wrath which expresses in a particularly vivid manner
its devastating effect, the metaphor of fire. When
Yahweh's holiness is violated, then his wrath is kindled,[1]
a fire flares up in his nostrils (Jer. xv.14, xvii.4; cf. Isa.
lxv.5), and smoke rises from them (Ps. xviii.9),[2] his
tongue is *like a devouring fire* in Isa. xxx.27.[3] The blazing
and consuming fire is by no means only a metaphor for
God in anger, but it also represents the wrath actually
at work: *the breath of Yahweh, like a stream of brimstone,
kindles it (tōpheth)* in Isa. xxx.33; cf. Deut. xxxii.22;
Ezek. xx.31. The use of metaphors and actual descriptions of the fire of wrath can also pass directly into each
other; cf. Ezek. xxi.31 [Heb. 36 f.]; Isa. xxx.27-33.
This shows to how small an extent these biblical statements are intended to be metaphors (in our sense).
Something similar to the metaphor of fire applies to
that of the storm which represents the destructive power
of wrath, even though it occurs more rarely than the
former in connection with wrath (Jer. xxx.23; cf. Isa.
xxx.30; Ps. lxxxiii.16[4] and also Isa. ii.6-22). Akin to
the conception of the storm of wrath is that of Yahweh
snorting in wrath, which lies behind the use of the word

[1] Usually *ḥārāh*, also *bā'ar* in Ps. ii.12(11), *yāṣat* in II Kings
xxii.13 and *yāqad* in Isa. lxv.5.

[2] In Deut. xxix.19(20) and in Ps. lxxiv.1 smoke actually takes the
place of wrathfulness.

[3] cf. also the etymology of *ḥārāh* and cf. p. 15.

[4] The LXX has significantly rendered with ὀργή both *storm*
(Ps. lxxxiii.15 [LXX, lxxxii.16]) and also *storm* and *tempest* (Jer.
xxx.23 [LXX, xxxvii.23]).

rūaḥ (cf. p. 18) and can be seen in the etymology of *'ānap* and *'ap* (cf. p. 14).

The wrath of God, in addition to being represented as heat, fire and storm, has another description, namely as a liquid. This occurs in the metaphor of *emptying out* and *drinking* the wrath. God pours out his wrath over the people of God and the foreign nations as water is poured out in Hos. v.10; cf. Jer. x.25; Ps. lxix.24(25) and especially Ezek. vii.8, xiv.19, xx.8 *et passim*. The metaphor of pouring out can be combined with that of fire: cf. Nah. i.6; Lam. ii.4 and in parallel verses or verse members in Ezek. xxi.31 [Heb. 36], xxii.31. It is impossible to decide whether the thought here is of representations of fire and brimstone (Ezek. xxxviii.22) or of streams of pitch (cf. Isa. xxx.33, xxxiv.9), or whether the piling up of metaphors is intended to make vivid the greatness and horror of the judgement of wrath. On the other hand the phrase about drinking the wrath as it occurs in Job xxi.20[1] and especially in the conception of the wine of wrath in Jer. xxv.15[2] and of the cup of wrath in Isa. li.17, 22; Jer. xxv.15 (cf. TWNT III, p. 168; V, p. 166)[3] is pure metaphor. It brings impressively before our eyes the fact that the wrath is inescapable and must be endured to the full.[4] The prophet offering the cup of wrath in Jer. xxv.15-28 calls up irrevocably the judgement of wrath on Jerusalem and the nations.[5]

[1] *Let him drink of the wrath of the Almighty.*

[2] *Wine of wrath* (*ḥēmāh*) occurs only here; the words are sometimes considered to be a gloss. But the LXX (τοῦ οἴνου τοῦ ἀρκάτου) tells against this; did it read *ḥemer* (*fermenting wine*) instead of *ḥēmāh*?

[3] The LXX renders *cup of wrath* (*ḥēmāh*) in Isa. li.7, 22 with τὸ ποτήριον (or τὸ κόνδυ) τοῦ θυμοῦ; in Rev. xiv.10 τὸ ποτήριον τῆς 'οργῆς αὐτοῦ appears with ὁ οἶνος τοῦ θυμοῦ.

[4] In Isa. li.17 *thou hast drunk to the dregs.*

[5] The metaphor of the winepress of wrath is also used once (Isa. lxiii.1-6).

The nations appear as the weapons of the wrathful God or as the instruments of his chastisement when they are spoken of as the *weapons of his indignation* (*za'am*) in Isa. xiii.5; Jer. l.25[1] and also as a *rod of anger* (*'ap*) or *staff of fury* (*za'am*) in Isa. x.5.[2] In this vivid metaphor is summed up the conception current throughout the whole OT that God can let his wrath be carried out by earthly powers. Beside it there appears the more abstract notion that he employs his arm as the instrument of his wrath in Isa. ix.12(11).

The metaphorical phrases for the onset and the cessation of God's wrath reveal something of the twofold use of the terms for wrath. When it is a question of the emotional disturbance, then the kindling or rising up of the wrath, or the fact that Yahweh will assuage his wrath, may have been used most frequently as in Ezek. v.13, vi.12; Lam. iv.11; when it was a question of wrath in action then the natural phrases are *raising wrath up* as in II Chron. xxxvi.16; *sending it* in Job xx.23; Ps. lxxviii.49; *carrying it out* in I Sam. xxviii.18; cf. Hos. xi.9. One might be inclined to infer the same twofold character from the differing use of the verb *return* (*šūb*) for the ending of the wrath: Yahweh *ceases from his wrath* in Exod. xxxii.12; II Kings xxiii.26; Jon. iii.9 (readily linked with *repent*) or he *turns away his wrath* in Jer. xviii.20; Ezra x.4; alternatively the *wrath is turned back* in Jer. iv.6; Isa. v.25; Hos. xiv.4(5). But this last phrase can also mean that the wrath has calmed down (not only that its judgement has come to an end), so that care must be exercised in making such distinctions

[1] Jer. [LXX, xxvii.25] has the literal rendering τὰ σκεύη ὀργῆς: Isa. xiii.5—no doubt in view of verse 4 (ἔθνος ὁπλομάχον) has οἱ ὁπλομάχοι (fighting with heavy weapons).

[2] Lam. iii.1 speaks of a *rod of wrath* (*'ebrāh*) as a metaphor for wrath in action; cf. Job. ix.34, xxi.9 and Prov. xxii.8 (of human wrath [*'ebrāh*]).

in view of the usage noted here. In the late period (of P and the Chronicler) the vaguer phrase *wrath comes* (*hāyāh*) is often used for the outbreak of the wrath (Num. i.53, xviii.5; Josh. xxii.20; I Chron. xxvii.24 *et passim*).

The basic effect of Yahweh's wrath is intended to be annihilation, complete obliteration. Thus it is said for instance in the exhortations of Deuteronomy: *the anger ('ap) of Yahweh would be kindled against you and he would speedily destroy you* (Deut. vii.4; cf. also ix.8, 19, 25 *et passim*) or in the Priestly writings: *I will consume them in a moment* in Num. xvi.21, xvii.10. The prophets too proclaim to Israel the all-consuming wrath of Yahweh (Ezek. xxii.31, xliii.8; Isa. xxx.28, xxxiv.2, 5, lxiii.1-3; Jer. l.13). Here we must notice that the prophets[1] describe the divine wrath not only in powerful metaphors, in part of cosmic proportions, and for this purpose bring into play the whole creation (Isa. xiii.13, xxx.30, xxxiv.2-4, lxvi.15 ff.; Ezek. xxxviii.22 *et passim*), but they bring it into relationship with actual historical events. Thus they interpret the affliction and the overthrow of their nation in past and present as the working of Yahweh's wrath which Israel comes to feel in separate onslaughts. Isaiah concludes his great poem of menaces with the refrain: *for all this his anger ('ap) is not turned away, and his hand is stretched out still* (ix.12 [Heb. 11], 17(16), 21(20); x.4, v.25).[2] According to him Yahweh hands over the people of his wrath to the Assyrian as the rod of his anger (x.5 f.; cf. ix.11(10) f.)[3]. For Israel the judgement of wrath consists above all in banishment from their land (*passim*). For the prophets,

---

[1] Just as in the Deuteronomic interpretation of history (see above).

[2] cf. Amos iv.6-12 (without the technical terms for wrath).

[3] With regard to other peoples too the nations become the weapons of his wrath (Isa. xiii.5; Jer. i.25) through whom he executes his judgement of wrath upon them, i.e. destroys them.

whether they look forwards or backwards, the exile is the chief example of God's wrath in action and in judgement. Similarly the early traditions, worked up and interpreted by the historians, record the destructive force and the terrifying dimensions of Yahweh's wrath, which achieves its purpose by drought and famine, pestilence and plague, wholesale slaughter of those affected, and abandonment to their enemies (Num. xi.1, 10, 33, xii.9, xvi.46 [Heb. xvii.11]; I Sam. vi.19; II Sam. xxiv *et passim*). With mysterious, irresistible power he falls upon them and lays low thousands[1] or strikes at individuals who presume to approach the Holy One (Exod. xix.1; II Sam. vi.7). It is of minor importance in this connection that at times the actual historical facts have perhaps not been reproduced in the same way as in the prophetic interpretation of history.

The proclamation of the prophets develops beyond the interpretation of events within history—perhaps in connection with earlier popular expectations[2]—more and more into the message of the final judgement of wrath in which Yahweh's claim to sovereignty prevails against all powers opposing him and brings history to an end. The prophets of the earlier period announce this judgement of wrath not only with regard to the 'nations', but also especially with regard to God's people which has turned away from its God.[3] In this sense they can speak of the Day of Yahweh, the 'day of wrath' as an eschatological event (Amos v.18-20; Isa. ii.6-21; Zeph. i.15, 18). From him no escape is

[1] In Num. xvi.49 (Heb. xvii.14), 14,700; in xxv.9, 24,000; in I Sam. vi.19, 50,070; in II Sam. xxiv.15, as many as 70,000 slain.

[2] cf. H. Gressmann, *Der Ursprung der israelitisch-jüdischen Eschatologie* (1905), pp. 144 f.

[3] It is not always possible to distinguish clearly in the prophetic writings (and elsewhere too in the OT) between the sway of the divine wrath within history or at the end of time; cf. therefore also p. 42.

possible for Israel—unless maybe that a few will be hidden from him by means of a timely repentance (Zeph. ii.1-3); nothing can avert the coming of the judgement of wrath. It rests entirely with Yahweh's love and merciful covenant to prevent wrath against Israel spending itself to the full and through the judgement of wrath to bring about the time of salvation which delivers Israel from the wrath. In the post-exilic period, especially in later Judaism, the coming judgement of wrath is expected in the first place on the nations (Ps. ix.17 f.; lvi.7[8]; lxxix.5-7[6-8]) and on the wicked and ungodly within the congregation (Ps. vii. 6[7]; xi.5 f., xxviii.4, xciv.2), whilst the godly amongst God's people believes that having experienced the forgiveness of his sins he is in safe keeping from the coming wrath (Ps. xxx.6, lxv.3 f., ciii.3). It is true that at this time too there can be no question of salvation being certain, of relying firmly on escape from the approaching judgement of wrath, especially since the weight of the wrath on the congregation and individuals amongst it—in spite of all experience of the forgiveness of sins— can never abolish the problem of the final appeasement of the divine wrath (cf. p. 50).

It may befall the individual godly man—as can be seen especially from the evidence of the later period[1]—to experience some shortening of life and a threat to his existence: sickness, oppression by personal enemies, the menace of premature death and the consciousness that God is far off, these are the signs of wrath (e.g. Ps. lxxxviii.16, xc.7, 9, cii.8[9], 10 f.[11], 23 [24]). This is displayed in a particularly impressive manner in the book of Job. Here the righteous man feels that he has been struck down by the wrath of God who has taken from him not only possessions and health, but also his

[1] The individual acts of wrath mentioned above (e.g. II Sam. vi.7) are here disregarded.

rights and his honour[1] and allows him in his wrath to discover the hidden nature of God (cf. below, pp. 37, 46).

iv. *The motives for divine wrath*

The search for the motives for divine wrath leads us to discuss God's inmost being and at the same time to fit the conception of his divine wrath into the presentation of God in the OT faith. A series of data in OT writings provides additional evidence that men saw themselves faced basically by an irrational and in the last resort inexplicable occurrence, befalling them with enigmatic and mysterious power.[2] Gen. xxxii.23-33 (Jacob's wrestling at the Jabbok) and Exod. iv.24 f. (Yahweh's attempt on Moses' life) betray an awareness of this. It is evident elsewhere too in various passages dealing with the sinister and fatal intervention of the holy God whom man may not see face to face (Exod. xxxiii.20; Judges xiii.22; Isa. vi.3), who destroys all that approaches his holiness too closely (Exod. xix.9-25, xx.18-21; Num. i.52 f.; I Sam. vi.19; II Sam. vi.7). In II Sam. xxiv.1 (Yahweh incites David to number the people), the motive for the unfounded and incomprehensible wrath of God is openly exposed (cf. also I Sam. xxvi.19=*if it is Yahweh who has stirred you up against me*). According to II Sam. xxi.14 Yahweh's wrath has been appeased; in xxiv.1 it breaks out again without any apparent reason; cf. also I Kings xxii.20 f. The change made in II Sam. xxiv by the Chronicler who replaces the wrath of Yahweh by Satan as the originator of David's temptation (I Chron. xxi.1), shows how vigorously later times repudiated such an interpretation. The lamentations of individuals in the

---

[1] cf. F. Baumgärtel, *Der Hiobdialog* (1933), p. 174.
[2] P. Volz, pp. 7-17.

Psalter and the book of Job in particular prove that the godly man was conscious of finding himself handed over to the wrath of Yahweh often for no reason. Thus the worshipper in Ps. lxxxviii, who has nothing to say about his guilt, complains to Yahweh whose *terrors I suffer from my youth up* that *thy wrath (ḥārōn) has swept over me* (verse 17), and Job rebels against God with the words: *He has torn me in his wrath ('ap) and hated me; he has gnashed his teeth at me* (xvi.9); *he has kindled (ḥārāh) his wrath ('ap) against me and counted me as his adversary* (xix.11). Admittedly this evidence from later times cannot be placed beside the early stories of sinister attack by divine wrath. The godly men of the post-exilic period measure their fate by the standard of strictly individual retribution which was not applied so consistently in earlier times. Nevertheless in the later as in the earlier period men were actively aware of being exposed to the behaviour of God which was so incomprehensible as to approximate to caprice and of which it may perhaps be more appropriate to say that the 'completely un-fathomable', 'the entirely other' is encountered, the *tremendum*.[1]

Here the element of Yahweh's inconceivable power and holiness outweighs other motives to be discussed later. But Yahweh's incomprehensible, terrifying be-haviour must not be explained as due to the absorbing of antiquity's faith in demons (cf. p. 25 n. 3), but it must be clearly stated that 'in the last resort "the demonic" in Yahweh has not been introduced into his nature, but is an original quality . . . is bound up with the inmost nature of this God and of his religion'.[2]

Yahweh's actions were indeed increasingly taken out of the sphere of the unaccountable and men were seeking more and more earnestly for an answer as to the

[1] Otto, pp. 21, 97. ET *The Idea of the Holy* (1928), pp. 19, 78; cf. Volz, p. 12 *et passim*.   [2] Volz, p. 33.

cause of divine wrath.[1] It appears to be a reaction to man's behaviour or failure. With Israel in view it is felt to be the wrath of the God who has made known his will to save by pledges and guidance and who requires absolute devotion from the people, that is to say, worship of himself alone, complete trust and fulfilment of the demands imposed. It is the wrath of the God of the Covenant who has given the promises and the Law and has thereby bound Israel exclusively to himself.

Thus wrath, according to all the sources of the Pentateuch, strikes the people, or individual groups among them, when they revolt against Yahweh's saving will, when they murmur against his leadership during the desert wanderings (Num. xi.1(E), xvi.41-50 [Heb. xvii.6-15] (P), xiii.25-xiv.38(JE); Deut. i.34-36). When Achan broke faith (Josh. vii.1; xxii.20) and Saul spared Agag, king of the Amalekites, the wrath of Yahweh was kindled.[2] The open apostasy of the people from their God, the turning towards strange gods, is a particularly constantly recurring motive for divine anger against Israel.[3] From Exodus xxxii ('the golden calf') and Num. xxv (Ba'al Pe'or) it pervades not only the exhortations of Deuteronomy (xi.16 f., xii.23-xiii.19, xxix. 15-17; Josh. xxiii.16), but also the presentation of the history

[1] The first series of Job's speeches too are pervaded by the 'wherefore', searching for an explanation of the wrath (Job [iii.11], vii.20, x.18, xiii.24).

[2] The Priestly historical writing and exhortation presents the whole sphere of ritual and cult as overshadowed by God's wrath: Nadab and Abihu who wished to offer *strange* (?unholy) *fire* before the Lord are devoured by the fire of Yahweh's wrath (Lev. x.1 f.); wrong behaviour on the part of the priests may easily bring wrath upon the congregation (Lev. x.6); similarly it can be provoked by the profanation of the Sabbath (Neh. xiii.18).

[3] A. Ritschl has pointed out correctly that the real cause of God's anger is *defectus a foedere*, even though he has argued this in too one-sided a manner.

during the period of the judges and the kings with its essentially Deuteronomic interpretation.[1] We meet it also in the well-known sequence; apostasy of the people, this provokes Yahweh, wrath of Yahweh who sells Israel to foreign nations, etc.[2]

This reveals the mainsprings of the action of divine wrath with regard to Israel. We find them in their greatest breadth and depth in the prophets. These never weary of emphasising what Yahweh has done for Israel by choosing and guiding them[3] and against this background deliver their message of Yahweh's wrath.[4] Behind all the individual accusations of the prophets, whether they refer to the cult[5] or to social injustice,[6] to the policy of preparing for war and entering into alliances,[7] or simply to the worship of other gods,[8] there stands in the last resort the *one* great accusation: the nation has forgotten its God, has turned away from him and thereby despised his love.[9] This is the deepest root of the conception of wrath and this explains the whole overwhelming force of the message; it is Yahweh's wounded, holy love which arouses his wrath.[10] His wrath is analogous to his holiness (*qōdeš*) and to his

[1] Deut. iv. 25, ix.18; Judg. ii.14, iii.8, v.7; I Kings xiv.15, xvi. 33; II Kings xvii.17, xxi.6, xxii.17 *et passim*.

[2] The Chronicler gives similar motives in II Chron. xii.1-7, xvi.7-12, xxv.14-18 *et passim*.

[3] cf. e.g. Amos ii.9-11, iii.2; Hos.xi.1-6; Isa. i.2, v.1 f., xvii.10; Jer. ii.1-3, xxxi.1-3; Ezek. xvi.4-14.

[4] e.g. Hos. v.10, viii.5, xiii.11; Isa. ix.11; Jer. iv.4, xvii.4; Ezek. v.13, vii.3, xx.8, etc.

[5] Amos v. 21-27; Hos. vi.6; Isa. i.10-17; Jer. vi.20, vii.21-28.

[6] e.g. Amos v.7, 10-12; Isa. i.15-17; Mic. iii.1; Jer. v.28 *et passim*.

[7] cf. Hos. v.13, vii.11; Isa. xxx.1-5, xxxi.1-3; Jer. ii.35-37; Ezek. xvi.23 *et passim*.

[8] Alternatively what appears to be the worship of Yahweh in alien cultic forms.

[9] cf. above n. 3.   [10] Eichrodt, p. 125 (ET, p. 259).

mercy (*ḥesed*), Yahweh's care for Israel, which con-
stitutes the foundation of the covenant relationship.
The not infrequent association of the conception of
Yahweh's jealousy (cf. TWNT II, pp. 880-882) with
that of his anger throws light on this fact.[1]

The jealousy of Yahweh is rooted in the relationship
between the holy God and his chosen people.[2] But
election includes within it God's gracious condescension
to Israel and his demand for the loyalty and obedience
of his people. If Yahweh's love finds no response from
his people and they turn to other gods, then Yahweh's
'jealousy' is kindled and this issues in wrath (Deut.
xxxii.20 f.; cf. Ps. lxxviii.58, lxxxix.5) and brings about
the rejection of Israel, his unfaithful wife (Ezek. xvi,
xxiii). The same term 'jealousy', however, can denote
Yahweh's concern for his people, as is attested from the
exile onwards. Yahweh, as loving husband, stands in
front of his people when they are threatened by other
nations (Isa. xlii.13, lix.17, lxiii.15), and in his wrathful
zeal brings destruction to the nations, but brings in
salvation for his own (Zech. i.14 f., viii.2 f.; Nah. i.2).

Many parts of the message of God's wrath against the
nations can be assigned to this motive. This is particularly evident in the post-exilic period when the
intervention of the nations in Israel's life was experienced, as in the hatred of Edom and the intention of
Babylon and other nations to destroy her;[3] in Israel
Yahweh himself is attacked; his people's honour is his

[1] *Jealousy* (*qin'āh*) is found in association with the terms for wrath
in: Deut. xxix.19; Ezek. xvi.38, xxxvi.6, and parallel with them in
Deut. vi.15; Ezek. v.13, xvi.42; Zeph. iii.8; Ps. lxxxix.5; Nah.
i.2.

[2] cf. F. Küchler, 'Der Gedanke des Eifers Jahves im AT', ZAW
28 (1908), pp. 42-52.

[3] Jer. x.25 (late): *Pour out thy wrath upon the nations that knew
thee not . . . for they have devoured Jacob*; cf. Zech. ii. 1-4; Mal. i.3 f.
et passim.

own honour (Isa. xlviii.9-11 and especially Ezekiel). Here a genuine concern of the prophets is expressed, though at times in the post-exilic period it is formulated in too exaggerated and one-sided a manner. The same motive already dominates the earlier historical writings when it is a matter of describing how Yahweh enforces his saving will against the enemies of his people (Exod. xviii.27-30; Josh. xxiv.12; Num. xxiv.18).[1] The basic foundation of this motive for Yahweh's wrath against the nations is his absolute claim to rule the whole world, a claim directed against the *hubris* of the nations (cf. Gen. xi) and their rulers, against their tyranny, and also against the infringement of his universally valid commandments. Thus Isaiah announces Yahweh's judgement to the Assyrian, called to be the rod of his anger against Israel, because he has over-stepped the limits of his authority (Isa. x.5-15; cf. xiv.4-6, xvi.6; Ezek. xxv.15-17, xxviii.1-17; Zech. i.15). In the same way his wrath strikes (Deut. xxix.23 [Heb. 22]) the immoral doings of Sodom and Gomorrah (Gen. xix), the Moabites' lack of awe (Amos ii.1) and the wickedness of Nineveh (Jonah i.2).[2]

Beyond all this we find that the OT proclaims the divine wrath in action throughout all human life. It interprets troubles and the finiteness of life as the result of the *hubris* of men and the guilt in which this involves them. From the fall of the first man (Gen. ii-iii) this train of thought leads through the increasing wickedness of men (Gen. vi-viii) and their plans to reach the heavens (Gen. xi) to the final verdict of the psalmist: *For we are consumed by thy anger ('ap); and by thy wrath (ḥēmāh) we are overwhelmed* in Ps. xc.7, which points to human sin to justify it (cf. verse 8); cf. also Job xiv.1-4:

---

[1] cf. Ritschl, *Rechtfertigung und Versöhnung* II, p. 128.

[2] The ethical motive by itself for Yahweh's wrath against the nations appears comparatively seldom in the OT.

*Man that is born of a woman is of few days and full of
trouble . . . who can bring a clean thing out of an unclean?*[1]
According to this all human life is a life of sin and is
subject to the ever active wrath of God.

v. *The onset, duration and averting of divine wrath*

When examining the onset of the wrath, its duration
and averting, we must again make a distinction between
its action within history and at the end of time. In this
section we are considering chiefly historical wrath (for
wrath as an eschatological occurrence cf. p. 34). Yahweh's wrath against Israel is carried into effect within
the history of his people by individual acts and in particular by the exile of the nation. In this sense the 'day
of wrath' which is expected or has already arrived can
be spoken of as an event within history (cf. TWNT II,
p. 947), in fact by remembering the fate of the nation
(Ezek. vii.19, xxii.24; Lam. i.12, 21, ii.1, 21 f.), and
also that of the individual (Job xx.28, xxi.30; Prov.
xi.4). Not infrequently, especially in the historical
writings of the OT, the onset of the divine wrath is
described as a sudden blow, as breaking in unheralded.
Like lightning it strikes those who have sinned against
Yahweh (Exod. xix.12; Num. xi.33, xii.9, xvii.6-11,
xxv.9-11; II Sam. vi.7).

On the other hand the OT testifies many times to
Yahweh's forbearance (cf. TWNT IV, pp. 378-381),
so that he does not allow his wrath free play, but restrains it and waits patiently (Exod. xxxiv.6 f.; Num.
xiv.18; Nah. i.3; Isa. xlviii.9; Ps. ciii.8). By means of
individual blows he warns Israel and exhorts them to
repent before he proceeds in his wrath to complete
annihilation. The prophetic writings contain proof of

[1] G. Hölscher, *Das Buch Hiob* (Handbuch zum AT I, 17, 1937)
ad loc. deletes the last words on the ground of rhythm ('metrically
unsatisfactory'), but this is scarcely correct; cf. Job iv.17. [But
cf. F. Horst, *Hiob* (1960 ff.), p. 207.]

this in many places, both in utterances of wrath (e.g. Amos. iv.6-11; Isa. ix.12 [Heb. 11] and parallels; Jer. iv.4), and also in the passages quoted above making a loving appeal (cf. p. 39 n. 3). When turning to Israel in his mercy,[1] Yahweh either prevents his wrath from taking effect (cf. especially Hos. xi.9)[2] or he shows kindness to his people.[3] By his forbearance he gives Israel an opportunity for penitence and repentance. This applies also to his forbearance towards Nineveh of which Jonah complained; whilst elsewhere in the case of the enemies of his people Yahweh's patient waiting (Jer.xv.15; Ps. vii.6 [Heb. 7], lxxvii.9 [Heb. 10] *et passim*) is due to the wish on the one hand to test and to chastise his people and on the other to bring more clearly into the open the guilt of their enemies.

Those who groan under the effects of the wrath as it is expressed in the course of history repeatedly ask how long it will endure. Jeremiah already puts the question into the people's mouth: *Will he be angry for ever, will he be indignant to the end?* (iii.5) and declares Yahweh's reply: *Return . . . for I am merciful. . . . I will not be angry for ever* (iii.12).[4] During the exile the hope is born that Yahweh's anger with his people has come to an end (Isa. xl.2; cf. Ps. ciii.9); in Deutero-Isaiah it is founded on the well-known passage: *In overflowing wrath for a moment I hid my face from you, but with perpetual mercy (ḥesed)[5] I will have compassion on you. . . . I have sworn that*

---

[1] Yahweh's forbearance is based on mercy (*ḥesed*) and compassion (*raḥᵃmīm*) (cf. TWNT II, pp. 475-479).

[2] *I will not execute my fierce anger . . . for I am God and not man, the Holy One in your midst and I will not come to destroy.*

[3] cf. Exod. xxxiv.6 f.; Num. xiv.18; Nah. i.3 (*and will by no means clear the guilty*).

[4] These verses do not belong to the same context, but their content may be brought together.

[5] The Isaiah scroll reads the plural, cf. *The Dead Sea Scrolls of St. Mark's Monastery* I (1950), Pl. 45.

I will not be angry with you (liv.8-10). And yet particularly after the exile the question of the duration of the
wrath is heard again and again in the psalms (Ps.
lxxix.5, lxxxv.5 [Heb. 6], lxxxix.46 [Heb. 47]) and in
the words of the prophets (Hag. i.5-11; Zech. i.3, 12).
To a greater extent than before the exile the congregation is aware from its life—just as the individual is
aware of it in his own lot—of the burden of God's
wrath. It is this experience which later produces in the
apocalyptic writings the recognition that the 'period of
wrath' prevails and must run its course, before the time
of mercy can dawn (Isa. xxvi.20; Dan. viii.19, xi.36;
cf. p. 17). This, it is hoped, will bring the wrath to an
end. On the other hand with regard to Yahweh's
enemies apart from Israel it can be proclaimed that his
wrath lasts for ever (cf. Nah. i.2), and in Mal. i.4 Edom
is described as *the people with whom Yahweh is angry for ever.*
Here the reflections on wrath within history and in the
eschatological sphere overlap. At the same time the
fact is expressed that Yahweh's wrath against the
nations is the reverse side of his care for Israel: the
enemies of Yahweh (and of the people) who thwart his
saving will, are destined for complete destruction.

The law was given with the purpose of warding off
Yahweh's devouring wrath and of preserving for Israel
the favour and mercy of its God, and this was largely
the aim too of the prophetic preaching,[1] for Yahweh is
a jealous God who punishes sins. Thus a warning in
the framework of Deuteronomy ends with the words
*lest the anger of Yahweh your God be kindled against you and he
destroy you from off the face of the earth* (Deut. vi.15). The
later period assigns to the cult and its servants the
crucial role of preserving the congregation from the

---

[1] The proclamation of inescapable judgement includes again
and again the call to repentance and penitence which alone gives
hope of preservation from the judgement of wrath.

threat of the divine wrath. The Levites are to encamp round the tent of the testimony *that there may be no wrath upon the congregation of the people Israel* (Num. i.53).[1]

Yet the people struck by God's wrath are denied the means of averting it, known and practised by Israel's neighbours, namely magical procedures for exorcising the deity.[2] On the contrary it was always evident that in the last resort Yahweh would avert his wrath of his own free will, and this would be an act of mercy and loving-kindness.[3] It is to Yahweh's mercy that the prayer to avert or curb his wrath is directed.[4] This has already appeared in the question about the duration of the wrath (cf. p. 43) and indications of it can be detected again and again elsewhere too,[5] for instance in the Deuteronomic formula.[6] Intercession for those threatened or struck by the wrath appeals to God's mercy. Thus Moses prays for the people in their backsliding (Exod. xxxii.11 f., 31 f.; Num. xi.1 f., xiv.11-13; Deut. ix.19; Ps. cvi.23) or for individuals who have become guilty (Num. xii.13; Deut. ix.20); Amos for Israel (vii.2, 5); Jeremiah for Judah (xiv.7-9, xviii.20); Job for his friends (xlii.7 f.). Such intercession is accepted by Yahweh and the effects of the wrath are

[1] This precaution surely does not merely express the fact that the sphere of the cult and the ritual is particularly exposed to God's wrath (Cr.-Kö. 812).

[2] Eichrodt, p. 126 (ET p. 261); M. Jastrow, *Die Religion Babyloniens and Assyriens* I (1905), ch. 16; cf. S. H. Hooke, *Babylonian and Assyrian Religion* (1953, 1962), pp. 71-79; Num. xvi.41-50 [Heb. xvii.6-15] describes a plan for expiation ordered by Moses.

[3] This does not mean that Yahweh does not demand punishment and expiation for the guilt incurred.

[4] cf. F. Heiler, *Das Gebet*[2] (1920), p. 87; ET *Prayer* (1932), p. 33.

[5] '*When the people cried to Yahweh, Yahweh raised up a deliverer for the people* in Judg. iii.9 *et passim* (cf. p. 39).

[6] cf. also the plea to restrain the wrath in Isa. lxiv.9 [Heb. 8]; Jer. x.24; Ps. vi.1 [Heb. 2]; xxxviii.2 and Yahweh's consent in Jer. xxx.11.

reduced (Num. xiv; Deut. ix) or averted altogether
(Num. xi; II Sam. xxiv). But the time may come when
Yahweh no longer yields to intercession (Amos vii.8,
viii.2; Ezek. xiv.14), and indeed forbids his servant
outright to offer it (Jer. vii.16). Then nothing can
avert the wrath any longer and it comes into action
irresistibly, overpoweringly (Ezek. viii.18, xiv.14). The
decisive motive for the intercession, the reference to
Yahweh's connection with Israel (Exod. xxxii.12; Num.
xiv.15 f.; Ps. lxxiv.2), his mercy and faithfulness to the
covenant (Num. xiv.18; cf. Deut. xiii.18), is occasionally supplemented by emphasising the weakness and
creatureliness of the object of his wrath. Thus Amos
substantiates his plea for Israel with the words: *How
should Jacob stand for he is small* in vii.2, 5 and the
Psalmist: *for we are brought very low* in lxxix.8.[1]

The book of Job brings out particularly clearly the
human creatureliness and the inability of man to with-
stand the onward rush of God's wrath. Admittedly
Job's speeches in the discourses testify rather to the fact
that man has succcumbed inescapably to God's wrath
and does not know about his love, with its readiness to
forgive, and could only come to feel the force of his
terrible power, so that in his defencelessness he begs that
God may let him off (Job vii.1-20, 21, ix.18-22, xiii.13-
22, xiv, especially verses 1-6). At the same time in view
of the present arrangement of the book of Job, it must be
observed that the reader is clearly told to start with that
Job's puzzling fate is not the consequence of the blind
fury of divine anger, but that his grievous lot has a
particular cause.[2]

[1] cf. also the reasons given for Yahweh's ceasing from wrath in Isa.
lvii.16; Ps. lxxviii.39; also F. Hesse, *Die Fürbitte im AT* (Diss.
Erlangen, 1950).

[2] J. Fichtner, 'Hiob in der Verkündigung unserer Zeit', in
Jahrbuch der Theologischen Schule Bethel (1950), pp. 71 ff., 88.

Since Yahweh's wrath is a manifestation of his holiness which has been violated by apostasy from the covenant and by infringement of his ordinances, he can combine his turning away from wrath and his gracious turning towards his people with punishment and reconciliation. Thus his wrath departed from Israel after their desertion to Ba'al Pe'or when the guilty had been slain (Num. xxv.1-5 (JE)), i.e. after Phinehas had given an example and pierced the wrongdoers caught in the act (Num. xxv.6-11 (P)).[1] The same thing happened after the extermination of Achan and his family who had stolen devoted objects (Josh. vii.1, 25 f., cf. II Sam. xxi.4). The OT speaks comparatively seldom of divine wrath being averted by propitiatory offerings (Num. xvii.11; II Sam. xxiv(17 ff.); Ps. lxxviii.38 and probably also I Sam. xxvi.19; cf. TWNT III, pp. 302-311). The prophets announce that Yahweh's wrath may perhaps still be averted by turning away from evil ways, by repentance and penitence (Jer. iv.4, 8, xxxvi.7; cf. Dan. ix.16 *et passim*), and Deutero-Isaiah promises the people in exile the end of divine wrath after it has expiated its guilt: *drunk to the dregs the cup of his wrath* (li.17, 22) and *received double for all her sins* (xl.2).

vi. *The relationship of divine wrath to God's holiness, his righteousness and his mercy*

Once only in the OT is the wrath of God singled out particularly as a feature of God's nature; this occurs in the context of God's wrath against his enemies, not against his own people in Nah. i.2: *avenging and wrathful.*[2]

---

[1] Phinehas by his action confirmed Yahweh's zeal for Israel (Num. xxv.11).

[2] *Jealous God* (*qannā*) (5 times in Exodus and Deuteronomy) and *qannō'* (twice) occurs more frequently. The phrase in Ps. vii.12 is not sufficiently well attested textually (cf. LXX).

This fact must not deceive us into supposing that the proclamation of God's wrath is not inextricably bound up with the whole message of the OT. God's wrath is the power of the holy God who asserts and enforces his absolute claim to rule. Even though—so far as the actual terminology is concerned—God's holiness is seldom associated with his wrath (cf. Ps. lxxviii.38-41),[1] yet in fact this association is incontestable. This is already demonstrated by God's wrath being again and again described in phrases and similes associated with those used for a theophany (cf. Ps. xviii; Exod. xix; Isa. xxx; Hab. iii). Thus divine wrath is conceived and described not as the consequence of an objective power controlled by fate, but of a subjective will controlled by a person. It describes an 'emotional disturbance' of God[2] and its expression by an attack on all the powers which oppose God's holy will. This formula covers completely Yahweh's wrath against Israel and the nations, against individuals and against mankind. With regard to God's people there is indeed a particularly deep-seated reason for Yahweh's wrath since by its means Yahweh's holy love and his reaction to the ingratitude and unfaithfulness of Israel in the face of his care for them is made known.[3]

Yet at the same time Yahweh's wrath is not simply identical with his righteousness as a judge. On the contrary it is significant that Yahweh's righteousness is never explicitly connected with his wrath, although in numberless passages the reasons adduced for the operations of the divine wrath are the commissions and

---

[1] Cr.-Kö. p. 810; in Hos. xi.9 Yahweh's holiness is contrasted with his wrath. [2] Weber, p. 11.

[3] If this can in the last resort be considered as the common denominator for God's wrath, yet we must not forget how varied are its representations in detail at different times and by different OT witnesses.

omissions of Israel (or of mankind), which affront God's sovereign claim and his concrete demands.[1] Job actually turns from the God who is angry with him and hostile to him to the God who as his advocate should procure him his rights, i.e. to the God of righteousness[2] (Job xvi.20 f.). These facts prove clearly that the men of the OT felt the divine wrath to be irrational, incalculable, subjectively wilful, whilst they themselves, having regard to God's righteousness see themselves directed rather to his revealed will. No doubt Yahweh's wrath has its reason and its occasion, but its effects, its duration and the escape from it cannot be foreseen, much less calculated or measured. Of course the reason and the occasion for God being angry may also remain completely in the dark and concealed;[3] thus so far as man can see, for example in the discourses in Job and in individual psalms, wrath and injustice approach each other. Perhaps this enables us to understand the request which we read occasionally (Jer. x.24; Ps. vi.1 [Heb. 2]; xxxviii.1 [Heb. 2]) that Yahweh may chasten 'in just measure', so to speak according to his justice and not in his overflowing wrath; hence the anxiety lest wrath should gain the ascendency in God's being, as suggested in the question of the Psalmist: *Has God forgotten to be gracious? Has he in anger shut up his compassion?* (Ps. lxxxvii.9 [Heb. 10]).[4] Yet it is hardly possible to use such passages and similar ones as the basis for the assertion that 'it is typical of the OT view of God that

[1] Eichrodt, p. 129 (ET, p. 266).

[2] cf. J. Hempel's remark: 'At the moment when God is under the sway of anger, it is needful that he should direct his thoughts to his true self' ('Das Problem des Hiob', ZSTh 7 (1929), p. 675, n. 2) is justified only with the meaning given by Job who does not know the occasion for his grievous lot and attributes it to the unwarrantable wrath of God.

[3] Or must first be discovered (e.g. Josh. vii).

[4] cf. Hab. iii.2: *In wrath remember mercy.*

love and wrath lie side by side in the divine nature, just as they do in an oriental ruler, without being harmonised in any way'.[1] On the contrary Yahweh's wrath with regard to Israel is the reverse side of his love for them; closely bound up with it is the conception of his jealousy (cf. p. 40). And when Deutero-Isaiah allows us to catch a glimpse of the struggle between wrath and compassion in God's heart, we do not look into the heart of a tyrant who dispenses wrath and love at random, but we see how mercy and compassion can restrain the overflowing wrath of Yahweh and how finally compassion retains the victory (Isa. liv.8-10; cf. Jer. xxxi.20). Thus the worshipper in Psalm xxx can confess: *his anger is but for a moment, and his favour is for a life-time* (verse 5 [Heb. 6])[2] and the song of praise in Isaiah xii can thank him for turning away his wrath. Beside these avowals of divine compassion there stand, it is true—especially in the earlier period—the declarations of an inescapable judgement of wrath on the people of God, and in the later times too, which expect God's wrath to fall mainly on the nations and the ungodly, there is even for the congregation no certainty that they will be saved from the approaching wrath which has overtaken all evil-doers (e.g. Jer. xxx.24; Isa. xiii.11).

[1] J. Lindblom, 'Zur Frage der Eigenart der alttestamentlichen Religion', BZAW 66 (1963), p. 135.

[2] Unless *stroke* (*nega'*) should be read for *moment* (*rega'*) with Halévy (thus H. Gunkel, *Psalmen* ([4]1926), p. 126); i.e. *his anger is a blow, his favour is life*.

III. GOD'S WRATH IN THE SEPTUAGINT

1. *The linguistic usage of the Septuagint*

i. ὀργή and θυμός

THE LXX uses primarily ὀργή and θυμός[1] for rendering the various Hebrew expressions denoting 'wrath' (pp. 14 ff.). By their etymology and the range of their meanings these two terms are clearly distinguished from each other. The difference between them is that ' θυμός denotes the emotion, ὀργή its outward appearance and expression. . . . θυμός is wrath rising up within, ὀργή wrath breaking out'.[2] But in the linguistic usage of the LXX the difference between ὀργή and θυμός is completely obliterated. This will be proved by the following survey of the use of ὀργή and θυμός and the verbs associated with them. In doing so it is not necessary to distinguish on principle whether the terms denote the wrath of God or of men. This will be indicated explicitly only in special cases.

(*a*) ὀργή and θυμός are found associated with each other; in Deut. ix.19 Moses refers to God's wrath against Israel as ὀργή (᾽*ap*) and θυμός (*ḥēmāh*); Ps. lxxviii [LXX, lxxvii], 49 places θυμός (*ʿebrāh*), ὀργή (*zaʿam*) and θλῦψις (*ṣārāh*) side by side; cf. also Ps. cii [LXX, ci], 10 [Heb. 11] Mic. v.15 [Heb. 14]; Isa. xiii.9; Jer. vii.20; Ezek. v.13 *et passim*.

(*b*) In the *parallelismus membrorum* both terms appear alternately in accordance with the laws of Hebrew poetry: so in Hos. xiv.11; Isa. xxxiv.2; cf. also Ezek.

---

[1] The ὀργή of God is mentioned well over 200 times, that of man about 50 times; the θυμός of God just 200 times, that of men 70 times. It is most noteworthy that in the LXX θυμός is used so frequently, and as a synonym for ὀργή, for God's wrath, whilst in secular Greek it never designates divine wrath (cf. Irmscher, pp. 3ff.).   [2] Cr.-Kö. 807; cf. p. 1.

vii.5; xxii.31, Ps. ii.5; vi.1 (Heb. 2), xxxviii (LXX, xxxvii), 1 (Heb. 2), xc (LXX, lxxxix), 11; Prov. xv.1, xxvii.4 *et passim*. The corresponding adjectives and verbs also appear in parallel members of a verse, as, e.g. in Prov. xxii.24.

(*c*) The two words connected by the genitive θυμὸς τῆς ὀργῆς (or θυμός ὀργῆς) and ὀργὴ τοῦ θυμοῦ (or ὀργὴ θυμοῦ) are used in exactly the same sense and both usually render *ḥᵃrōn 'ap* : Exod. xxxii.12; Num. xxxii.14; Jer. iv.26; Ps. lxix (LXX, lxviii), 24 (Heb. 25) *et passim*; occasionally they stand for a single Hebrew term: in Job iii.17, xxxvii.2; Ezek. xxxiii.25; Ps. cvi (LXX, cv), 23 (Codex Vaticanus); Isa. ix.18, xiii.13.

(*d*) The combination θυμοῦσθαι ὀργῇ (Gen. xxxix.19; Josh. vii.1; Isa. v.25) is frequently found; less often ὀργὴ θυμοῦται (I Sam. xi.6; II Kings xxiii.26). The latter is always, the former is almost without exception, the translation of *ḥārāh 'ap*. The construction θυμοῦσθαι θυμῷ or θυμόν does not occur in the LXX according to Hatch and Redpath.[1] More frequent than θυμοῦσθαι ὀργῇ is the phrase ὀργίζεσθαι θυμῷ (e.g. in Exod. xvii.24; Deut. vii.4; Judges ii.14; Ps. cvi [LXX, cv], 40). Like the very rare θυμὸς ὀργίζεται (Judges vi.39; Ps. lxxiv [LXX, lxxiii], 1; cxxiv [LXX, cxxiii], 3) it is almost always a rendering of *ḥārāh 'ap*. The construction ὀργίζεσθαι ὀργήν in Zech. i.2, 15 corresponds to *qāṣap qeṣep* in the Masoretic text; in the form ὀργίζεσθαι ὀργῇ it occurs in II Chron. xxix.8 for *hāyāh qeṣep*.

(*e*) The number of phrases formed with ὀργή or with θυμός to reproduce the Hebrew original is astonishingly great. We are only offering a selection of them and as far as possible are giving equal consideration to both terms in our references to the passages.[2] The following

---

[1] *Concordance to the Septuagint* (1897-1906).

[2] The first passage in each case attests ὀργή (or ὀργὴ θυμοῦ) the second θυμός (or θυμὸς ὀργῆς).

verbs can be used with ὀργή and θυμός as the subject:
ἀναβαίνειν (Ps. lxxviii [LXX, lxxvii], 21; Ezek. xxiv.8);
γίνεσθαι (Josh. xxii.20; Lam. iii.47); εἶναι (II Chron.
xix.10; Lev. x.6); ἔρχεσθαι (Job iii.26, xxxvi.18 [Codex
Alexandrinus]);[1] ἐκκαίεσθαι (Deut. xxix.20 [Heb. 19];
Jer. xliv [LXX, li], 6); παύεσθαι (Job xiv.13; Isa. i.24);
ἀποστρέφειν (intransitive. Hos. xiv.5; Jer. xxiii.20);
ἀποστρέφεσθαι (Num. xxv.4; Dan. ix.16); εὐχεῖσθαι (II
Kings xxii.13; Jer. vii.20 [Codex Alexandrinus]) and
others. ὀργή and θυμός are found in the accusative of the
object and governed by ἐγείρειν (Prov. xv.1; Ecclus.
xxxvi.7); ἐκκαίειν (Ps. lxxviii [LXX, lxxvii], 38); Job
iii.17 [Codex Vaticanus differs]); ἐξαποστέλλειν (Ps.
lxxviii [LXX, lxxvii], 49a and b); ἀποστρέφειν (Prov.
xxix.8; Ps. lxxviii [LXX, lxxvii], 38); συντελεῖν (Ezek.
v.13; Lam. iv.11); ἐκχεῖν (Zeph. iii.8; Ezek. ix.8).
Other phrases with ὀργή or θυμός as the object are rare.
Both are found depending on the adjective πλήρης in Isa.
xxx.27; Wisd. v.22[2]; they are also used as attributes to
the noun ἡμέρα (Job xx.28; Zeph. ii.2)[3]; καιρός (Ecclus.
xliv.17; Jer. xviii.23); πῦρ (Ezek. xxi.31, xxxvi.5);
πλῆθος (Ps. ix.25; Isa. xxxi.4) and ῥάβδος (Isa. x.5).

In contrast to this considerable quantity of phrases
which can be formed equally well with ὀργή or θυμός,
there is a substantially smaller number of constructions
attested with ὀργή alone and not with θυμός, and vice
versa. None of these cases taken either singly or as a
whole, provides a criterion for distinguishing the concepts of ὀργή and θυμός. So they are not adduced here
in extenso.[4] It is striking how often ὀργή and θυμός are

---

[1] Compounds of ἔρχεσθαι are also found.

[2] Both are also found with the same prepositions.

[3] ἡμέρα θυμοῦ occurs only in Zeph. ii.2 and Prov. xi.4 (LXX,
Vaticanus and Sinaiticus omit); elsewhere always, including other
passages in Zephaniah, ἡμέρα ὀργῆς is found.

[4] Most of the phrases in question are used once only.

interchanged in the manuscripts of the LXX.[1] If there were a distinction between the two concepts, based on their meaning, or even only on their usage, these frequent interchanges would hardly have been possible. All this goes to show that ὀργή and θυμός, as well as the verbs associated with them, can be used completely indifferently, and are in fact so used in the LXX.

ii. ὀργίζω (θυμόω), παροργίζω, παροργισμός

Active forms of ὀργίζω and θυμόω, both meaning *to make angry, to provoke to wrath* (trans.) are each attested reliably only once (Job xii.6 [Alexandrinus]; Hos. xii.14 [Heb. 15]). On the other hand the passive form of ὀργίζω is found in nearly 80 passages, that of θυλόω in more than 60, often emphasised by θυμῷ or by ὀργῇ (cf. p. 52), always with the meaning *to grow angry, to be wroth*. Either God or man can be the subject of ὀργίζομαι and θυμόομαι. Similarly the active παροργίζω,[2] used in more than 50 passages, has the transitive meaning of *making angry, provoking to wrath*. It is surprising how seldom the LXX uses the two associated nouns παροργισμός (6 times) and παρόργισμα, not found in the NT, (3 times). They mean *provocation, cause of anger* (I Kings xv.30; II Chron. xxxv.19c [not in Hebrew text]), and also in the wider sense denote an action provoking wrath (LXX, II Esdras xix.18 [=Hebrew Neh. ix.18]; I Kings xvi.33). The subject of παροργίζειν is man (except in Deut. xxxii.21).[3] παροργισμός and παρόργισμα too when in the active mood are only used of man. In two passages παροργισμός is used with a passive meaning: II Kings xiv.3 and Jer. xxi.5.

---

[1] cf. Isa. x.4; Jer. x.25; Lam. iv.11; II Chron. xxix.8 *et passim*.

[2] Not in the active only in Dan. xi.36 and Ecclus. iv.2.

[3] Here the occasion is the contrast with Israel's provocation.

iii. ὀργίλος and θυμώδης

ὀργίλος occurs as an adjective 4 times (Ps. xviii [LXX, xvii], 49 and 3 times in Proverbs), as an adverb once (IV Macc. viii.9); θυμώδης is found 8 times (5 times in Proverbs, twice in Ecclus., once in Jer xxx [LXX, xxxvii], 23). Thus both are used predominantly in the Wisdom literature. They mean *inclined to anger, passionate*, and apart from Jer. xxx [LXX, xxxvii], 23, denote only a human quality.

iv. (κότος), χόλος, and μῆνις

These three terms which are used in secular Greek only to signify divine wrath,[1] are in the LXX not employed for the wrath of God. κότος is not found at all, χόλος in 5 passages only (Prov. xvi.28 [Sinaiticus]; Eccles. v.16; II Macc. iii [Alexandrinus], 28; III Macc. v.1, 30) and the verb (ἐκ) χολᾶν only in III Macc. iii.1. In all 6 passages the wrath of man is meant.[2] Μῆνις occurs 4 times (Gen. xlix.7; Num. xxxv.21; Ecclus. xxvii.30, xxviii.5); μηνίαμα or μήνιμα[3] only in Ecclus. xl.5; the associated verb μηνίειν 5 times (Lev. xix.18; Jer. iii.12; Ps. ciii [LXX, cii], 9; Ecclus. x.6, xxviii.7). In 8 of these 10 passages human wrath is meant; only in Jer. iii.12 and Ps. ciii.9 is the verb connected with God and in both cases it must be noted that an irreconcilable μηνίειν by God is explicitly denied. All these facts lead to the conclusion that the Greek translators considered κότος, χόλος and μῆνις and their derivatives were too definitely tainted by their use as the expressions for the wrath of the (Greek) gods and

---

[1] In secular Greek they are used almost exclusively in poetic language (Kleinknecht).

[2] In Eccles. v.16 it stands for *qeṣep*, in Prov. xvi.28 there is no Hebrew counterpart; the other passages are in II and III Macc.

[3] The LXX has μήνιμα (Sinaiticus and Alexandrinus) or μηνίαμα (Vaticanus).

were not suitable technically; in consequence they avoided them intentionally when it was a matter of indicating the wrath of the God of the Scriptures.

2. *Interpretations given in the Septuagint*

On the whole the LXX translators have reproduced correctly the original Hebrew in the OT passages dealing with wrath. It must be admitted that in so doing they worked at times somewhat mechanically; for instance they rendered *ḥēmāh*, one of the chief Hebrew terms for wrath[1] by θυμός even in those passages where it means the *poison* of snakes or of arrows (Deut. xxxii.24; Ps. lviii.4 [Heb. 5]; Job vi.4); only in Ps. cxl [LXX, cxxxix], 3 (Heb. 4) do we read ἰός which we should expect. *Ka'as* (*ka'aś*) found 25 times in the OT and usually meaning *annoyance, resentment, trouble*, is rendered in the LXX almost exclusively by ὀργή (9 times),[2] θυμός (8 times), παροργισμός (twice) and παρόργισμα (once), thus with typical terms for wrath; only quite seldom do other translations appear: I Sam. i.16 (Alexandrinus), ἀθυμία; Prov. xxi.19 γλωσσώδης (beside ὀργίλος) and in Eccles. i.18 probably γνῶις. *Rūaḥ* is translated in some passages with ὀργή (Prov. xvi.32) or θυμός (Zech. vi.8; Prov. xxix.11), in others, where this rendering would be at least equally obvious, with πνεῦμα (Judges viii.3; Isa. xxv.4, xxx. 28); *mērūaḥ 'appō* (*at the blast of his anger*) in Job iv.9 with ἀπὸ πνεύματος ὀργῆς. The LXX has several times replaced the concrete means or effects of God's wrath in action by the abstract word *wrath*, thus in Jer. xxx [LXX, xxxvii], 23 *storm of God* is replaced by ὀργή; similarly—and perhaps more strikingly because the context here does not deal with God's wrath—in Ps. lxxxiii [LXX, lxxxii], 16.

---

[1] When meaning *wrath* it is rendered 70 times by θυμός and 25 times by ὀργή.

[2] In addition once by ὀργίλος.

The translation of *'ap* in two cases, where it does not mean *wrath*, but *nose*, is particularly characteristic. When it is a question of a man's nose (Prov. xxx.33) or the snout of an animal (Prov. xi.22), the LXX can say μυκτήρ or ῥίς; it is said of idols too (Ps. cxv.6 [LXX, cxiii.14]).[1] On the other hand the phrase in Ps. xviii (LXX, xvii), 8 (Heb. 9) evidently aroused the translators' scruples; so they rendered it with ἀνέβη καπνὸς ἐν ὀργῇ αὐτοῦ. Similarly they translate verse 15 (Heb. 16): *at the blast of the breath of thy nostrils* with ἀπὸ ἐμπνεύσεως πνεύματος ὀργῆς αὐτοῦ. Clearly they can endure more easily the anthropopathic phrase about God's wrath than the anthropomorphic one about God's nose given in the Hebrew text. In other passages the Greek aversion to the passions (πάθη) suggests to the LXX translators the replacement of the conception of God's wrath by other concepts. Thus several times instead of speaking of God's wrath, they have mentioned human sin which provoked it. Cf. Job xlii.7; Num. i.53; similarly Isa. lvii.17; I Esdras vi.14 (15) [cf. Ezra v.12] (TWNT I, p. 289).[2] Mal. i.4 also contains a change in the interpretation. The apocalyptic punishment is not said to be as stated in the Masoretic text: *the people with whom the Lord is angry for ever*, but the LXX has substituted for it: *the people against whom the Lord stands prepared for battle so long as the world endures*. In Isa. lxvi.14 the Masoretic text reads: *and his* (Yahweh's) *indignation against his enemies*. The LXX has altered both conceptions and has thereby made allowance for the more ethical and rational idea of God in Hellenism. Perhaps the greatest change is in Zech. i.12: κύριε

[1] In Amos iv.10 the words *the stench of your camp into your nostrils*, obviously the result of a misreading, are understood quite differently in the LXX.

[2] cf. Weber p. 155 for such changes of interpretation in the Targum as well.

παντόκρατωρ, ἕως τίνος οὐ μὴ ἐλεήσῃς τὴν Ἰερουσαλημ καὶ τὰς πόλεις Ἰουδα, ἃς ὑπερεῖδες (Heb. zā'am have indignation) τοῦτο ἑβδομηκοντὸν ἔτος; here undoubtedly national pride is playing a role in addition to the changed conception of God. In Hab. iii the whole chapter is involved. In the Masoretic text it is a psalm about the manifestation of the wrathful God. In the LXX this recedes behind the revelation through his word. By what appears to be a double translation in verse 2 (cf. BH³) this statement is produced: *when my soul is confused by* (God's) *wrath then thou wilt remember thy mercy.* Thereby the remark interjected into the Masoretic text, which is perhaps after all only a gloss, becomes a principal sentence. In verse 5 the terrible weapon of pestilence (*deber*) is replaced by revelation through the λόγος (*dābār*). Whilst in the Masoretic text Yahweh is the subject throughout the whole chapter, in the LXX λόγος becomes the key-word in verses 5-9. Not until later are the statements about it put into God's mouth by the λέγει κύριος in verse 9. Again in verse 12 we read: ἐν ἀπειλῇ ὀλιγώσεις γῆν καὶ ἐν θυμῷ κατάξεις ἔθνη. ἀπειλή (*threat*) is substituted for za'am (similarly in Prov. xix.12 for za'ap also; here it is used for the king's wrath), so that it is no longer the question of an emotional disturbance in God, but of an expression (revelation) of it to the earth. θυμός in the second half of the verse must now be interpreted to correspond. It refers to the will, the intention of God. Hence the meaning given to the sentence by the LXX is like that of Ps. xxxiii.9: *By* (thy mere) *word the earth was made small* (*subject*), *by* (thy mere) *command thou dost overthrow nations.* It is not the God of Sinai, manifesting himself in nature's catastrophes, but the spiritual God who is being praised here. The LXX endeavours to bring out its knowledge of God partly by writing in Deut. xxxii.22 not: *a fire is kindled in my anger ...,* but ἐκ τοῦ θυμοῦ μου, which is probably intended to mean *in consequence of my wrath* or more generally *according to my will*. The LXX has also simply taken over the statements in the Psalms: cf. Ps. ii.12; lxxviii (LXX, lxxvii), 38 (God does not allow his wrath to take full effect); lxxix (LXX, lxxviii), 5; lxxxix (LXX, lxxxviii), 47). Ecclus. xlviii.1 also speaks of God's wrath being mediated. The statement does indeed in the first place refer to Elijah, but from what follows it is clear that it is really God who speaks and acts (verse 3). Thus the passage resembles the prophet's description of the manifestation of God's wrath in Isa. xxx.27; cf. Isa. lxv.5; Jer. iv.4, vii.20, xv.14, xliv [LXX, li], 6. The point of these passages too is the effect brought about by the wrath.[1]

[1] pp. 58 f. are by Bertram.

IV. GOD'S WRATH IN LATE JUDAISM

1. *The Apocrypha and Pseudepigrapha*

THE post-canonical Jewish literature continues on OT lines, in the Diaspora as well as in Palestine.

(*a*) Where the original Hebrew has been preserved (in Ecclus. and in the Zadokite Document [CD]) the words used for wrath (God's) are *'ap* (Ecclus. v.6; CD i.21 [i.17] *et passim*): *ḥēmāh* (Ecclus. xvi.6, 11; xxxvi.6 ; CD ii.5 [ii.4]); *za'am* (Ecclus. v.7, xxxi.23); *rōgez* (Ecclus. v.6). In the Greek texts ὀργή with its derivatives[1] dominates the field as the designation for God's wrath; so too we find θυμός[2] without any material difference of meaning and as the equivalent of the same Hebrew words (obviously preferred in Macc. IV): with θυμόομαι (in the Sibyllines only). The combinations ὀργὴ θυμοῦ (I Macc. ii.49; Gr. Enoch v.9) or θυμὸς καὶ ὀργή (Ecclus. xlv.18) correspond to the duplication *ḥaʾrōn 'ap* (CD ix.4, 6 [x.2, 4] *et passim*) and are to be considered like similar expressions in Eph. (τὸ κράτος τῆς ἰσχύος in i.19, vi.10, etc.; ἀρχὴ καὶ ἐξουσία in i.21, vi.12, etc.) as a rhetorical piling up of concepts. Other words are rare: ἀγανακτέω in IV Macc. iv.21; παροξύνω Bar. iv.7; Ps. Sol. iv.21; Test. Asher ii.6; χόλος in

---

[1] ὀργίζομαι in Ps. Sol. vii.5; Gr. Enoch xviii.16; Gr. Bar. iv.8, ix.7; Apoc. Mos. viii.16, 18, 21; ἀποργίζομαι in II Macc. v.17; ἐποργίζυμαι in II Macc. vii.23; παροργίζω in Judith viii.14, xi.11; Test. Levi iii.10 *et passim*; παροργισμός Ps. Sol. viii. 9; διοργίζομαι III Macc. iii.1, iv.13.

[2] cf. R. Smend, *Griechisch-syrisch-hebräisches Index zur Weisheit des Jesus Sirach* (1907), s.v. ὀργή and θυμός; cf. p. 74. The range of meaning of θυμός is rather narrower, in so far as it has not shared in the development reaching the meaning of *judgement of wrath* (pp. 63, 87).

Wisdom xviii.22; μηνίω in Prayer of Manasseh 13. The last two with their derivatives are obviously preferred in the epic language of the Sibyllines[1] to ὀργή and θυμός.

(b) Wrath in men is considered in a very different light according to whether it is judged from its association with God or whether alien standards are substituted. In the first case it can be considered as a justifiable wrath, if it is kindled by infringement of the law or by blasphemy against God; thus particularly in the Maccabees (I Macc. ii.24, 44; vi.59; II Macc. iv.40; x.35). The wrath of a pagan ruler can also be approved if it is directed against a sinner (cf. II Macc. iv.38; I Macc. ix.69; III Macc. vi.23, cf. p. 75 n. 3); in that case it can even be aroused against God (II Macc. xiii.4; cf. Gr. Bar. xvi.2). The just wrath of a king—as among the Rabbis (cf. p. 68)—serves to illustrate divine anger (Slav. Enoch xlvi.1). According to this view only unrighteous anger is unjustifiable (Ecclus. i.22). But in most cases wrath is condemned as a passion leading to sin and disaster (cf. Wisdom x.2; Ps. Sol. xvi.10; Sib. III.377; CD ix.4, 6 [x.2, 4]); especially in Ecclus. (e.g. x.18, xx.2) and in the XII Testaments (Dan i-vi; Gad v.1; Judah xiv.1; Simeon iv.8; cf. also ii.11; Zebulun iv.11). When frequently disapproval of the fierce rage of the pagan rulers is expressed,[2] this is usually because it is directed against the people of God, but also because it is a sign of the arrogance of man; for in fact wrath befits God alone (Ecclus. x.18). Therefore it is the

[1] χόλος in III.51, 556, 561; IV.160, 169; V.130, 373, 456, 508; Fr. 3, 19; χολόομαι in III.766; μηνίω in IV.51; μῆνις IV.135; μήνιμα in III.632, 811; ὀργή in IV.162; V.76; θυμός in III.309; Fr. 3.19; θυμόομαι in V.298, 358.

[2] Tob. i.18; Judith v.2; Ps. Sol. ii.23 f.; xvii.12; Syr. Bar. xlviii.37, lxiii.2; Sib. III.660 f.; and especially also in the books of the Maccabees.

wrath of man which arouses the wrath of God so greatly (Dan. xi.36[1]; Ecclus. v.18 f.; Slav. Enoch xliv.2; Apoc. Abr. xvii (Bonwetsch, p. 28; cf. G. H. Box [1918]), pp. 57 ff.). It is always a sign of God's wrath when he turns away (p. 132); cf. Ecclus. xxviii.3, 5: he who is angry can expect neither ἴασις nor ἐξιλασμός from God; for μῆνις and ὀργή are βδελύγματα in the sight of God (Ecclus. xxvii.30).

When the criteria of reason take precedence over those of religion, wrath is usually condemned (cf. e.g. Ecclus. xxx.24); according to Gr. Enoch (text of Syncellus), viii.3 Semjaza, a leader of the fallen angels, taught men 'to be angry contrary to reason'. Wisdom (x.1 ff.) especially places ὀργή in complete opposition to σοφία. On the other hand in IV Macc. it is significant that θυμός is subordinated to λογισμός (ii.15 ff.) which can cure the former (βοηθῆσαι iii.3). IV Macc. shares with Greek philosophy the problem of mastering wrath (cf. Sen. De Ira II 2, 1 ff.); so does the Letter of Aristeas in the only passage in which it speaks of wrath (253 f.). In addition to the critical and favourable verdicts passed on wrath, the literature contains also many neutral statements about the wrath of man.[2]

(c) In view of the prevailing depreciation of wrath in man, it is striking that almost the whole apocryphal and pseudepigraphical literature speaks without any embarrassment of God's wrath (but cf. p. 65). The only exception, due to its principles, is made by the Letter of Aristeas written under Stoic influence: God rules the

---

[1] The play upon words which is more than that: παροργισθήσεται (i.e. Antiochus IV) . . . ἕως ἂν συντελεσθῇ ἡ ὀργή (i.e. of God) dates only from the Greek translator. Here too postcanonical apocalyptic is merely continuing the line of the canonical apocalypses.

[2] e.g. Tob. v.14; Ecclus. xxv.15; II Esdras x.5, and especially in Jub. (xxvi.8, xxvii. 3, 6, xxviii.4 et passim).

world without wrath of any kind (254).[1] It appears to be due to chance that Tobit and III Macc. are exceptional in making no mention of God's wrath. It is especially noticeable that a writing so definitely tinged with Hellenism as IV Macc. reckons quite unconcernedly with the just wrath of God (iv.21, ix.32; p. 65), and that the most passionate delineation of divine wrath to be found in this literature happens to occur in the Sibyllines (IV. 59: χόλῳ βρυχῶν).

ὀργή, like θυμός, μῆνις and χόλος with the verbs derived from them, means in the first place the passionate emotion itself, when for instance the kindling (e.g. Ecclus. xvi.6) or calming (Ecclus. xlviii.10) of wrath is mentioned, or when it is said (Eth. Enoch xcix.16): the Lord *will arouse the spirit of his indignation* (cf. p. 64). We may call this an 'anthropopathism', but we must also take into account the fact that it is expressing here on the one hand God's personal nature,[2] and on the other his holy abhorrence of all evil. But in not a few cases ὀργή describes the outcome of divine wrath in its verdict on man, that is to say, the judgement of wrath, when for example the great wrath in the Apoc. Mos. xiv is interpreted as death which dominates our whole race, or in Vit. Ad. xlix as the catastrophes of water and fire, falling upon the descendants of Adam and Eve (p. 111), or when Jub. xxxvi.10 speaks of a daily renewal of the judgement in wrath and fury. Particularly when ὀργή is used in the eschatological sense, it often means the judgement of wrath, thus in Jub. xxiv.30 and especially

[1] This opinion determines also in the subsequent centuries the Alexandrian tradition in Philo (p. 71), Clement of Alexandria (p. 7) and Origen (*Cels.* IV.71 ff.).

[2] We can also gather this from the phrase 'to anger the name of God' (Palaea on Apoc. Abr. xxix, see N. Bonwetsch, *Die Apk. Abr.* (1897), pp. 63 f.; cf. also p. 63 (top); G. H. Box, *The Apoc. of Abr.* (1918), pp. 77 f.).

in Gr. Enoch xiii.8: ἴδον ὁράσεις ὀργῆς,[1] as well as in phrases resembling a hendiadys, such as *wrath and punishment* (Eth. Enoch lv.3; xci.7, 9; Jub. xli.26). Often the two ideas can both be detected, namely the upsurge of divine anger and the punishment which it inflicts, thus e.g. in Judith ix.9; I Macc. iii.8; Ecclus. vii.16, xlvii.20; Ps. Sol. xv.4; Test. Reuben iv.8; Test. Levi vi.11; Sib. V.76.[2] This applies especially to some cases in which God's wrath is personified in various ways, as when wrath is said to send (Eth. Enoch ci.3), to go forth (Ecclus. v.7)[3] and to rest (verse 6). But elsewhere personifications of this kind have the direct effect of detaching the reaction of wrath from God himself, thus in Eth. Enoch xcix.16 (the spirit of his indignation); CD ii.5 (ii.4: ḥēmāh gᵉdōlāh as the angel of destruction, cf. p. 69); similarly in Wisdom xviii.22, 25 (wrath as κολάζων and ὀλεθρεύων which Moses resists and conquers).[4] ὀργή as well as denoting the effect of wrath can also describe the occasion for it, as it does obviously in Ecclus. xxvi.8; cf. xxv.22.

The above exposition enables us to recognise the motives for the theodicy. They are also equally evident in the many other statements about God's ὀργή, as for instance in those about the relationship to the mercy, the forbearance and the justice of God (pp. 47f., 87ff.).

[1] cf. also Bar. iv.9, 25; I Macc. i.64; Gr. Enoch x.22; Eth. Enoch cvi.15; Ass. Mos. viii.1. A similar meaning must be given in the Sibyllines to χόλος in III.51; V.130 *et passim*) and to μήνιμα (III.811). Even θυμός in Ecclus. xlviii.10, if it is original here, stands clearly for the eschatological judgement.

[2] The same applies to χόλος in Sib. III.556, 561; and θυμός in Ecclus. xviii.24.

[3] cf. also verse 6c, if we should really read ἐλεύσεγαι instead of ἔλεος καί; cf. V. Ryssel in Kautzsch, *Apokryphen und Pseudepigraphen*, I, p. 253.

[4] cf. also the somewhat enigmatic passage in Apoc. Abr. xxv in which God says: *the statue which you saw is my wrath which is aroused in me by the people issuing from you* (i.e. Abraham).

Ecclus. v.6[1] xvi.11 places wrath and mercy side by side as a single quality of God with many tensions: ἔλεος καὶ ὀργὴ παρ' αὐτῷ. It appears similarly in the Prayer of Manasseh 5 f. Particularly with regard to Israel, God's wrath can be seen as the effect of his chastening mercy and love.[2] This is the way to look at things according to II Macc. v.17, 20, vii.33 and Wisdom xi.9, xvi.5, xviii.20-25 (cf. Ps. Sol. vii.5). On the other hand God's forbearance is shown when he withholds his wrath[3] (Syr. Bar. lix.6; cf. Rom. ix.22; pp. 88 f.). God's wrath can be seen too to be in full agreement with the justice when it is kindled by the transgressions of sinners,[4] indeed it may then be directly called a function of divine justice. This is specially clear in IV Macc. iv.21; cf. ix.32.

Only a few apocalyptists consider that God's justice and mercy exclude the effects of his wrath. II Esdras for instance, in which the image of God is defined on the one hand by passionless justice, on the other by boundless mercy, offers several motives for the restraint of wrath; the small number of the righteous (viii. 30), the ignorance of the masses which resemble the cattle, and the general sinfulness which makes it seem unreasonable and unjust to be angry (viii.34; cf. verse 35).[5] The

---

[1] But cf. p. 64, n. 3.

[2] With regard to the pagans on the other hand an ἀνελεήμων θυμός (Wisdom xix.1) holds sway.

[3] cf. by contrast Ecclus. vii.16.

[4] cf. Sjöberg, pp. 197 f., 224-227.

[5] II Esdras iv.29 does not belong here, irrespective of a preference for the reading *comminatio* or *indignatio*, because here God's powerful action in cosmic catastrophes is meant (the idea that these are a form of God's judgement of wrath is beside the mark here); Syr. Bar. xxi.6, xlviii.8 is similar (here 'to be angry' appears as the original reading instead of 'to threaten'; Ryssel in *op. cit.* (p. 64, n. 3), II, p. 428 has based his translation on a conjecture of Charles, without indicating this fact). (*Apocrypha and Pseudepigrapha* II (1913), p. 493.)

ideas in Syr. Bar. (xlviii.14, 17) are analogous: the complete frailty and insignificance of man inhibits wrath, although it is uncertain whether this is due to God's justice or to his mercy. In the background of the Apoc. Abr. too there stands the problem of God's justice: why is God angry about the evil which he has himself made subject to his decree? (p. 90).

The wrath of God is discharged in two phases: in the historical and in the eschatological sphere (p. 97).[1] Ecclus. (cf. xviii.24)[2] and the Zadokite Document mention only historical wrath. It falls on all mankind (cf. Eth. Enoch lxxxiv.4; CD ii.21 [iii.7]: on individuals: thus on Cain as the first υἱὸς ὀργῆς[3] (Apoc. Mos. iii),[4] and on Adam and Eve especially (Apoc. Mos. viii f.; Vit. Ad. iii, xxxiv); on individual groups and nations: thus the Egyptians (Wisdom xix.1) or 'the scornful man', 'the man of derision' with his company in the Zadokite Document (i.21 f. [i.17]; v.16 [vii.17], viii.13 [ix.22 = Text B, xix.26], viii.18 ix.26]=Text B, xix.31]; on Israel whose chief sin provoking wrath is idolatry (Apoc. Abr. passim; Eth. Enoch lxxxix.33). But whilst God remains angry with others until the end (cf. Wisdom xix.1) in the case of Israel he limits his wrath (cf. xvi.5, xviii.20) and does not destroy utterly (cf. Gr. Enoch v.9: οἱ ἐκλεκτοὶ . . . οὐ μὴ ἀποθάνωσιν ἐν ὀργῇ θυμοῦ); yet cf. Syr. Bar. lxiv.4 and especially Jub. xv.34, where an everlasting wrath even against Israel is mentioned (cf. xxxvi.10). In addition other created things are the objects of his wrath, thus the vine (Gr.

---

[1] Both are denoted side by side by ὀργή and θυμός at random rather than on principle in Ecclus. xlviii.10; but cf. p. 80.

[2] cf. V. Ryssel (p. 64, n. 3) ad loc.

[3] cf. Sib. III.309; Eph. ii.3.

[4] If it is not Cain's wrath against Abel which is meant (the name qain being thought to derive from qānē'); cf. the textual variations in C. Tischendorf, Apocalypses apocryphae (1866), p. 2.

Bar. iv.9) because of its seductive effect,[1] the moon (Gr.
Bar. ix.7)[2] and the stars (Gr. Enoch xviii.16); beings
hostile to God: the devil (Vit. Ad. xv f.; Jub. iii.23);
the hosts of Azazel (Eth. Enoch lv.3), the fallen angels
(Gr. Bar. iv. 8; Eth. Enoch lxviii.4: . . . *because they act
as if they were the Lord*; Jub. v.6); perhaps the disobedient
sons of God of Gen. vi (Gr. Enoch xvi.4, text of Syncellus; xxi.6).[3]

All the operations of wrath within history point forward to the eschatological operation. All the historical
periods of wrath (Ecclus. xliv.17; CD i.5 are
preludes to *the* day of wrath (e.g. Jub. xxiv.28, 30,
xxxvi.10; cf. p. 98), to the ὀργὴ πυρός (Ecclus. xxxvi.8)
in the καιρὸς συντελείας (xxxix.28). The eschatological
wrath strikes two groups, according to whether the
national or the individual aspect predominates. It is
directed against the pagans (Ecclus. xxxvi.6; Ass. Mos.
x.3; Apoc. Abr. xxiv; probably also Eth. Enoch xc.15,
18; and especially Jub. xxiv.28; here the Philistines are
the object of the historical as well as of the eschatological wrath[4]), and against the sinners who do not
repent, whether pagans or Israelites, the mighty ones of
the earth, on whom the wrath of the Lord of the spirits
rests (Eth. Enoch lxii.12), the oppressors of the orphans,
widows and strangers (Slav. Enoch l.5 [Text A], etc.;
cf. Wisdom v.17–23; Ps. Sol. xv.5; Jub. xxxvi.10, etc.).
The very things which appear as the objects of the

---

[1] Another conception, containing an allusion to the Holy
Communion, cuts across this one and is probably the result of a
Christian interpolation.

[2] According to the Greek text, because the moon shone through
the serpent, when Adam was tempted; according to the Slavonic
text because the moon laughed when the serpent seduced Adam
and Eve and made them conscious of their nakedness.

[3] cf. Stauffer, *Theologie*, p. 199, ET *NT Theology* (1955), pp. 220.

[4] In this 'divine wrath' the Jews give vent to their all too human
national wrath.

divine wrath in action in history can also be his tools: men, especially the pagan oppressors and persecutors (IV Macc. iv.21; Ass. Mos. viii.1), various creatures (Wisdom v.22,[1] xvi.5; cf. xi.18), and angels employed against the fallen angels (Jub. v.6).

Judaism too was troubled by the question as to how God's wrath could be overcome and averted; it found a variety of answers, but without knowing the only final one (pp. 129ff.). The answers given are: by prayer (Apoc. Abr. xx [p. 31 Bonwetsch; cf. p. 62; cf. Box, pp. 65 f.]), through services of worship (Slav. Enoch xviii.8 [Text A]; cf. Wisdom xviii.20 ff.), through righteousness (Ecclus. xliv.17), through the vicarious intercession of Moses and Elijah (Wisdom xviii.21; Ecclus. xlviii.10); through vicarious suffering (II Macc. vii.38), through the wrath of the elements, working as an antitoxin (Ecclus. xxxix.28), through God's own saving action (Wisdom xvi.5; Num. xxi). In this last instance Judaism came nearest to the NT; yet it is just here that the veil covering it is clearly seen.

2. *Rabbinic thought*

In the Rabbinic literature too the thought of God's wrath is quite familiar. No trace of any aversion to it can be detected. On the contrary it belongs to those theological matters which are taken for granted. Passages from the OT dealing with God's wrath are quoted without any attempt to re-interpret them. It is often said that God is angry, that he is provoked to wrath, etc. Comparisons are used in which divine wrath is portrayed exactly like that of men; it is described as though a father were angry with his son, a king with his subjects, a husband with his wife.[2] There is no hesitation

---

[1] Here is a remarkable description of the wrathful God putting on his armour.

[2] cf. e.g. J. Taan. II 65 b 43 (Str.-B. III, p. 30); M. Exod. xiv (Horovitz p. 98); S. Lev. ix.4 f. (Weiss, p. 43a); cf. Sjöberg, p. 63.

here in including in the representations of divine
wrath the irrational quality of chance which charac-
terises human wrath; like the latter, it bursts out perhaps very violently and then after a time it dies down
again;[1] sometimes God is more angry, sometimes less so.[2]
Admittedly these descriptions are tied down to interpretations of biblical passages, but it is worth remarking
that those which might well be omitted are given quite
naturally. All this is the more striking since Rabbinism too
condemns wrath against one's neighbour[3] (although it
recognises that wrath against a sinner is justifiable).[4]

If in some, rather late, passages wrath in various
forms is hypostasised into angels,[5] the reason for it is
definitely, judging by what has been said, not the wish
to avoid anthropopathisms. On the contrary it is due
on the one hand to the preference for a concrete and
vivid method of presentation, peculiar to Rabbinism,
and on the other to the growth of speculations about
angelology in general.

In spite of the freedom with which divine wrath has
been depicted on the pattern of human wrath, Rabbinism asserts firmly on principle that it does not abolish
justice. It is essential to Rabbinism, as to the rest of
Judaism (p. 90) that God never acts contrary to
justice. Thus we read for example on Deut. xxxii.41:
*When I whet my glittering sword, this means, when I deliver the
judgement, it is swift as lightning, but nevertheless* (it is
written) *my hand maintains what is right.*[6]

[1] cf. in addition to the passages in the previous note Str.-B. III,
pp. 409, 685, 687.

[2] M. Exod. xvii.4 (Horovitz 174); S. Num. 90 on xi.10. See
also S. Deut. 305 on xxxi.14; R. Nathan: on account of his love
for Israel God will not be angry with their actions.

[3] Str.-B. I, pp. 276 ff.

[4] Str.-B. III, pp. 602 f.; cf. also Str.-B. I, pp. 365 f. (*b* and *c*).

[5] Str.-B. III, pp. 30 f.

[6] S. Deut. 331 on xxxii.41. Cf. Sjöberg, p. 4.

In other ways too the wrath of God is distinguished from that of men. An angry man may perhaps strike out in fury having lost control of himself; but God does not forget to care for the world in kindness and mercy even in the hour of his wrath.[1] If sin is in the world, divine wrath is there too[2]; but it is not there alone. Divine mercy is in action also. This means that God does not forget to be kind to the righteous because he is punishing those who provoke his anger. But his mercy is at work for sinners too. It reveals itself especially in forbearance and in good gifts which he bestows on them in spite of their sin, so that there is often occasion to cry: *If God acts thus towards those who provoke him to wrath, how much more will he give to those who do his will?*[3] If he is like this in the hour of wrath, how much more gracious will he be in the hour of good-will.[4]

But the idea that wrath is linked with mercy is by no means always present. Sometimes it is simply said that sin provokes God's wrath and leads to punishment. Occasionally this thought can be carried so far as to say that *sin makes the merciful one* (=God) *cruel.*[5] It holds good particularly at the last judgement, after death or on doomsday, that the sinner will be struck by God's wrath alone without finding mercy.[6] The judgement of

[1] M. Exod. xv.3 (Horovitz, p. 130).

[2] Midr. Tannaim on Deut. xiii.18 (Hoffmann, p. 69); S. Deut. 96 on xiii.18.

[3] See, e.g. M.Exod. xv.1 (Horovitz, pp. 122 f.); xvi.13 (Horovitz, p. 165); S. Deut. 43 on xi.16, 320 on xxxii.19. cf. Sjöberg, pp. 62-71, 86-94, 110-117.

[4] S. Num. 105 on xii.10, 137 on xxvii.14. Here it is speaking of those who are righteous in other respects, but on account of some sin have provoked the wrath of God.

[5] M. Exod. xv.6 (Horovitz, p. 134); S.Num. 175 on xxxi.16.

[6] Mek. R. Sim. on Exod. xx.5 (Hoffmann, p. 105): *A jealous God: This teaches that they saw the figure which in the future will demand requital from the sinners; a jealous God: a God who judges, a hard God, a cruel God.*

Gehenna is a judgement of wrath,[1] and the day of judgement is a day of wrath—although this particular phrase hardly ever occurs.[2] Yet the idea that the judgement is just occupies a much more prominent place than the one that it is executed in wrath.

3. *Philo*

Philo's position between the OT and Stoicism, or rather his attempt to live and to think in both, is reflected also in his statements about wrath. But here too Stoic and Alexandrian ways of thought are in complete control. He admits with biblical and non-biblical antiquity that human wrath against evil and the wrongdoer is justified[3]; but fundamentally he (like the Letter of Aristeas) considers with the Stoics that wrath is an emotion which must be suppressed and controlled by reason.

This makes it intelligible that a certain contradiction appears too in his statements about divine anger: when Philo speaks of ἄζια ὀργῆς he may be thinking of divine as much as of human wrath (*Somn.* II, 179). In such matters it is 'permissible' to speak of God becoming angry[4] and Philo is aware of the real effects of God's wrath on affairs of this earth[5] as well as on the fate of man.[6] Yet on the other hand—and this is the prevailing line in Philo—God's outbursts of wrath are not real—in so far as pagan statements are concerned—but poetical additions,[7] like everything ἀνθρωποπαθές which the pagans attribute to the 'divine' in their poetry (*Sacr. A.C.* 95); for in the case of God there is no real

---

[1] S. Deut. 320 on xxxii.22; see also Str.-B. I, pp. 115 f.

[2] No Rabbinic passage is quoted by Str.-B. III, p. 804 on Rom. ii.5 nor on Rev. vi.17; but cf. p. 98.

[3] cf. Leisegang II, pp. 591 f.

[4] *Somn.* II, 177; cf. also *Spec. Leg.* I, 265.

[5] *Vit. Mos.* I, 6 (of harvest failure in Egypt), cf. also *Vit. Mos.* I, 119.   [6] *Somn.* II, 179.   [7] *Sacr. A.C.* 96.

πάθος.[1] Indeed such features are therefore mere *mythical fictions* (*Deus Imm.* 59). But this interpretation does not hold good in those cases where Moses himself *describes* . . . *his jealousy, his wrath, his moods of anger, and the other emotions similar to them . . . in terms of human nature* (*Deus Imm.* 60), i.e. with regard to the OT as a whole. The numerous passages in which such things are mentioned in the OT present to Philo a cause of offence and a theological problem. He finally interprets them as an accommodation of the divine word to the receptive capacity of the foolish who are incapable of true knowledge of God; this is a means of helping them to have right ideas[2]; accordingly there is no reality corresponding to such statements, yet they are of value to the learner.[3]

4. *Josephus*

Josephus differs from Philo in that he stands under the influence of the OT and the Rabbinate of his time.[4] Like the LXX he knows ὀργή as both divine and human wrath. In addition he mentions χόλος (e.g. *Bell.* 7, 34, 332), μήνιμα and μῆνις (*Ant.* 15, 243; cf. 15,299), which are found in the LXX almost only in Ecclus. and reveal the influence of Greek thought. On the other hand he never uses θυμός and θυμόομαι,[5] perhaps because θυμός

---

[1] *Abr.* 202: Similarly too Clement of Alexandria, *Strom.* V,11, 68, 3 (cf. the formal identity of expressions with Philo, *Sacr. A.C.* 96; *Somn.* I.285 etc.).

[2] *Deus Imm.* 52. Cf. also Orig. *Cels.* IV.71 f.: to speak of the anger of God is only the Bible's way of speaking for the sake of the uneducated; since what is forbidden to men cannot be ascribed to God.

[3] *Somn.* I, 235. cf. also *Deus Imm.* 53 f. with its contrasting sentences: *God is not as a man—God is as a man* and the appended remark: the first sentence expresses what is real, the second one on the other hand *is introduced for the instruction of many.*

[4] cf. B. Brüne, *Flavius Josephus* (1913), pp. 151-153.

[5] Schlatter, *Theologie des Judentums*, p. 40.

=ḥēmāh did not seem to him to be worthy of God, unless we are to think as with Philo of the psychological meaning of the Platonic θυμός; but this is less likely. He takes over the ὀργὴ θεοῦ from the OT where it is associated with illegal actions and infringements of the law (*Ant.* 11, 141: *lest God conceive anger at all of them alike and again bring misfortune upon them*; 11, 127: *in order that the deity may not conceive any anger against me . . .*, cf. 3, 321: *fear of the law and of the wrath*). In popular opinion the house of Herod stands subject to the divine wrath (*Ant.* 15, 376: *This cannot escape the notice of God, and at the close of your life his wrath will show that he is mindful of these things*; in 15,334: Herod's sickness *had been brought upon them by God in his anger*). Herod's great misfortune in the thirteenth year of his reign seems to be the result of *God's being angry or because misfortune occurs in cycles* (*Ant.* 15, 299); his illness was *just punishment inflicted by God for his lawless deeds* (*Ant.* 17, 168). It is true that Josephus, no doubt under Greek influence, readily replaces the personal ὀργή of God by the impersonal δίκη which 'like εἱμαρμένη (*destiny*) develops into an independent power'.[1] The division into parties in Jerusalem, *being between criminals, might be called a blessing and the work of justice* (*Bell.* 5, 2). When Simon bar Giora was punished it is the case that *villainy does not escape the wrath of God nor is justice weak* (*Bell.* 7, 34). *Simon, in retribution for his cruelty to his fellow-citizens . . . was delivered by God into the hands of his deadliest enemies* (7, 32). Hyrcanus asked the Pharisees *what punishment they thought this man* (Eleazar) *should have . . . in accordance with what was right* (*Ant.* 13, 294). Everywhere belief in God's wrath supplies the foundation, but its limits are set by δίκη; its instrument in Josephus' day is the Romans, whose world power rests on God's plan.

[1] Schlatter, *op. cit.* pp. 40 f. whence the following examples are taken.

V. THE WRATH OF MAN AND THE WRATH OF GOD IN THE NEW TESTAMENT[1]

1. *The wrath of man*

Apart from the root word ὀργή, all derivations from the root ὀργ- are used the in NT to denote only human wrath.[2] Where ὀργή itself is employed in this way it is generally done interchangeably with θυμός (cf. pp. 1; 51 ff.; 80 ff.). Nevertheless, where the sudden blazing passion of wrath and fury is to be described, θυμός is preferred (Luke iv.28; Acts xix.28), although owing to the derivation of ὀργή, it would seem particularly appropriate for just this purpose (cf. p. 1). Yet this word includes an element of set purpose, even of deliberation, which is missing in θυμός; in James i.19 (βραδὺς εἰς ὀργήν) for instance ὀργή could hardly be replaced by θυμός. Παροργίζω and παροργισμός go further than ὀργή and denote the wrathful indignation which threatens to become a lasting bitterness[3]; cf. Eph. vi.4, iv.26, where the change from ὀργίζομαι to παροργισμός is no doubt quite intentional. But elsewhere παροργίζω can be merely the active mood of

[1] In the following pages passages with the synonyms: θυμός, θυμομαχέω, θυμόομαι, ἀγανακτέω, ἀγακάκτηεις, ἐμβριμάομαι, παροξύνομαι, etc., are also taken into consideration in order to go beyond the partly merely fortuitous usage of the words with the stem ὀργ- and to produce as complete a picture as possible of the NT statements concerning human and divine wrath. For detailed discussion of the above words, cf. TWNT *ad loc.*

[2] In the case of ὀργίζομαι in Matt. xviii.34 and xxii.7 human anger is used as a picture of divine wrath; παροργίζω occurs in the NT only twice (in Rom. x.19; Eph. vi.4); παροργισμός and ὀργίλος only once each (Eph. iv.26; Titus i.7). The same applies to θυμόομαι which in the NT is also used for human wrath alone (Matt. ii.16).   [3] cf. Philo, *Somn.* II, 177.

ὀργίζομαι (as in Rom. x.19), as it usually is in its frequent use in the LXX.

i. The conditional justification for wrath in man

In the NT there is no uniform opinion on the question of man's giving way to anger. It differs from Stoicism (cf. pp. 2 f.), because a complete condemnation of human wrath is not possible where the wrath of God receives serious consideration. For if every stirring of wrath is automatically condemned, then statements about God's wrath must be explained away.[1] But if on the contrary these statements are taken seriously, then in the human sphere too at least a certain limited right to wrath must be recognised (yet cf. Rom. xii.19; cf. pp. 78, 104). The NT is acquainted with a holy wrath, hating what God hates, and demonstrates it most of all by Jesus himself (Mark iii.5: μετ' ὀργῆς; cf. John xi.33, 38, both times ἐμβριμᾶσθαι; cf. Paul in Acts xvii.6: παρωξύνετο τὸ πνεῦμα αὐτοῦ ἐν αὐτῷ). When Jesus is angry God's own wrath manifests itself (cf. pp. 92 ff.). Yet whilst this wrath, simply by reason of its close association with derivatives from the root δικ-[2] (Rom. i.18, iii.5, xii.19, xiii.4) appears as a δικαία ὀργή (cf. pp. 2, 90), human wrath is never described in the NT by this word.[3] Wrath is God's right; but it is not right for man (James i.20; cf. p. 77).[4] Whilst God's love

[1] As is done in Stoicism (cf. p. 5), Philo (cf. p. 71). Origen (Cels. IV, 71 ff.), etc.

[2] Righteousness in this series (1951, 1959), esp. pp. 13 ff.

[3] On the other hand instances of just wrath are found amongst the Greeks (cf. p. 2), in the OT (cf. p. 18) and amongst the Jews. In the last case it is found not only towards the ungodly (cf. the passages in Str-B. III, pp. 602 f.), but also—according to the Jewish attitude towards the alien (cf. TWNT V, pp. 11 ff.) —towards non-Jews (cf. S. Lev. xix.18 (352a) in Str-B I, p. 366).

[4] Something similar may be said of ἐπιτιμᾶν (cf. TWNT II, pp. 620 ff.), one of the forms in which ὀργή expresses itself.

includes wrath (cf. pp. 87 f.), in man love and wrath
exclude each other (cf. I Cor. xiii.5: ἀγάπη . . . οὐ
παροξύνεται). Only in two passages in the NT does
human wrath appear as having a definite value. In
Rom. x.19: ἐπ᾽ ἔθνει ἀσυνέτῳ παροργιῶ ὑμᾶς. This
παροργισμός differs in meaning from its use in the passage quoted there (Deut. xxxii.21)[1] by being a salutary
wrath; God himself brings it about in order to move
Israel to self-examination. In II Cor. vii.11 ἀγανάκτησις
(only here in the NT) stands beside ἐκδίκησις amongst
the seven fruits of repentance and clearly denotes the
well-founded wrathful indignation over the ἀδικήσας
(verse 12) or their own attitude which hitherto has been
so mistaken.[2]

ii. *The condemnation of human wrath*

Everywhere else in the NT the wrath of man is condemned. We can see this already in the gloomy pic-
tures of the angry man (wherever Christ or God himself
is not meant, cf. pp. 95 ff.), in the parables, stories
and visions of the NT, e.g. in that of the elder brother
in Luke xv.28. Here is the antithesis of Jesus, for his
anger is merciless as contrasted with holy merciful
wrath (Mark iii.5). God's wrath is that of wounded
love (cf. pp. 88, 124, 95), man's wrath is that of indignant
selfishness (cf. Luke iv.28).

Selfish wrath such as this is necessarily directed
against God, as it is in Luke xv.28 (apart from the very
transparent imagery here) and in iv.28 (ἐπλήσθησαν
πάντες θυμοῦ) and it is especially so in the case of the
Gentiles (Rev. xi.18; cf. Acts xix.28: γενόμενοι πλήρεις

[1] cf. also Ezek. xxxii.9 and especially Gr. Bar. xvi, a passage
perhaps interpolated from Rom.x.19. But here the helpless anger
of the Jews is not shown the prospect given by Paul, that it will be
the means of leading them back to God.
[2] cf. H. Windisch, *Kommentar z. 2. Korintherbrief* ([9]1924) *ad loc.*

θυμοῦ; Heb. xi.27: [Moses] μὴ φοβηθεὶς τὸν θυμὸν τοῦ βασιλέως). The final concentration of anger against God is that of the devil (Rev. xii.17; cf. verse 12: ἔχων θυμὸν μέγαν); he is full of fury with God's victorious preparations for salvation[1] and at the same time because his own scheme for damnation has been defeated. The historical antitype to the wrathful devil is Herod (Matt. ii.16: ἐθυμώθη λίαν), likewise because his scheme, intended to frustrate God's plan of salvation, proved unsuccessful.[2] These concealed causes of hostility to God constitute a main reason for Jesus' verdict, like that in James i.20: ὀργὴ . . . ἀνδρὸς δικαιοσύνην θεοῦ οὐκ ἐργάζεται i.e. the angry man cannot stand before God. Perhaps we can understand Jesus' saying about being angry in the Sermon on the Mount (Matt. v.22: πᾶς ὁ ὀργιζόμενος τῷ ἀδελφῷ αὐτοῦ ἔνοχος ἔσται τῇ κρίσει in this sense, if verse 22b and c were added only later; in that case ἔνοχος τῇ κρίσει means to come under the final judgement of God. But since the tripartite logion must for several reasons be considered genuine, κρίσις must be given the meaning of the local court of justice, and the logion itself receives the grotesque quality characteristic of so many sayings in the Sermon on the Mount. For what human judge can indict anger before his court, unless it has incriminated itself by concrete expressions (as some people have indeed conjectured to be Jesus' meaning)? But it is just this grotesque quality which shows—as elsewhere too—the absolute nature of Jesus' demands. Anger which has not yet made itself known even by a word is put on a par with homicide; anger is

[1] The wrath of the devil with the attempts of the first men to recover their salvation is a kind of prototype (*Life of Adam and Eve*, ix).

[2] The NT shows us another furious Herod (Acts xii.20), though without explaining the reason of his θυμομαχεῖν. If we might connect it with the immediately preceding narrative, then here too it would represent wrath at the failure of a godless plan.

the first step in murder.[1] Jesus, even more than OT
(cf. p. 21) attributes to ὀργή the full seriousness of sin.
Paul too and his followers share this view. In Col.
iii.8 and Eph. iv.31 ὀργή is included in the condemnation of the κακία, and in fact here again, as in James
i.19 (beside λαλῆσαι), it is clearly chiefly a sin of the
tongue.[2] Whilst refraining from wrath is called giving
place to God (Rom. xii.19),[3] being angry leads to
giving an opportunity to the devil (Eph. iv.26 f.).
Indeed if it grows into revenge it becomes an usurpa-
tion of God's exercise of his wrath (cf. p. 104) and of his
rights as a judge (Rom. xii.19). The anger of man is
therefore met by the wrath of God (cf. Col. iii.8 with
verse 6 and especially Rev. xi.18; cf. p. 118)[4] in the
time of the judgement.[5] Hence the exhortation not to
be angry oneself (Col. iii.8; Eph. iv.31, cf. p. 2) nor
to provoke others to anger (Eph. vi.4); for that means
leading them into sin (σκανδαλίζειν) and this is just as
bad as ἁμαρτάνειν or even worse (cf. Matt. xviii.6).
Anger is therefore banished particularly from the
proximity of God, thus in I Tim. ii.8: βούλομαι . . .

[1] cf. amongst others H. Huber, *Die Bergpredigt* (1932), pp. 76-
85.

[2] Similarly θυμοί in Gal. v.20 belong to the ἔργα τῆς σαρκός
and in II Cor. xii.20 to the catalogue of vices, for the most part
sins of the tongue. These statements differ in this respect from
Matt. v.22 where ὀργή and sins of the tongue are clearly distinguished.

[3] Rom. xii.19 is completed by I Peter ii.23 which uses Jesus as
an example in accordance with his own words in Matt. v.38 ff., 44.

[4] A good parallel is found in Livy 8, 6, 2 f.: Annius is angry
with Jupiter and in consequence he is himself slain by the wrath
of the gods.

[5] The same thought occurs in B. Ned. 22a (in Str.-B. I, p. 277):
He who is angry is subject to all the punishments of Gehenna; for
Gehenna is the place of the judgement of wrath. Conversely
according to Gr. Bar. xvi when God becomes angry man replies by
getting angry too.

προσεύχεσθαι τοὺς ἄνδρας ... χωρὶς ὀργῆς καὶ διαλογισμοῦ¹;
Titus i.7: δεῖ ... τὸν ἐπίσκοπον ἀνέγκλητον εἶναι ... μὴ
αὐθάδη, μὴ ὀργίλον. If a man is θεοῦ οἰκονόμος (of the
household of God), wrath is not compatible with the service in the sanctuary,² for where wrath is found God
does not wish to dwell (Ign. Phld. viii.1).

This almost general condemnation of wrath in man
explains the greater reserve adopted by the NT than by
its environment towards concessions which can be
found at most in Eph. iv.26 and James i.19. In Eph.
iv.26 (ὀργίζεσθε καὶ μὴ ἁμαρτάνετε) ὀργίζεσθε does not
have the full emphasis of the imperative, not merely
because it is a quotation (Ps. iv.5) but because it is
given in the rendering of the LXX;³ i.e. instead of *be
angry so far as I am concerned, but do not sin*, it would be
better to render it *if you must be angry, beware lest you sin*.
Anger is not actually called sin, but the thought is
suggested; when a man is angry, sin lies in wait at the
door.⁴ So it goes on to say: ὁ ἥλιος μὴ ἐπιδυέτω ἐπὶ
παροργισμῷ ὑμῶν. This quotation must also be read in
the light of the saying which follows 5 verses later (verse

---

¹ In the case of ὀργή, as well as in that of διαλογισμός, it is
open to question whether it is directed against God (cf. Plut.
De Ira Cohibenda 5 (II, 455d; cf. p. 2): *we are angry even with the
gods*) or against men. In the latter case it would be parallel to
Mark xi.25 (cf. Matt. v.23 f.). The rabbinic parallels (in Str.-B.
III, p. 643) make the latter more probable at any rate in the case
of ὀργή (thus also G. Wohlenberg, *Kommentar z. d. Pastoralbriefen*
(1906), p. 112.

² In substance Ign. Phld. i.2 says the same thing: *his incapacity
for anger* (i.e. of the bishop). But the word is in the neuter and the
related expressions (*steadfastness, virtuous, reasonableness*: τὸ
ἀνίκητον, ἐνάρετος, ἐπιείκεια) suggest the influence of Stoicism
on the ideas; cf. W. Bauer in Handbuch z. NT, *Die Apostolischen
Väter* (1923) *ad loc.*

³ For other renderings see Str.-B. III, p. 602.

⁴ The thought in B. Ber. 29b is similar; *Do not flare up, lest you
sin*, etc.

31), in which πᾶσα ὀργή is rejected. The continuation quoted above (Eph. iv.26b) forms a counterpart to James i.19: ἔστω δὲ πᾶς ἄνθρωπος . . . βραδὺς εἰς ὀργήν (cf. verse 20), inasmuch as here too wrath is not re- jected absolutely to start with and the thoughts in the two passages complete each other: first, take a long time before you allow yourself to be angry (James), and then, do not take long in suppressing your anger (Eph.)[1] The phrase βραδὺς εἰς ὀργήν might be considered as the parallel and equivalent of *longsuffering* ('*erek* '*appaim*) beside μακρόθυμος (cf. pp. 22, 103). In that case this would be a recommendation for the imitation of God and his longsuffering, and since this is very similar to his grace (cf. pp. 88 f.) this exhortation would approxi- mate to the demand to forgive instead of being angry. Here too, as in Eph. iv, the apparent concession is followed by the sentence in verse 20 already quoted above: *for the anger of man does not work the righteousness of God.*[2]

2. The wrath of God

i. Differences from contemporary usage

(a) Linguistic differences. Unlike Josephus,[3] but certainly following the lead of the LXX,[4] the NT never

[1] This behaviour is practised in both senses by those who *hold righteous indignation in reserve*, the phrase used in praise of the Essenes by Josephus in *Bell.* 2, 135.

[2] For the meaning of δικαιοσύνη θεοῦ in this passage, cf. Pirke Abot v.11: (*He who is*) *hard to provoke and easy to pacify, he is pious.* When considering expressions like this, one should picture to oneself how different were the conditions in vogue at that time outside the world of those thinking in biblical categories (cf. Athenag. Suppl. 21). On the one hand concern for culture, on the other for righteousness and piety; on the one hand concern for men, on the other for God.

[3] cf. A. Schlatter, *Wie sprach Josephus von Gott?* (1910), p. 59.

[4] cf. Wetter, p. 16.

employs μῆνις[1] and χόγος,[2] terms used in Greek poetry for the inexorable wrath of the gods (cf. pp. 2 f., but it denotes God's anger only by ὀργή and θυμός,[3] θυμός appearing only in Rom. ii.8 and in Revelation (xiv.10, 19; xv.1, 7; xvi. 1, 19; xix.15).[4]

It cannot be decided confidently whether a feeling for the difference in quality between θυμός and ὀργή influenced the apostle Paul or the seer John in their choice of words.[5] The piling up of concepts in several of these passages (Rom. ii.8 f.: ὀργή καὶ θυμός,[6] θλῖψις καὶ στενοχωρία; Rev. xvi.19: τὸ ποτήριον τοῦ οἴνου τοῦ θυμοῦ τῆς ὀργῆς; similarly xix.15; xiv.10), serving to increase the shattering impression of the tremendous reality of divine wrath (cf. pp. 23, 60), does not permit a more precise differentiation in the meaning between θυμός and ὀργή. But it might perhaps be said that θυμός, to which clings the concept of passion breaking out, is well suited to represent the vision of the seer, but not to denote the Pauline conception of God's wrath.

[1] But the LXX does used the verb μηνίζω (μηνίω) for God as well, e.g. Ps. ciii.9 [LXX, cii.9].

[2] But significantly in Sib. VIII.93 (inexorable).

[3] cf. von Jüchen, pp. 49 f. The reason for this may be purely linguistic, namely, that already at that time the other terms were felt to be predominantly poetic and strange in prose. On the other hand it may be due not so much to the fact that these words have lost their forcefulness (cf. Wetter, p. 16) as because the conception and the understanding of the difference between the wrath of the gods and that of God had become clarified.

[4] cf. TWNT III, pp. 168, 7 ff. For the use of derivatives, cf. p. 74 and n. 2; also pp. 54 f.

[5] cf. pp. 1 f. and on this especially also Philodemus, De Ira, 32 ff. (Wilke, p. 90), as well as the passages quoted in the apparatus there about the meaning of ὀργή and the difference between ὀργή and θυμός. Cf. also Trench, pp. 123 ff.

[6] So also Aelianus, Var. Hist. 13, 2 (in A. Fridrichsen, 'Observationen zum NT aus Ael. Var. Hist.': Symbolae Osloenses 5 (1927), p. 63); Isoc. 12, 81, etc.

The meaning of ὀργή can be defined more exactly by observing the terms with which it is used together or in contrast in the NT (cf. p. 98). The fact that it stands beside ἐκδίκησις (Luke xxi.22; Rom. ii.5; cf. TWNT II, pp. 442 ff.) and δικαιοκρισία (Rom. ii.5) (cf. p. 75; cf. TWNT II, p. 229; *Righteousness* in this series [1951], p. 73) excludes the idea of unbridled and therefore unjust vengeance when it is applied to God. That it has as parallels θλῖψις (Mark xiii.19 and par.; Rom. ii.8 f.), στενοχωρία (Rom. ii.8 f.) and ἀνάγκη (Luke xxi.23) shows that in the majority of the NT passages the effect of the wrath rather than the emotion itself predominates in the meaning of the word (p. 87; cf. pp. 26 f.).

(b) Differences in meaning

Jesus and the Baptist (Luke iii.18) bring a gospel which includes the announcement of the ὀργὴ θεοῦ (cf. Matt. iii.7 and par.; Luke xxi.23), and like them Paul, the Gospel and the Revelation of John testify to a message which proclaims not only the grace and mercy, but also the wrath of God (cf. e.g. Rom. i.18; John iii.36; Rev. xiv.10). The wrath of God is therefore to be regarded by no means as a piece of the OT religion of the law, dragged in as an irrelevance, as though speaking of God's anger belonged by its nature to the OT, whilst speaking of his love similarly belonged exclusively to the NT. For the OT proclaims the love and the mercy of God beside his wrath as impressively as the NT preaches the wrath of God together with his mercy (cf. pp. 87 f.).

Although the world into which the men of the NT were born and that to which they spoke regarded the wrath of God as something to be reckoned with, yet the NT is in this respect characteristically distinguished from the values of the world before their time and of that surrounding them. It is true that a profound cause of divine wrath is the same in both, namely the *hubris* of men which fundamentally despises God and at any rate wants to live its life without him (cf. Rom. ii.4 ff., i.18 ff.; cf. pp. 101, 104). But when in the pagan world everlasting enmity appears in consequence between gods and men,[1] there remains in the NT beside and above the wrath the love of God, and its wounding continually supplies fresh occasions for his wrath (cf. p. 76). It is in accordance with this that nowhere in the NT is God's wrath described with the colouring of psychic or natural passion, which appears so frequently in the OT. The NT does not contain any trace of those enigmatic, irrational outbursts of wrath, and the divine wrath does not burn for ever (cf. pp. 105 ff.). In the NT a theological concept of ὀργή clearly outweighs the psychological one.[2] Closely associated with this is the fact that consideration of the effect plays a larger part in the NT than consideration of the 'psychic reaction' (cf. p. 103).

ii. *The place of wrath in the NT conception of God*

(a) In the biblical conception of God, and hence in that of the NT as well, wrath is an essential feature which cannot be omitted. Behind all the passages—and this applies to the whole NT—which are aware that it is a terrible thing to fall into the hands of the living God (Heb. x.31), that he is able to save life and to destroy it (James iv.12), and that he is feared because after he has killed he has authority to cast into hell (Luke

---

[1] cf. von Jüchen, pp. 33, 47 f.

[2] This is shown in phrases such as ἐπιφέρω ὀργήν (Rom. iii.5), ὀργὴ ἔρχεται (Rev. xi.18) or φθάνει (I Thess. ii.16), θησαυρίζω ὀργήν (Rom. ii.5), etc.; cf. Pohlenz, p. 14.

xii.5; Matt. x.28),[1] there lies the awareness of God's wrath.[2]

(b) At times in the NT also wrath does seem (pp. 24, 69) to be, as it were, detached from God, like an independent active power, indeed almost personified as a terrible demon. It is undoubtedly striking that Paul in 15 out of 18 passages speaks of ὀργή without the qualification (τοῦ) θεοῦ.[3] A theory based on this and some other observations[4] has been propounded that Paul, like Judaism, considers ὀργή to be an independent being standing beside God.

Traces of such an 'absolute' usage of ὀργή occur already in the OT (cf. Ezra vii.23; Dan. viii.19). The personification of ὀργή was also prepared for in the OT by the simile of the *weapons of wrath* (Isa. xiii.5; Jer. l.25; cf. p. 32),[5] as well as by all kinds of figurative

[1] It seems to me that there can be no doubt that in this logion Jesus is thinking not of the devils but of God; cf. the commentaries *ad. loc.*

[2] In some passages this wrath seems to have 'numinous' features (e.g. Mark xi.14; Heb. xii. 29). Thus Otto, pp. 99 ff. (ET, pp. 88 ff.) attempts to fit a series of NT passages and narratives, particularly that of Gethsemane (cf. p. 131 and p. 114 n. 2), into the picture sketched by him of the phenomenon of numinous wrath. But there is no room either in the portrayal of Jesus or of God in the NT for divine wrath as an irrational, *mysterium tremendum*. Besides, in all passages of this kind the real subject under consideration is the holy wrath of Jesus Christ and of his father (cf. P. Althaus, *Die christliche Wahrheit* II (1948), p. 163.

[3] Some textual witnesses supply the θεοῦ which they find missing in several passages: Western evidence in I Thess. ii.16, Chrysostom on Rom. xii.19. By contrast, Marcion suppresses the genitive in Rom. i.18, because it does not fit into his image of God.

[4] cf. Wetter, pp. 16-55; the same is hinted at also in Pohlenz, p. 15. Böhmer, pp. 320-322 discusses the same observations and similar conclusions with regard to the OT.

[5] Hebrew: $k^ell\bar{e}$ $za'am$, LXX Jer. xxvii.25 (= l.25 in the Masoretic text): σκεύη ὀργῆς, clearly weapons which God takes out of his armoury (θησαυρός); cf. also Isa. x.5: ῥάβδος τοῦ θυμοῦ μου

phrases, as for example, the sending, coming, passing over of wrath (e.g. Isa. x.6, xxvi.20; cf. p. 64), or when God says in Isa. lxiii.5: *my wrath upheld me*. But Judaism goes appreciably further on this road, as already in numerous passages in the Apocrypha and Pseudepigrapha (cf. Wisdom xviii.21: [Moses] ἀντέστη τῷ θωμῷ). Apoc. Abr. xxv speaks in a rather enigmatic manner of a statue of God's wrath[1] *with which the people issuing from thee* (i.e. Abraham) *and coming to me provoke me*. For Rabbinic Judaism 'the wrath' is one of the two fundamental forces (*Middoth*) associated with God.[2] On the other hand *'ap* and *ḥēmāh* or the angel of wrath (*mal'ak za'ap*)[3] appear as independent angels of destruction (cf. p. 103 n. 2; p. 64). On the one hand it is thought that the 'absolute' construction of ὀργή in the NT may be recognised as a continuation along this line; on the other hand it is seen as a form of the fatalism of antiquity, a counterpart to the εἱμαρμένη (*destiny*) of the Greeks and the *Fatum* of the Romans, although it is

καὶ ὀργῆς. But in Isa. xiii.5 the LXX renders *kēlē za'am* which figure in God's battle-array at the judgement of the world by ὁπλομάχοι. For the whole question, cf. Böhmer, pp. 320 ff.

[1] Obviously the 'statue' stands till the end as a memorial of the judge, for the human sacrifices to idols are called a *witness to the last judgement*.

[2] cf. Bousset-Gressmann, pp. 350 f. 'Wrath' corresponds to *quality of justice* (*middat haddīn*). According to S.Num. 71a; Targum Ps. lvi.11 and other passages, the name Elohim belongs to this, whilst the name Yahweh belongs to *quality of mercy* (*middat hāraḥᵃmīm*); cf. also Weber, pp. 145, 259. In the light of this conception, it is not only possible, but significant that the Midrash reads Ps. vii.6 [Heb. 7] in the form: *Arise, Yahweh, against thy wrath*, (instead of *in thy wrath*) and that in B. Ber. 7a God is said 'to pray': *May it be my will that my mercy may restrain my wrath*.

[3] cf. B. Shab. 55a; Deut. R. 3 (200c). J. Taan. 2, 65b 43 (cf. p. 103) in Str.-B. III, pp. 30 f.; cf. Bousset-Gressmann, pp. 350 f.; Weber, pp. 154, 172; Böhmer, p. 321.—Tanch. 155b (in Str.-B. III, p. 30).

admitted that the ὀργή of the NT differs from these deities of fate by the fact that it is always subject to God and guided by him.[1]

It must be stated in contradistinction to these alleged prototypes and counterparts of the NT ὀργή that (1) the conception of transcendent personifications of wrath (such as the prophets' *weapons of wrath* (cf. pp. 32, 108 f.) or the angels of wrath) is unknown to the NT; for the angels in the book of Revelation who pour out the bowls of wrath, etc., are merely messengers and those who carry out God's will in accordance with the nature of all the angels in the NT. (2) Although the coming of the wrath (yet never its sending, etc.) is mentioned several times in the NT, yet the *coming* in this context is merely a technical term for the coming of that which is to come, i.e. the last things.[2] (3) The NT has nothing to do with two basic motifs of the religiosity of that period, namely fatalism and dualism. It can easily be demonstrated that in none of the NT passages is ὀργή a rigid principle acting independently of God, but that it stands everywhere in the closest connection with him and in fact with the God whose personal reaction it is.[3] It must not be concluded from the fact that θεοῦ is frequently lacking that ὀργή is felt even by Paul to be an independent hypostasis. On the contrary this usage enables the power to be recognised which makes all men conscious of God.[4] The independent use of ὀργή is altogether in line with that of χάρις in Paul and his successors[5] who likewise take for granted its meaning of God's grace.

[1] Wetter, pp. 46-55.

[2] cf. Cr. Kö. pp. 445 f. *sv*; TWNT II, pp. 666 ff.

[3] cf. Braun, p. 42.

[4] Thus A. Schlatter, *Kommentar z. Matthäusev.* (1929), p. 71.

[5] cf. especially Rom. v.20 f., vi.14 f.; Phil. i.7; Heb. iv.16; also, e.g. in the (introductions and) endings of the letters; thus in I Peter i.2; Col. iv.18; I Tim. vi.21; II Tim.iv.22; Heb. xiii.25.

(c) But in spite of the fact that the NT ὀργή cannot be detached from God, we must not dismiss the question: does this idea really imply the idea of an emotional disturbance in God (cf. p. 26)? Is it not rather the act of punishment inflicted by God in his wrath?[1] (cf. pp. 2, 63, 82). Now Origen (Cels. IV, 72) is undoubtedly right: a passion cannot be 'stored up' (Rom. ii.5 f.). In most of the NT passages ὀργή is in fact the working out of God's wrath, its infliction and its judgement (thus in Matt. iii.7 and par.; Rom. ii.5, xii.19, etc.). But it cannot be denied that some NT passages using ὀργή imply the conception of an actual divine behaviour, just as it is possible that they do in the case of ἀγάπη[2] and ἔλεος;[3] so in Rom. i.18, ix.22; Rev. vi.16 and most definitely in the quotation from the OT in Heb. iii.11, iv.3. As in the OT (cf. p. 32), so also in the NT ὀργή is both things: God's indignation at evil, his 'passionate' aversion to all wills which are contrary to him,[4] as well as his intervention in judgement on them.

(d) Objections have been raised again and again to the assertion that the ὀργὴ θεοῦ is an integral part of the biblical message. This is based particularly on the belief in God's love. It is said that if God really is love, surely he cannot be angry.[5] But already the period

[1] Thus R. Bultmann, pp. 283 f. (ET pp. 288 f.).

[2] cf. Love in this series (1949), esp. pp. 54 ff.

[3] cf. Althaus, op. cit. (cf. p. 84 n. 2), II, p. 164.

[4] cf. P. Kalweit, article on 'Zorn Gottes' in RGG [2]V, 2137. In the Enlightenment, such conceptions were called 'crude anthropopathisms of an uneducated age' (quoted by Ruegg in RE[3] 21, p. 719). But they are in no way more anthropopathic than the biblical statements about God's love as a father; they all belong inseparably to the biblical image of a personal God.

[5] This conclusion was drawn, e.g. already by Marcion for his 'good God'; cf. Tertullian, Marc. I. 27: Deus melior inventus est, qui nec offenditur nec irascitur nec ulciscitur. (He discovered a better god, who is neither offended, nor does he get angry, nor does he take vengeance.)

before the NT knew that in God wrath and love do not
exclude each other, but in fact include each other.[1] In
the NT as in the OT, in the case of Jesus as in that of
the prophets, in the case of the apostles as in that of the
rabbis, the preaching of God's mercy is accompanied
by the announcement of God's wrath (cf. p. 82). Only
he who knows the greatness of the wrath is overwhelmed
by the greatness of the compassion. Again it is equally
true that only he who has experienced the greatness of
the compassion can realise how great the wrath must be.
For God's wrath springs out of his love and his compassion (cf. p. 39): where this compassion encounters
man's hostile will instead of faith and gratitude, good
will and answering love, then love is turned into wrath
(cf. Matt. xviii.34; Mark iii.5; Rom. ii.5). Christ is the
touch-stone which divides mankind into those who are
exempt from wrath because they have allowed themselves to be rescued by his compassion, and those who
remain under wrath because they scorn his compassion.
Simeon (Luke ii.34) and John the Baptist (Matt.
iii.12) had announced this about Jesus from the outset.
This was the effect of his words and actions, as he himself had seen (cf. Luke xx.18; Mark iv.12); and at the
last by dying between the two criminals he demonstrated in his own person this divisive power for all to
see (Luke xxiii.39 ff.).

(e) How is the ὀργή related to God's forbearance
(μακροθυμία, cf. TWNT IV, pp. 378 f.)? This becomes
the burning question in the exegesis of Rom. ix.22:
εἰ δὲ θέλων ὁ θεὸς ἐνείξασθαι τὴν ὀργὴν κτλ. The

[1] cf. Prayer of Manasseh 5 f. The same is summed up twice
over more tersely in Ecclus. v.6 = xvi.11 (in the second passage at
least the text must be considered original owing to the parallel in
the other half of the verse, cf. pp. 64 f., n. 3). For a more
recent discussion, cf. K. Barth, *Kirchliche Dogmatik*, II, 1 (²1946),
pp. 407, 442-446; ET, *Church Dogmatics*, II, 1 (1957). Althaus,
op. cit. (p. 84, n. 2), II, pp. 32 f.

forbearance of God appears in a somewhat different light according to whether θέλων is taken here to be causative[1] or concessive.[2] Is it a servant of his wrath or a means of his compassion? Probably it has a double function: it is primarily the outpouring of love (cf. I Cor. xiii.4) and of pity, giving the sinner time for repentance (cf. Rom. ii.4; Rev. ii.21; II Peter iii.9) and consequently an aid to salvation (II Peter iii.15; cf. I Tim. i.16) whereby even the σκεύη ὀργῆς can become σκεύη ἐλέους[3] and thus it is a way to the final manifestation of the glory for the vessels of mercy. But when the patience of God is slighted and misused (cf. I Peter iii.20), it serves merely to increase the divine wrath and to render more certain the perdition to which the σκεύη ὀργῆς are destined (cf. Ign. Eph. xi.1). God's forbearance has the same mysterious twofold effect as all demonstrations of God's grace—e.g. the miracles of healing and Jesus' parables, even Jesus himself (cf. p. 97). They cause some to fall, others to rise again. Thus we may paraphrase Rom. ix.22 as follows: *But if God bore with great forbearance with the vessels of wrath, created for destruction, because he wished to use them for demonstrating his wrath and making known his power (yet he did this) nevertheless also[4] in order that he might make known the riches*

---

[1] Zahn, Schlatter, Kühl, Lietzmann, Althaus, etc.

[2] Thus B. Weiss, *Römerbrief* ([9]1893), *ad loc.* A. Jülicher in *Schriften des NT*, ed. J. Weiss ([3]1917 *ff.*) *ad loc.* and the translations of Weizsäcker, Menge, the Zürich Bible, etc. Cf. here text and margin of NEB.

[3] The possibility which repentance turns into reality is open to the σκεύη ὀργῆς just as much as for the τέκνα φύσει ὀργῆς. See Eph. ii.3 (cf. pp. 109 f.). The NT knows of no rigid predestination to eternal perdition (cf. p. 109, n. 2). On this particular matter another view is held by T. Zahn, *Römerbrief* (1910), p. 459 (but cf. p. 461), H. Lietzmann, *Römerbrief* ([3]1928) on ix.22, etc. (cf. p. 90, n. 1).

[4] καί is lacking here in B Vulg. etc.; if it is understood as *also* the construction is difficult but not impossible. So too T. Zahn,

*of his glory through the vessels of his grace which he had pre-
pared for glory long ago.* Here too the idea of Rom. i.17 f.
and iii.23 lies in the background, that the manifestation
of wrath is the indispensable foil for the manifestation of
grace.[1]

(*f*) The tension between wrath and justice, with
which antiquity was acquainted in spite of the fact that
the judge was permitted on principle to display wrath,[2]
reveals its own special set of problems in the theological
thought of the NT. Here God's wrath dominates the
sin of mankind, but it is just the ἀδικία of men which
actually promotes the triumph of his δικαιοσύνη[3] (Rom.
iii.4 f. ὅπως). If there were no sin there could not be the
miracle of the *sola gratia*, on which not only our salvation, but also God's glory depend (verse 7). Hence the
question seems to be justified (Rom. iii.5): μὴ ἄδικος ὁ
θεὸς ὁ ἐπιφέρων τὴν ὀργήν; indeed when the inter-
weaving of causes and of effects in the working of ὀργή
is examined more closely, it becomes necessary to amplify
the question: Is it right for God to be angry with the
chaos of sin into which he himself thrusts God-forgotten
mankind[4] (cf. pp. 120, 126 f., 128 f.). Paul's answer to
these questions is to begin with (Rom. iii.6) an argument

Römerbrief (1910), p. 458, n. 24; P. Althaus, *Römerbrief* (NTD) *ad
loc.*, etc.

[1] A somewhat different interpretation in J. Chr. K. von Hofmann,
Die heilige Schrift NTs III (1868), pp. 401-406 and cf. TWNT
IV, pp. 377 ff. (Horst); especially p. 385; both reject the possi-
bility considered in p. 89, n. 3.

[2] cf. p. 2; Pohlenz, p. 15, n. 3 and Hirzel, p. 417 refer to
Demosth. 24.118 and Aeschines 3.197, where there is a discussion
of the manner in which the offence can be matched with the
judge's wrath.

[3] cf *Righteousness* in this series (1951), esp. pp. 40 ff.

[4] cf. Apoc. Abr. xxvii (Bonwetsch, p. 36) with xxv (p. 35) where
the metaphor of God's wrath with Israel passes over unnoticed
into the idol with which Israel arouses God's wrath; i.e. God's
wrath always produces fresh wrath (cf. pp. 126 f.).

of Jewish theology: God is the judge of the world; thus he cannot be other than just. Today we should modify this argument somewhat as follows: When a man knows himself to be a sinner who deserves to receive from God nothing but wrath, from the final judgement nothing but condemnation, he sees that God's judgement is raised high above all questionings; for he recognises that God's wrath, being his repugnance against unrighteousness is simply an expression of his righteousness.[1]

This idea is already the basis of Paul's exposition in Rom. i.18 ff. But the introductory parallelism of verses 17 and 18 contains a quite different answer to this question, expressing an astonishing agreement between God's wrath and righteousness which man cannot explain.[2] Just because (γάρ verse 18) God must feel anger against the whole world, not only the Gentiles, but also the Jews, and indeed every individual (chapter ii), therefore he bestows righteousness ἐκ πίστεως εἰς πίστιν (i.17, iii.21 ff.) and proves himself to be the just judge in his recognition of this righteousness (iii.26).

But this produces a fresh problem: If God is angry with those who do not pursue the way of faith, is this just? This problem is only one of the many in the continuous dialectic of the Bible which cannot be solved by reason. Everything is established according to God's will and plan, and yet this does not diminish the guilt of everything opposed to God, and therefore the wrath of God provoked by it is righteous without any qualification. There is only one refuge from this conclusion: Christ and faith in him (cf. p. 130).

---

[1] cf. Althaus, op. cit. (p. 84, n. 2), II, p. 163.
[2] cf. Schrenk, pp. 14 ff.

iii. The manifestation of divine wrath

(a) In the portrayal and message of Jesus

Wrath is an integrating feature in the gospel's picture of Jesus.[1] It is true that it is only seldom mentioned *expressis verbis* (ὀργή in Mark iii.5; ὀργίζομαι Mark i.41 (in a variant reading); cf. ἐμβριμάομαι in Matt. ix.30; Mark i.43; John xi.33, 38), but the fact itself appears more often.

That Jesus felt anger is firstly a sign that he was a human being of flesh and blood.[2] Yet it is never a merely human anger; it always implies something of the manner of God's anger. This is seen above all in those things at which and because of which Jesus is angry. His anger is aroused by hostility to God shown by various forms of powers and forces under the control of a will: he addresses Satan imperiously (Matt. iv.10, xvi.23)[3]; he censures the demons wrathfully (ἐπιτιμάω) in Mark i.25, ix.25; Luke iv.41); he confronts with

[1] cf. J. Ninck, *Jesus als Charakter* (1925), pp. 22-23; P. Feine, *Jesus* (1930), pp. 245 f.

[2] He does not resemble the Stoic with his 'inhuman' (cf. Sen. *Ep.* 99, k5: *inhumanitas, non virtus*) ἀταραξία (*impassiveness*). So there is nothing artificial when he becomes angry, as some have wished to deduce from the reflexive phrase ἐτάραξεν ἑαυτόν John xi.33; cf. Aug. in *Joh. Ev. Tract.* 49, 18; W. Heitmüller in *Die Schriften der NT ad loc.;* W. Bauer, *Kommentar z. Johannisev.* (²1925) *ad loc.*; H. J. Holtzmann, *Lehrbuch der neutestamentlichen Theologie* II (²1911), p. 193, n. 1; cf. R. Bultmann, *Johannisev.* (1941), p. 310, n. 4 and especially the completely misleading exegesis of the passage by H. J. Holtzmann, in *Handkommentar zum NT* IV (³1908) *ad loc.* The phrase means no more than the reading of the Western text, given also in P⁴⁵: ἐταράχθη τῷ πνεύματι (also xiii.21) ὡς ἐμβριμούμενος, that is to say, an intense and direct personal reaction (for its cause, cf. p. 94 and n. 1). On the other hand τῷ πνεύματι with ἐμβριμᾶσθαι, or with ταράττεσθαι can probably be taken with T. Zahn, *Johannisev.* [3][4] 1912), *ad loc.* to be so pregnant with meaning, as though it expressed that fact in Jesus God himself was roused to anger.

[3] Jesus regards Peter as actually a tool of Satan who conceals himself in him; cf. Stählin, *Skandalon* (1936), pp. 162 f.

bitter anger (ὀργισθείς)[1] the terrible disease of leprosy (Mark i.41), he is deeply shocked by the diabolical behaviour of men (John viii.44), especially of the Pharisees (as πονηροὶ ὄντες in Matt. xii.34, as the murderers of God's messengers in xxiii.33, as untruthful hypocrites xv.7 et passim). This is the wrath of the Lord of creation who is roused to indignation by those who indignantly spurn him. Furthermore he is incensed (ἐμβριμάομαι) against those whom he has healed and whose disobedience he foresees[2] (Mark i.43[3]; Matt. ix.39); and against the disciples and their lack of faith

---

[1] The reading, ὀργισθείς of D, it. (a, ff², r) Tat. is to be preferred to the usual σπλαγχνισθείς which is more easily accounted for (perhaps the origin of the one or the other is to be explained by the confusion of the gutturals (in an Aramaic original: 'trḥm-'tr'm); cf. E. Nestle, Philologica sacra (1896), p. 26; R. Harris, 'Artificial variants of the Text of the NT', Exp. 24 (1922), pp. 259-261; so also J. Schniewind, Markus (NTD) ad loc. Ὀργίζεσθαι denotes Jesus' 'embittered' grappling with the death-like disease, and is thus equivalent to ἐμβριμᾶσθαι in John xi.33, 38 and στενάζειν in Mark vii.34. It is very much less likely that Jesus is indignant with the leper because he approached him contrary to the law (cf. J. Weiss in Die Schriften der NT on Mark i.41) or because he said doubtfully if thou wilt (Ephraem. Evangelii concordantis expositio, translated by J. B. Aucher [1876], p. 144), or that the anger had originally been attributed to the leper (change of subject after ἥψατο, thus K. Lake, "Ἐμβριμησάμενος and ὀργισθείς in Mark i.40-43', HThR 16 (1923), pp. 197 f.).

[2] We might also reflect that Jesus would be angry because he foresees that many will be tempted to have a superficial faith due to the miracles wrought on those who were healed.

[3] It is natural to attempt the reconstruction of an inner link between the ὀργίζεσθαι before and the ἐμβριμᾶσθαι after the healing of the leper, perhaps by referring to the unprecedented emotional expenditure of power which appears in the θέλω (verse 41) and in the ἐξέβαλεν (verse 43). But these are considerations scarcely applicable to Jesus (cf. above and notes 1 and 2). On the other hand the ἐμβριμησάμενος of verse 43 cannot be excised because it does not fit into the theory of prophetic frenzy (which can occur only before

(xvii.17). He is distressed at the unbelieving Jews who give way in his presence to unrestrained grief although he has just acknowledged that he is the resurrection and the life (John xi.32), and immediately afterwards he is once more provoked by the spiteful remarks arising from their lack of faith and understanding (verse 38).[1] This is the wrath of the Lord to whom lack of faith and disobedience are affronts to his majesty. Above all Jesus is filled with sorrow mingled with wrath (μετ' ὀργῆς συλλυπούμενος in Mark iii.5)[2] at the Pharisees. It has no doubt a twofold cause: first the wrath of the merciful one towards the legal-minded who will not accept mercy as the new way of salvation, and who therefore allow themselves to be driven to mercilessness and actually to deadly enmity (verse 6).[3] It is at the same time the wrath of love which seeks to win the

the cure); thus C. Bonner, 'Traces of Thaumaturgic technique in the miracles', HThR 20 (1927), pp. 178-181) who regards ἐμβριμησάμενος as the original reading in verse 41; this would then have become *iratus* in the Itala and by retranslation ὀργισθείς in D.

[1] There has been much discussion concerning the reason for Jesus' distress in the story of Lazarus; for the various conjectures see F. Godet, *Commentar zu dem Ev. Joh.* ([3]1890), p. 401; H. J. Holtzmann, *op. cit.* (cf. p. 92, n. 2) *ad loc.*, Bauer, *ad loc.*; Bultmann *ad loc.* who explains ἐμβριμάομαι (like ταράσσω and στενάζω) as the *vox mystica* for the spiritual perturbation of a θεῖος ἄνθρω πος(in dependence on Bonner, *op. cit.* [p. 93, n. 3], pp. 176 ff.). Probably the most natural explanation is wrath on account of lack of faith, because Jesus' distress is mentioned both times obviously in connection with the behaviour of the Jews.

[2] cf. Schlatter, *Mark. ad loc.* In the parallels the reference to Jesus' ὀργή and λύπη is lacking. On the other hand an analogous association of grief and anger occurs in Jos. *Ant.* 16, 200.

[3] An astonishing parallel to the relationship of the Pharisees to Jesus is that of the Romans to Caesar whom they will not accept and finally kill, just because he is *lenissimus* (cf. his own declaration in Cic. *Att.* 9, 7 C 1, as well as *pro sua humanitate, indulgentia*, etc., cf. *ib.* A 2; further Sen. *De Clementia*). They do not want the new way of kindness and reconciliation, as Caesar himself emphasises

Pharisees too for the kingdom of mercy and to which they respond with hatred because they desire not mercy but law. So divine compassion[1] for their piety which is so remote from God is combined with holy wrath. It is the same wrath which Jesus illustrates in the parable of the master of the house (Luke xiv.21: τότε ὀργισθεὶς ὁ οἰκοδεσπότης) whose generous invitation is spurned by those who had received it. But an incomparably graver wrath is described in the case of the wicked servant (Matt. xviii.34: καὶ ὀργισθεὶς ὁ κύριος αὐτοῦ) whose reply to the boundless mercy shown to him was an incomprehensible lack of mercy.[2] In all these cases it is the holy wrath of rejected mercy and wounded love which is discharging itself. Lastly, Jesus is filled with terrible wrath for the towns which had refused to listen to the call for repentance (Matt. xi.20 ff.) and for the traders in the temple who by dishonouring the house of God showed that they did not take God himself seriously (Matt. xxi.12 ff.; cf. John ii.13 ff.),[3] and in a symbolic act which is strange to the modern reader[4] he

energetically. Cf. now E. Stauffer, 'Clementia Caesaris' in *Schrift und Bekenntnis, Zeugnisse lutherischer Theologie* (1950), pp. 174-184, especially pp. 182 f.

[1] This is indicated by the compound συλλυπέομαι, cf. Pr.-Bauer *sv*, etc.

[2] The Baptist still keeps the door open for the Pharisees (cf. Matt. iii.8) and Jesus himself does so even more; his divine love sorrows for each one who is lost (cf. Luke xix.41 ff.; perhaps also John xi.38) and maintains to the end the promise of salvation to the Pharisees as well (cf. Luke xiii.35). On the other hand the disciple who has been forgiven but refuses forgiveness suffers final condemnation of wrath; the reason for this judgement in Matt. xviii.34 is the same as that in Heb. vi.4-6.

[3] Here the φραγέλλιον in verse 15 is both the symbol and the weapon of the divine wrath, announced already by the prophets for the cult which had become completely externalised.

[4] When Jesus cursed the fig-tree in anger, the question as to whether his anger was just is raised in regard to him too; for the time when figs ripened was long past (cf. the commentaries). This

reveals his wrath for those who withhold from him the fruits of repentance (Mark xi.14; cf. Luke xiii.7). This is the wrath of the eschatological judge who has authority to destroy, to exclude from the community of God (ἐκβάλλω in Matt. xxi.12; cf. xxii.13, xxv.30; Luke xiii.28), to thrust down into Hades (Matt. xi.23), and who is already exercising this authority.

It can be seen from what has just been said that Jesus was conscious of the fact, and often demonstrated it in his sayings and parables, that when his anger is provoked, it is fundamentaly already the manifestation of the eschatological wrath of God. It is one trait in the rich picture of the last things fulfilled in Jesus' coming. It is he who is the enraged Lord of the Last Judgement (cf. Ps. ii.12),[1] he who refuses all knowledge of those against whom his wrath is aroused (Matt. vii.23, xxv.12, Luke xiii.27),[2] he who destroys his enemies in his rage (Luke xix.27, xii.46 and parallels; cf. Matt. xxii.7, and allows those who are rejected to be thrown εἰς τὴν κάμινον τοῦ πυρός (Matt. xiii.42; cf. verse 49 f., xxv.41) and εἰς τὸ σκότος τὸ ἐξώτερον (xxii.3, xxv.30), or into imprisonment for debt without hope of release (xviii. 34). This must be mentioned here although the key-word ὀργίζομαι is used only twice in the passages referred to (Matt. xviii.34, xxii.7). It needs all the more emphasis since, with a correspondence to the

is probably one of the many traits in Jesus' parables and symbolic acts which shock us and the only purpose of which is to direct our attention to what is described and to emphasise its real importance.

[1] On the other hand it is worth noticing that in Luke xiii.9 Jesus says ἐκκόψεις (you can cut it down), not ἐκκόψω (I will cut it down). When judgement is passed in the historical era the parts to be played by the wrathful judge and the merciful intercessor are divided between the Father and the Son.

[2] The sevenfold 'woes' in Matt. xxiii expresses something similar; with this word Jesus as the judge at the present time pronounces God's sentence of wrath.

opening sections of the New Testament, the last book takes up again with its characteristic intensity and vividness the picture of the wrathful king and judge of the last days. Thus, for example, there is the picture in Rev. xix.15 which presents the King of Kings and Lord of Lords himself treading the winepress of the wrath of God the Almighty in a garment drenched with blood and with a sword issuing out of his mouth (cf. pp. 102, 115), and again the particularly striking phrase of the ὀργὴ τοῦ ἀρνίου in Rev. vi.16[1] (cf. also xiv.10). In the case of this apparently impossible mixture of images, we must consider firstly that ἀρνίον (in contrast to ἀμνός in John i.29, etc.) is also associated with the image of a strong young ram; secondly, and above all, that it is the same Christ who, defenceless as a lamb, had once to submit to the judgement of men, but who will then himself as a wrathful judge pass judgement on men with terror (cf. especially Rev. xix.11 ff.). His wrath will come in the first instance upon those who scorn the 'lamb's' offering of himself.

(b)   At work in history and at the end of time

Like many other NT concepts and important ideas— βασιλεία, δικαιοσύνη,[2] σωτηρία—ὀργή is a concept which

---

[1] The authenticity of the phrase καὶ ἀπὸ τῆς ὀργῆς αὐτοῦ has been challenged (E. Vischer, *Die Offenbarung Joh.* (1881), pp. 40 f.; F. Spitta, *Die Offenbarung des Joh.* (1889), pp. 27 f.; J. Weiss in *Schr. NT* on Rev. vi.16; E. Sievers, 'Die Johannesapokalypse klanglich untersucht und herausgegeben', ASG 38, 1 (1925), p. 31, etc. So also Procksch in the first form of this article on Wrath. This view is maintained firstly because the phrase is tagged on to the end of the phrase ἀπὸ προσώπου τοῦ καθημένου ἐπὶ τοῦ θρόνου, secondly because in verse 17 the majority of the witnesses read αὐτοῦ instead of αὐτῶν. Nevertheless a later interpolation of the phrase seems to me improbable; Christ is at once both saviour and Judge—the words *wrath of the lamb* express this in terse impressiveness and the day of judgement is the day of *his* (αὐτοῦ) wrath in verse 17.

[2] cf. *Basileia* (1957) and *Righteousness* (1951) in this series.

can possess both a decidedly eschatological character
and a decidedly contemporary one.[1] As in the case of
those central ideas, ὀργή applied to contemporary situ-
ations assumes a different and provisional quality in
comparison with its eschatological counterpart. Both
of these descriptions are of about equal importance in
the NT, if not numerically, yet in actual fact.

(i) Eschatological wrath is distinguished by some
typical adjuncts, antitheses and metaphors. The following eschatological technical terms occur in connection
with ὀργή: the verbs ἔρχομαι (I Thess. i.10; cf. Eph.
v.6; Rev. xi.18) and μέλλω (Matt. iii.7), especially
their present participles (cf TWNT II, pp. 666 ff.), also
σώζω (Rom. v.9) and ἀποκαλύπτω (Rom. i.18; cf.
TWNT III, p. 586; but cf. p. 101, n. 1), and in
particular ἡμέρα as the designation coined by the prophets for the day of Yahweh[2] (e.g. Zeph. i.15; cf. Ps.
cx (LXX, cix), 5 et passim, cf. pp. 34 f., 71 but also p. 42),
which reappears in the Pseudepigrapha (e.g. Jub.
xxiv.28, 30) and in the Talmud (B.AZ, 18b; B. BB, 10a;
cf. p. 110 n. 2), and is also taken up into the NT (Rom.
ii.5; Rev. xi.17). The following antitheses to the eschatological ὀργή occur: ζωὴ αἰώνιος (Rom. ii.7; cf. verse 5)
and περιποίησις σωτηρίας (I Thess. v.9). Amongst the

---

[1] cf. L. Pinoma, 'Der Zorn Gottes', ZSTh 17 (1940), p. 590.
Ritschl, Rechtfertigung und Versöhnung', p. 153, thought he could
prove that the conception of God's wrath in the NT is only applied
eschatologically and is no longer (as in the OT [pp. 33 ff.] and in
Judaism [pp. 66 f.]) used in judging contemporary phenomena and
that thereby he demonstrated that it is no longer binding for the
Christian faith. But this kind of consistently eschatological
interpretation is also one-sided and leads to wrong conclusions
(cf. F. Weber, passim; Cr.-Kö. pp. 813-816; P. Feine, p. 207;
R. Bultmann, Johannisev., p. 121, n. 4).

[2] Occasionally in the OT ἡμέρα ὀργῆς is also used for historical
disasters; cf. II Kings xix.3 and in the parallel text in Isa. xxxvii.3;
probably also in Job xx.28, xxi.30.

images for divine wrath (cf. pp. 108 ff.) those of fire
(Matt. iii.10-12), of the cup (Rev. xiv.10) and of the
winepress (xix.15) bear an eschatological stamp.

The significance of eschatological wrath for the NT
message is demonstrated most clearly by the fact that
the NT, following directly in the wake of the OT prophets (cf. p. 34), starts with the announcement of the
ὀργὴ μέλλουσα (Matt. iii.7) and ends on the same theme
(Rev. up to chapter xix). John the Baptist, with his
preaching of the coming wrath of God[1] (Matt. iii.7,
10-12) and with his baptism which aims at deliverance
from it (cf. pp. 111, 129), provides the prelude and in
this matter Jesus followed him. Jesus seldom speaks
expressis verbis of divine wrath (cf. p. 92); the noun ὀργή
occurs in one passage alone, in the Lucan form of the
discourse concerning the future (xxi.23), and the verb
ὀργίζομαι is found in this eschatological sense only a few
times in parables (in Matt. xxii.7; somewhat differently
in Luke xiv.21; cf. also Matt. xviii.34). But the thing
itself is a unifying feature in Jesus' picture of the future,
just as it is in that of his apostles, particularly in that of
Paul and of the seer John (cf. p. 100). In fact there are
two points in the picture of the future at which the
eschatological ὀργή has its appropriate place, i.e. in the
period of distress before the end and in the distress
during the judgement at the end itself.

Jesus' only statement containing the word ὀργή (Luke
xxi.23) occurs in the description of the messianic woes,
where it is almost synonymous with ἀνάγκη,[2] and where
in the synoptic parallels (Matt. xxiv.21; Mark xiii.19)
θλῖψις is found. These are all technical terms for the

[1] According to the account of the evangelist John not only the
first words of John the Baptist, but also his last ones (iii.36), dealt
with the wrath of God.

[2] cf. for this close association of *ira deum* and *fatum* amongst the
Romans, e.g. Tac. *Hist.* IV 26. Cf. p. 11.

eschatological distress, the chief event of which is the destruction of Jerusalem (cf. verses 21, 24). We are therefore concerned here with an activity of ὀργή in historical times, and consequently with one of limited duration, verse 24: ἄχρι οὗ πληρωθῶσιν καιροὶ ἐθνῶν.

The Rabbis already used 'wrath' occasionally as a designation for the judgement of Gehenna itself.[1] Similarly in Paul's writings ὀργή can have the same meaning as ἀποκάλυψις δικαιοκρισίας τοῦ θεοῦ (Rom. ii.5) and in Revelation as καιρὸς τῶν νεκρῶν κριθῆναι (xi.18). Clearly ὀργή here is not so much the righteous wrath of the judge of the world himself as that which he inflicts (cf. p. 87), the ἐκδίκησις (cf. Luke xxi.22 f.), the opposite of δικαίωσις that is to say the 'refusal of salvation'.[2] Therefore the last day is named from its most salient feature ἡμέρα ὀργῆς (Rom. ii.5; Rev. vi.17). The fact that in the first place where ὀργή appears in Revelation we read: ἦλθεν ἡ ἡμέρα ἡ μεγάλη τῆς ὀργῆς shows that the whole drama of wrath in the Revelation takes place on this one 'day' of judgement. In a succession of ever fresh calamities wrath is poured out: when the sixth seal is broken (vi.12 ff.); when the last trumpet is sounded (xi.18); when each of the seven bowls of wrath is poured out (xv f.); when judgement is pronounced over Babylon (xvi.19), and at the parousia of the Lord and Judge who himself treads the winepress of his wrath (xix.15).

(ii) In the NT wrathful condemnation at the present time is found in a varied relationship to the eschatological judgement of wrath. We have already seen (pp. 95 f.) how the Jesus of the gospels, when provoked to anger in this world, appears already as the person in whom the messiah and judge of the last days, indeed the holy God himself, is present. Further, Jesus displays

[1] cf. Str.-B. I, pp. 115 f. Cf. p. 110, n. 2.
[2] Cr. Kö. p. 814.

in different ways in his discourses wrath in action in
history (e.g. in Luke xiii.2 ff.). Paul too speaks plainly
in several contexts about the effect of God's wrath in
this era. The first passage to be named here is Rom.
i.18: ἀποκαλύπτεται γὰρ ὀργὴ θεοῦ ἀπ' οὐρανοῦ ἐπὶ πᾶσαν
ἀσέβειαν καὶ ἀδικίαν ἀνθρώπων τῶν τὴν ἀλήθειαν ἐν ἀδικίᾳ
κατεχόντων. There can hardly be any doubt that
this is an announcement of a contemporary manifestation of God's wrath.[1] It is manifested at the same time
in every detail in a manner analogous[2] to the δικαιοσύνη
θεοῦ. Moreover the two manifestations are connected
by a significant γάρ. The fact that apart from πίστις
there is only ὀργή for all mankind (cf. iii.9 ff., 23) is the
indispensable presupposition of δικαιοσύνη being manifested only ἐκ πίστεως.[3] The significance of the γάρ is
the same as that of the double γάρ in iii.22 f. or of the
ἵνα in Gal. iii.22. But the twofold manifestation of
God's wrath and righteousness depends exclusively on
Christ; since the time when he came into the world the
eschatological judgement of the world is taking place,
the acquittal (justification) as well as the condemnation
in wrath.[4] For the term ἀποκαλύπτω stamps the message
as an eschatological act of salvation.[5] At the same time
ἀποκαλύπτω indicates in both cases a veiled manifestation,

[1] The present tense must be taken neither as bringing the future
vividly into the present nor as the gnomic present of a doctrine of
things to come, derived from prophecy (thus Ritschl, *Rechtfertigung
und Versöhnung*, pp. 142-147), as is certainly the case in I Cor. iii.13
(ἡ ἡμέρα . . . ἐν πυρὶ ἀποκαλύπτεται); since this interpretation
is excluded in the case of i.17, it must be rejected also for the
verse immediately following (Cr. Kö. p. 815).

[2] cf. especially A. Schlatter, *Römerbrief*, p. 46 and for the dialectic
of the relationship of the two manifestations W. Elert, *Der Christliche Glaube* (1940), pp. 170-176.

[3] cf. A. Schlatter, *Römerbrief*, p. 52; cf. p. 91.

[4] cf. the contemporary judgement in John and on this G.
Stählin, 'Zum Problem der johanneischen Eschatologie', ZNW 33
(1934), p. 238; Cr. Kö. pp. 814 f.   [5] Bornkamm, p. 239.

i.e. one that is manifested only to the believer. This applies just as strictly to the ἀποκάλυψις ὀργῆς as to the ἀποκάλυψις δικαιοσύνης. Admittedly the ἐν αὐτῷ in Rom. i.17 is not to be linked formally with i.18; but only in the sphere of the gospel is it manifest that the abysmal sinfulness of the world is a manifestation of divine wrath.[1] Yet every such veiled manifestation in time points to a complete manifestation at the end. Hence beside the proclamation of the present manifestation of wrath there stands necessarily that of the future wrath (ii.8), just as the message of the present justification (iii.24, 28) is accompanied by a promise of it in the future (verse 30).

Corresponding to this, in the other case in which Paul speaks of the ὀργή (θεοῦ), beside the eschatological factor a contemporary one can usually be identified (thus in Rom. ii.5, 8, ix.22). Contrariwise where wrath in action at the present time is mentioned (as in Rom. iii.5, iv.15, xiii.4 f.; I Thess. ii.16), the eschatological aspect is never completely lacking.[2] In Rom. iii.7 τί ἔτι κἀγὼ ὡς ἁμαρτωλὸς κρίνομαι is parallel with μὴ ἄδικος ὁ θεὸς ὁ ἐπιφέρων τὴν ὀργήν; in verse 5. The present ἐπιφέρων points back to the manifestation of God's wrath in the present in i.18 f.; but κρίνομαι, likewise in the present tense but undoubtedly eschatological, does lend to ὀργή the quality of eschatological wrath.[3]

[1] Bultmann, p. 271, ET p. 275; Elert, op. cit. (see p. 101, n. 2).

[2] The case is different in Heb. iii.11, iv.3. Here in the quotation from Ps. xcv.11 it is the completely uneschatological divine wrath of the OT which from time to time raged over Israel and the pagan nations.

[3] Wetter, p. 29 explains Paul's argument as follows: if God is already the future judge of the world (verse 6), his present exercise of authority as judge is certainly also just, that is to say, a conclusion a maiori ad minus. But the present and future operations of his wrath cannot be divided up in this way; cf. T. Zahn, Römerbrief (1910), ad loc.

(iii) A striking postponement of the judgement of wrath is noticeable in the NT. God himself appears to observe the rule required of men: ἔστω πᾶς ἄνθρωπος . . . βραδὺς εἰς ὀργήν in James i.19. This explains why so often we cannot see any effect of his wrath where it would be most expected.

The theme of wrath's delay is found in a variety of modifications already before the NT; amongst the Greeks (Homer, Solon, cf. pp. 4 f.), in the OT, particularly in the form of the vivid expression 'erek 'appaim (=μακρόθυμος etc., cf. TWNT IV, p. 378; cf. p. 14, n. 2; pp. 42, 80),[1] and in Judaism (e.g. Syr. Bar. lix.6). Here it is admittedly constricted by particularism to serve either as a one-sided means for the salvation of Israel (e.g. J. Taan. 2, 65b, 44 ff.; especially 50-58[2]), or as an expression of θυμός against the nations (e.g. II Macc. vi.14). Both are combined in B. Erub. 22a: *slow to wrath against the righteous, slow to wrath against the wicked.*[3]

In the NT the idea of delayed wrath forms the background to three passages in the letter to the Romans,[4] and in two of them a double effect can be observed,

[1] In addition, cf. Jer. li.33 (*yet a little while* denotes the period of time which the wrath of God allows itself before it breaks out into judgement [= harvest]), perhaps also in Nahum i.2 f.

[2] 'erek 'appaim (in Joel ii.13) is understood here in the sense of *keeping wrath at a distance* and explained by the conception of wrath personified as two angels of destruction—two owing to the dual 'appaim—, 'wrath' and 'resentment', ordered to go far away. Thus Israel is able to repent during the long period until they approach from the distance (cf. Str. B. III, p. 30).

[3] Here the dual is explained as two faces of God, the one friendly, the other resentful (L. Goldschmidt, *Der babylonische Talmud* II (1930), p. 69, n. 132).

[4] It can also be found in some of Jesus' parables: e.g. in Matt. xiii.24 ff. the postponement of the judgement serves to preserve the δίκαιοι; in Luke xiii.8 it affords an opportunity for the fruits of repentance.

similar to that in the rabbinic sayings. In Rom. ix.22 (cf. pp. 88 f., 108 f.) the postponement of the judgement of wrath serves on the one hand to demonstrate all the more powerfully the might of God's anger against the σκεύη ὀργῆς, on the other hand an all the more glorious manifestation of his compassion for the σκεύη ἐλέους. In Rom. ii.4 we see clearly how the twofold function of postponing God's wrath (ἀνοχὴ καὶ μακροθυμία) can take effect not only in different people, but in one and the same person. It can lead to μετάνοια and thereby to δικαιοσύνη ἐκ πίστεως and thus also to the ἔργον ἀγαθόν. On the other hand it can lead to an accumulation of the store of wrath until in the ἡμέρα ὀργῆς καὶ ἀποκαλύψεως δικαιοκρισίας τοῦ θεοῦ the time arrives when the payment of the whole large sum is required (cf. pp. 115f.). Lastly in Rom. xii.19 man is urged, by practising retribution on himself, to seek to forestall the divine wrath whilst it delays (but cf. p. 122, n. 1).

(iv) Thus a historical survey of the doctrine shows the following result. Salvation history is divided into two periods, one marked by ὀργή, the other by δικαιοσύνη θεοῦ. There are two αἰῶνες, οὗτος and ἐκεῖνος, which nevertheless overlap in the time of Christ between the two parousias. Therefore during this period the two-fold manifestation of Rom. i.17 f. occurs simultaneously. The manifestation of wrath turns our eyes in two directions. It discloses the history of mankind as standing under ὀργή since the fall of man, and on the other hand precisely on that account, as being the anticipation of the world judgement. In fact it is like the tinder at which the ὀργή of the aeon of wrath is kindled, namely the law: ὁ νόμος ὀργὴν κατεργάζεται in Rom. iv.15. The law too, like the gospel, is a gift of God's love,[1] and as indifference to the goodness and forbearance of God

[1] Orthodox Jews to this day regard the law in this light.

in the gospel arouses ὀργή, so also does indifference to the law. This is not the purpose of the law[1]—it only looks like it to the transgressor. When God is provoked to anger by the law's infringement, that too is the reaction of neglected love which intended the law to be a benefit to men.[2]

(v) When eschatological events are anticipated in history, a transference takes place, as it were, from the instantaneous to the gradual. Events turn into conditions, the μέλλουσα ὀργή becomes the ὀργὴ μένουσα. In John iii.36 we read: ὁ ἀπειθῶν τῷ υἱῷ οὐκ ὄψεται ζωήν, ἀλλ' ἡ οργὴ τοῦ θεοῦ μένει ἐπ' αὐτόν. What does this mean? Does wrath remain until the end or to eternity? The second alternative would mean that in view of the present judgement of wrath the expectation of the future one is completely cancelled. But as John's views on eschatology are not exhausted by his picture of fulfilled eschatology,[3] the answer may be given here that the μένουσα ὀργή will be superseded by the μέλλουσα ὀργή.[4] But beyond this the question remains: is there in the view of the NT an eternal ὀργή?

The answer of the Greek world to this question is yes, that of the OT no. The myths for example of Sisyphus and of Prometheus tell of the eternal raging of the gods' μῆνις (wrath).[5] On the other hand the Lord of the Bible says: *I will not be angry for ever* (Jer. iii.12: cf. Ps. ciii.9 ff.,

---

[1] Nor is it an unalterable decree (cf. Wetter, p. 39, etc.). This is the somewhat one-sided view of Paul (cf. p. 126).

[2] cf. von Jüchen, pp. 33 ff. and above p. 39.

[3] cf. G. Stählin, *op. cit.* (p. 101, n. 4), pp. 253-257.

[4] So also Procksch; Cr. Kö. p. 814.

[5] Definitions of antiquity distinguished between θυμός and ὀργή as temporary and long-lasting (thus Pseudo-Ammonius, *De adfinium Vocabulorum Differentia sv*). But there is no suggestion here that ὀργή will last for ever. The same is true of analogous definitions in Diogenes Laertius VII l, 63, Greg. Naz. *Carmina* II 34, 44, and Theodoret on Ps. lxviii (Masoretic text lxix), 25.

etc.).[1] Judaism occasionally mentions eternal wrath, thus in Sib. III.309 (conjecture of Geffcken): *and to the children of wrath eternal perdition*, and Jochanan ben Zakkai (B. Ber. 28b): *the king of kings whose wrath when he is provoked is an everlasting wrath.* But in this matter Jewish opinions are not unanimous; e.g. according to Sanh. 10, 6d the heat of divine wrath hangs over the world only so long as there are wicked men in it[2] and B. Ber. 7 dilates on the fact that God is indeed provoked to anger daily, but each time only for a fleeting moment.

In the NT itself there are passages which speak of a definite limit to the duration of wrath (thus Luke xxi.23, cf. p. 99) beside others which appear to reckon with an anger which burns eternally, as in Matt. iii.12: the πῦρ ἄσβεστον is here a metaphor for ὀργή (similarly in Mark ix.43 ff.); the same applies to the πῦρ αἰώνιον of Matt. xviii.8, xxv.41; Jude 7. In Matt. xviii.34 the wrath of the king vents itself upon the wicked servant in a manner implying eternal duration, for whilst in prison for debt when could he discharge his endless debt? Similarly the wine of wrath in Rev. xiv.10 (*et passim*) is obviously parallel to the torments in the sulphurous lake which last εἰς αἰῶνας αἰώνων (verse 11; xx.10). But in all the last named cases it is a question not of the wrath itself, but of the punishment inflicted by it, which according to the main line (cf. TWNT I, p. 390: ἀποκατάστασις) of NT statements is certainly of eternal duration. It is only in this sense that one can

[1] But cf. p. 44. See p. 107, n. 2 on the frequent mention of wrath εἰς τέλος in the OT.

[2] Occasionally the Rabbis also reckon in a theologically untenable manner on wrath coming to an end; thus in various comments on Ps. xcv.11 by means of which they apparently wish to avoid the conclusion of Heb. iv.3 ff.: Num. R. 14 (177c) in Str. B. III, p. 685; T. Sanh. 13, 10 f. (435) in Str. B. III, p. 409. Midr. Qoh. 10, 20 (49b) in Str. B. III, pp. 678.

speak of eternal ὀργή in the NT.[1] But God's wrath too,
as such, is certainly something enduring, because it is
not a quickly evaporating passion, but the holy repugnance to all that is not holy; it endures until the last
will opposed to God is subdued (Rev. xx.10, 14, xxi.8).
The question concerning the eternal duration of the
ὀργὴ θεοῦ is posed directly in I Thess. ii.16 where it is
said of the Jews: ἔφθασεν (or ἔφθακεν) ἐπ᾽ αὐτοὺς ἡ
ὀργὴ εἰς τέλος. What does εἰς τέλος mean? *Until the end*
(and then no longer)[2] or *for ever?* It might mean: owing
to the continuous serious transgressions of the Jews,
God's wrath has been in operation again and again
until the last days which are now dawning. But probably we
have here merely the very ordinary and already somewhat hackneyed εἰς τέλος with which the LXX renders
the Hebrew.[3] εἰς τέλος can certainly have the serious
meaning of εἰς τὸν αἰῶνα, e.g. in Ps. ciii.9 [LXX, cii.9]:
οὐκ εἰς τέλος ὀργισθήσεται οὐδὲ εἰς τὸν αἰῶνα μηνιεῖ, but
probably I Thess. ii.16 does after all mean *for ever,*
without any thought being given to what is involved in
the eternal duration of this wrath.[4] Reflection might
indeed suggest that, because the Jews had rejected
Christ and deliverance in him from the ὀργὴ θεοῦ, they
would be handed over to eternal wrath.[5] But in that

---

[1] cf. Althaus, *op. cit.* (p. 84, n. 2), II, p. 31.

[2] τέλος is perhaps used in the sense of annihilation, as in the
parallel (is it the original of this passage? or is it derived from it?)
in Test. Levi vi.11: *The wrath of the Lord came upon them* (i.e. the
Shechemites) *to bring annihilation.* Annihilation causes wrath to
cease as well.

[3] The frequent combination of εἰς τέλος with ἕως πότε, e.g. in
Ps. lxxix.5 [LXX, lxxviii.5]: ἕως πότε, κύριε, ὀργισθήσῃ εἰς τέλος;
shows that εἰς τέλος was used merely as a rhetorical expression.
(Cf. also on *lānesaḥ*, D. Winton Thomas, JSS 1 (1956), pp. 106-109.)

[4] Thus for example in Jub. xxiv.28 (*cursed be the Philistines unto
the day of wrath and indignation*) the thought of the end of the curse
is of no importance. It means quite simply: *as long as the earth
lasts, for ever.*   [5] Thus Pr.-Bauer *sv*; Dibelius, *Theologie ad. loc.*

case the passage would be in irreconcilable contradiction to Rom. xi where Paul expounds the principles of his eschatological views concerning the Jews. These principles may be regarded as determining the interpretation of other passages dealing with the Jews, such as I Thess. ii.14 ff. This 'anti-Semitic' section cannot therefore be accepted as authority for views of an ὀργή which lasts for ever.

iv. The wrath of God in the imagery of the NT

The statements in the NT concerning God's wrath are, like those in the OT (cf. pp. 29 f.) clothed to an extraordinary extent in metaphors. As in the case of other NT concepts, the images provide all kinds of indications to enable the ideas associated with these concepts to be more clearly grasped. This is true of the concept of ὀργή although many of these images have become trite figures of speech from having been used over and over again.

(a) Images of the man provoked to anger occur in some of Jesus' parables (Matt. xviii.34, xxii.7; cf. Luke xiv.21). In these the ὀργίζεσθαι of the king or the master always indicates the turning point in the story, and going beyond the story to the rejection of the Jews and all who go the same way. The same wrath of the judge, but without the actual words ὀργή or ὀργίζομαι appears in the parables of the fig-tree (Luke xiii.6 ff.; Mark xi.13 f.; cf. pp. 95 f.), as well as in the great picture of the judgement in Matt. xxv, which emphasises the wrath at the contempt of God, at actual affronts to him (verses 24, 26, 30), and at the complete lack of love (verses 41ff.).

(b) Metaphors for those struck by wrath. The metaphor of σκεύη ὀργῆς in Rom. ix.22 (cf. p. 104) is derived from the LXX (Jer. l.25 [LXX, xxvii.25]) and occurs again in Symmachus (Isa. xiii.5). But corresponding to the breadth of meaning of its Hebrew equivalent kᵉlē, σκεῦος (ὀργῆς) in the Greek OT means the instrument with which, or rather in the NT that on which, God's wrath operates. In the former they are weapons out of God's arsenal of wrath (Jer. l.25 [LXX, xxvii.25]) or soldiers in God's army at the world judgement (Isa. xiii.5). In the latter they are the vessels into which God's wrath is, so to speak, poured so as completely to fill up their destiny of being devoted to destruction.[1] The counterpart is the σκεύη ἐλέους which are similarly filled with compassion. Yet a change in the contents is possible before the τέλος which brings about the final dispensation of the ὀργή when Christians experience in themselves that from being τέκνα φύσει ὀργῆς they become τέκνα θεοῦ (Eph. ii.3), and vice versa when the wicked servant doubtless from being a σκεῦος ἐλέους becomes a σκεῦος ὀργῆς, or when the Jews from being υἱοὶ τῆς βασιλείας (Matt. viii.12) become υἱοὶ γεέννης (xxiii.15).[2]

The phrase τέκνα ὀργῆς in Eph. ii.3 similarly has some pre-NT prototypes.[3] It belongs to the large group

[1] For this distinction between the meanings of σκεύη ὀργῆς, cf. von Hofmann, op. cit. (p. 90, n. 1). A different view is held by T. Zahn, Römerbrief (1910), ad loc. who will accept here too only the meaning of instrument. But there is no doubt that the image of the potter naturally first suggests vessels. Yet it is correct that the meaning of σκεῦος passes imperceptibly from the active meaning of σκεῦος εἰς τιμήν (verse 21; cf. II Tim. ii.20) = utensil, vessel for an honourable purpose—to the passive one. Thus a vessel out of which the wrathful judgement of God is poured out over others, such as Pharaoh, is after all itself permanently suffering from the effects of this wrath and in particular is itself destined for the endless judgement of wrath.

[2] Similarly Elert, op. cit. (p. 101, n. 2) p. 563: '"Children of wrath" too, who are probably none other than the "vessels of wrath", can be promoted in Christ Jesus into the heavenly nature (Eph. ii. 3-6).'

[3] Apoc. Mos. iii (Tischendorf, p. 2): Cain = ὀργῆς υἱός; Sib. III.309 (cf. p. 106): καὶ θυμοῦ τέκνοις αἰώνιος 'ἐξολόθρευσις,

of words denoting close relationship with τέκνον or υἱός (so that there can no longer be a question of any imagery). The imperfect ἤμεθα τέκνα φύσει ὀργῆς means: although φύσις seems to express the original, the natural condition of lying under the judgement of wrath (cf. Gal. ii.15; Rom. xi.21, 24), yet it has become a matter of the past, it has been replaced by a new ζωοποίησις, by another 'φύσις'; for in the sight of God there is, as it were, a change of family (John i.12; Matt. xxiii.15) through adoption, a fresh υἱοθεσία, and thus also a change of φύσις (cf. Rom. vi.5).[1]

(c) The images or wrath itself are taken mainly from three spheres:

(i) The image of fire (πῦρ)—used originally for the passionate outburst of wrath (cf. pp. 14, 30), then for the judgement of wrath—combines several conceptions: an image of the terrors and torments at the end, a conception of the final judgement itself (e.g. I Cor. iii.13, 15) and that of the 'fires of hell' (Matt. v.22, xviii.9), of the πῦρ αἰώνιον (Matt. xviii.8, xxv.41; Jude 7). This is the threefold background to the threefold image of fire with which the Baptist in Matt. iii.10-12 develops his saying concerning the μέλλουσα ὀργή (verse 7).[2] Closely connected with this there is in Matt. iii.10

i.e. *for the children of Babylon there comes eternal perdition.* T. Zahn, *Römerbrief* (1910), p. 457, n. 22 compares also the completely literal statement ἀνὴρ ἐπιθυμιῶν (*longed for*) in Dan. x.11 (Theodotion).

[1] σύμφυτος *like by nature, kindred* (Plat. *Phileb.* 16c), *conformed* (= συμμορφιζόμενος in Phil. iii.10), as happened in the case of Stephen, the prototype (Acts vi.15, vii.59 f.). If a man receives a share in Jesus' mortal body, he will also have a share in the body of his resurrection (cf. Rom. viii.29; Phil. iii.21; cf. TWNT V, p. 192). This exegesis of σύμφυτος must at least be considered beside the usual one of *grown together.*

[2] Verse 9 disturbs the continuity and probably did not belong here originally. On the other hand verse 8 forms the presupposition of verse 10 which with ἤδη is directly linked with the μέλλουσα

and parallels the saying about the axe. This is another image for the impending divine wrath. Whilst Matt. iii.10 refers to the eschatological wrath, Luke xiii.7 (Codex Bezae, cf. verse 9) applies to the historical situation (cf. p. 96 n. 1).

(ii) In the Baptist's preaching, as already occasionally in the OT, the image of water-floods (cf. Job xl.11) is mingled with that of fire (cf. Ezek. xxi.31 [Heb. 36]; xxii.31; cf. p. 31). This combination of the images is suggested by the twofold tradition of the flood and of the rain of fire on Sodom and Gomorrah, as well as by the expectation, corresponding to the fundamental biblical conception of the similarity of the primeval and the final days,[1] that at the end there will be a great universal fire and also a great universal flood.[2] This connection is the result of observing that the Baptist links not only the image of baptism by fire, but also his baptism by water with the μέλλουσα ὀργή (Matt. iii.7). Water shares with fire—as 'beneficent' as it is 'terrible' —and other elemental forces,[3] an ambivalent nature; it can be death-bringing or life-giving.[4] This is the basis

ὀργή of verse 7. How closely wrath and fire were seen to be associated already in Judaism is shown by the rabbinic sayings in which '(day of) wrath' is regularly interpreted as hell-fire; cf. B. AZ 18; B. BB 10 and on these note 360 in Goldschmidt (p. 103, n. 3), VIII, p. 38; also B. Ned. 22a (Goldschmidt V, p. 410). For the baptism of fire, cf. C. M. Edsman, *Le Baptême de feu* (1940).

[1] cf. H. Gunkel, *Schöpfung und Chaos in Urzeit und Endzeit* ([2]1921).

[2] cf. Vit. Ad. xlix. A contradiction between the expectation of an eschatological flood and of the promise of Gen. ix.11 appears only if the emphasis on the phrase 'never again all' is ignored. For a part of mankind will be saved from the final flood. cf. R. Eisler, Ἰησοῦς βασιλεὺς οὐ βασιλεύσας (II, 1933), pp. 101 ff.

[3] cf. the opposite effects in the case of ὀσμή (II Cor. ii.16), λίθος (Luke xx.17 f.), etc.

[4] Their interchangeability is the salient point in the Adapa myth (AOT ed. 1, pp. 36 f.; ANET, pp. 101 ff. Cf. *Chant de la Saussaye* I, p. 600; K. Galling, article on Water in RGG[2] V, 1770 f.).

of the fact—and not only the rite of immersion—that
baptism can be already for Jesus the symbol of death,
and indeed of his own death (Mark x.38; Luke xii.50).[1]
By contrast, the meaning of salvation arises from the
conception of the water of life as well as from the act of
emerging, typifying the resurrection or new birth. Baptism is one of the numerous symbolic actions of the
gospel which are not only ambiguous, but which often
have in fact two or more meanings. Already for John
the Baptist it is clearly just as much a symbol pointing
forward to baptism of the spirit, as it is a preliminary
image anticipating the judgement of annihilation at the
end.[2] In the first sense it awards the gift of salvation of
the last days (ϵis $\check{a}\phi\epsilon\sigma\iota\nu$ $\dot{a}\mu a\rho\tau\iota\hat{\omega}\nu$ in Mark i.4; cf. Acts
ii.28 where in the same way baptism, forgiveness and
the gift of the spirit are linked together). In the second
sense it procures deliverance from the baptism of fire[3]
of the last judgement. Therefore whoever desires baptism, hopes to escape from the future wrath (Matt.
iii.7). Yet that on which from the beginning the power

[1] This conception, which occurs both in the Marcan tradition
and in the material peculiar to Luke, no doubt belongs to the
basic stock of Jesus' sayings. Like the logion about the ransom, it
must not be prised by critical manipulation out of the original
core of the Jesus-tradition.

[2] This is the meaning of Matt. iii.11 where—at any rate according to the evangelist's interpretation ($\pi\hat{v}\rho$ must be understood in
verse 11 as in verses 10 and 12 to be the fire of judgement)—baptism
by water is contrasted with the double baptism performed by him
who comes. The voice from heaven too (verse 17) apparently
assumes the connection of John's baptism with the final baptism
of wrath. He who of his own free will placed himself under $\dot{o}\rho\gamma\dot{\eta}$
stands in reality under $\epsilon\dot{v}\delta o\kappa\acute{\iota}a$ (cf. p. 132).

[3] For the expectation of a river of fire ($\pi o\tau a\mu\dot{o}s$ $\pi v\rho\acute{o}s$, diluvium
ignis) at the end cf. also Sib. II.196 ff., 315, 252 f.; Pseudo-Melito
12, in J. C. Th. von Otto, Corpus Apologetarum Christianorum Saeculi
Secundi IX (1872), p. 432 and on this Eisler, op. cit. (p. 111, n. 2),
p. 109.

of baptism rests, still remained concealed, namely its association with Jesus' death and redemptive power. Since by his death Jesus took upon himself God's whole wrath against the world (p. 131), the power to deliver from his wrath lies in the baptism's sacrament of death. But whilst John's baptism awards this gift only as a promise, the baptism of Christ awards it in actual fact.

(iii) The third group of images, comprising the symbols of the cup and the bowl, the wine and wine-press of wrath, also stands in a certain family relationship to the two groups of water and of fire.[1] In the NT (cf. p. 31) the image of the cup of wrath[2] and of the wine belonging to it ranks amongst the favourite metaphors of the book of Revelation, and indeed it describes two different (cups and) wines of wrath corresponding to the two main effects of divine wrath (cf. p. 128). The one kind symbolises the punishment of $\beta a \sigma a \nu \iota \sigma \mu \acute{o}s$ (Rev. xiv.10, here as an epexegetical parallel $\beta a \sigma a \nu \iota \sigma \theta \acute{\eta} \sigma \epsilon \tau a \iota$ $\acute{\epsilon} \nu \pi \upsilon \rho \grave{\iota} \kappa a \grave{\iota} \theta \epsilon \acute{\iota} \omega$, cf. xvi.19). The other is the judgement of wrath on apostasy which proceeds according to the fundamental principle that God's wrath punishes sin by means of sin; thus in Rev. xiv.8; (Babylon) $\mathring{\eta} \ \acute{\epsilon} \kappa \ \tau o \hat{\upsilon}$ $o \mathring{\iota} \nu o \upsilon \ \tau o \hat{\upsilon} \ \theta \upsilon \mu o \hat{\upsilon} \ \tau \hat{\eta} s \ \pi o \rho \nu \epsilon \acute{\iota} a s \ a \mathring{\upsilon} \tau \hat{\eta} s \ \pi \epsilon \pi \acute{o} \tau \iota \kappa \epsilon \nu \ \pi \acute{a} \nu \tau a \ \tau \grave{a}$ $\acute{\epsilon} \theta \nu \eta$ who has made all nations drink the fierce wine[3] of her

---

[1] The frequent metaphorical phrase *to pour out wrath* (cf. p. 31) can be understood by combining the metaphors adduced in (ii) and (iii); in the NT, cf. especially Rev. xvi.1 ff.

[2] The image occurs also in the recently discovered Qumran manuscripts, 1 Qp Hab XI (on Hab. ii.16); cf. O. Eissfeldt, 'Der gegenwärtige Stand der in Palästina gefundenen Handschriften 2,' Th LZ 74 (1949), col. 96. For the origin of the image, cf. H. Gressmann, *Der Ursprung der isr.-jüdischen Eschatologie* (1905), pp. 129 ff. and P. Volz, *Der Prophet Jeremia* (1928), pp. 392 f.; cf. TWNTV p. 166, n. 26.

[3] The interpretation given here is not unchallenged. Usually $\theta \upsilon \mu \acute{o}s$ is understood in the sense of *passion*, thus perhaps *the wine of her passionate ungodliness*. But xviii.6 $\acute{\epsilon} \nu \ \tau \hat{\omega} \ \pi o \tau \eta \rho \acute{\iota} \omega \ \mathring{\omega} \ \acute{\epsilon} \kappa \acute{\epsilon} \rho a \sigma \epsilon \nu$

fornication, similarly in xviii.3.[1] It is the wine and cup of staggering of the OT (e.g. Ps. lx.3 [Heb. 5]; lxxv.8 [Heb. 9]; Isa. li.17, 22) which is brought here to its eschatological fulfilment. It is God who really acts when Babylon in its ungodliness takes or gives God's wine of wrath, as it is described in Jer. li.7 with the same imagery: *Babylon was a golden cup in the Lord's hand, making all the earth drunken; the nations drank of her wine, therefore the nations went mad.* This means that God's wrath itself offers the cup of fornication, i.e. of apostasy from God, and punishes all who drink it. Rom. i.18-32 is the commentary on this thesis.[2]

κεράσατε αὐτῇ διπλοῦν makes it probable that the οἶνος τοῦ θυμοῦ in xiv.8 and 10 are similar. It may be said that we have here a certain mixture of metaphors. But it is the same cup of wrath, even though filled with different kinds of wine of wrath. The interpretation that θυμός = *poison* (as, e.g. in Deut. xxxii.33) is quite unlikely, for although in Rev. xiv.8, xviii.3 the wine might be poison, yet it could not be this in xiv.10, xvi.19, xix.15; similarly W. Bousset, *Kommentar z. Apokalypse* ([6]1906), p. 385; E. Lohmeyer, *Kommentar z. Apokalypse* (1926), pp. 121 f.; F. Büchsel in TWNT III, 168; a different view in H. Seesemann, TWNT V, p. 167.

[1] On the other hand in xvii.2 the wine (οἶνος τῆς πορνείας) is only a metaphor for the seductive power of ungodliness which confuses the senses.

[2] Is the cup which Jesus asks his almighty father to take away from him (Mark xiv.36: παρένεγκε τὸ ποτήριον τοῦτο ἀπ᾽ ἐμοῦ) also God's cup of wrath? In that case Jesus would fear that this cup would bring to an end the loving intercourse on which his existence rested. Then the cry from the cross that God had forsaken him (Mark xv.34 and parallels) would be the indication that he had nevertheless been obliged to drink it (so Procksch, cf. p. 132). Now it is true that in the OT such a cup with no further description is occasionally the cup of wrath (e.g. Jer. xlix.12). But apart from the fact that it is hardly possible to distinguish between the cup of anger and that of suffering (TWNT III, p. 168), it is more probable from Jesus' own usage of the image (Mark x.38; John xviii.11) that in Gethsemane he means the cup of death. Cf. also Asc. Isa. v.13.

The different form of the metaphor represented by the seven bowls of wrath[1] (Rev. xvi.1 ff.) agrees with the first conception of the cup of wrath ($=\beta\alpha\sigma\alpha\nu\iota\sigma\mu\acute{o}s$). These bowls, the third of the great apocalyptic groups of seven, are poured out over the earth. The contents of the $\dot{\epsilon}\pi\tau\grave{\alpha}$ $\phi\iota\acute{\alpha}\lambda\alpha\iota$ $\tauο\hat{v}$ $\theta\upsilon\muο\hat{v}$ $\tauο\hat{v}$ $\theta\epsilon ο\hat{v}$ are *the wrath of God who lives for ever and ever* (xv.7); they are actually in the form of the seven last plagues with which the wrath of God is consummated.

The metaphor of the wine-press appears in the book of the Revelation in two passages.[2] In xix.15 it is again the same wine of God's wrath (as in xiv.10, xvi.19) which Christ on his return himself prepares, treading the wine-press. In xiv.19 f. it is the grapes full of men's sins which are pressed out in the $\lambda\eta\nu\grave{o}s$ $\tauο\hat{v}$ $\theta\upsilon\muο\hat{v}$ $\tauο\hat{v}$ $\theta\epsilon ο\hat{v}$ and the wine is their blood which streams from the wine-press and becomes a great lake (verse 20).

(iv) Lastly we must mention once more the phrase $\theta\eta\sigma\alpha\upsilon\rho\acute{\iota}\zeta\epsilon\iota\nu$ $\dot{o}\rho\gamma\acute{\eta}\nu$ (Rom. ii.5; cf. p. 104) which hints at the paradoxical metaphor of a store of wrath[3] accumulated in heaven. It forms the counterpart to the conception of a completely different 'treasure in heaven' (Matt. xix.21, vi.20; Luke xii.33 f.). Whilst the interest on this store from profit and earnings is already enjoyed in this life according to Jewish ideas and only the capital remains to be handed out at the end, the store of wrath grows until the last day in order to be paid with

---

[1] Their prototype in the OT is probably the threat of the seven-fold chastisement of wrath in Lev. xxvi.18, 21, 24, 28, or even the six men of Ezek. ix.2.

[2] Their OT prototype is Isa. lxiii.1-6; Joel iii [Heb. iv], 13; cf. G. Bornkamm, TWNT IV, pp. 260-262.

[3] It may also be found in rabbinic writings, e.g. J. Peah, 1, 15d 64: . . . *four things punished in a man in this world, while the store remains in that world—idolatry, adultery, bloodshed, blasphemy.* So also T. Peah, 1, 2 (cf. W. Bauer on Peah 1, 1b; G. Schlichting, *Der Toseftatraktat Pea* (Diss. Tübingen, 1936), *ad loc.*).

compound interest. Hence that day is called ἡμέρα ὀργῆς (Rom. ii.5).[1]

v. The objects and the instruments of divine wrath

(a) Its objects

In the NT too God is not provoked to anger arbitrarily; wrath is not a trait of the divine nature (cf. p. 26). As in the old historical works and in the prophets (cf. pp. 26 ff.), the first object of God's anger is the ancient people of God, the Jews. Already the Baptist's preaching speaks of this (Matt. iii.7 and parallels): *Do you think that you can escape from the wrath to come?* Jesus takes up the idea (Luke xxi.23): ἔσται ἀνάγκη μεγάλη ἐπὶ τῆς γῆς καὶ ὀργὴ τῷ λαῷ τούτῳ. This means: *the messianic distress will come upon the whole earth*[2] *and God's wrath will fall particularly upon this people.* Elsewhere too when Jesus speaks about anger, he is referring to the Jews (cf. Mark iii.5; Luke xiv.21; Matt. xxii.7 and probably also xviii.34), and Paul too sees things at first in the same

[1] Many of the images mentioned have a trait of gruesome irony of their own: a treasure is really a joyful thing (Matt. vi.21 and parallels; xiii.44), the harvest (Matt. iii.12) and the vintage in particular (Rev. xiv.18 ff.) are times of rejoicing (cf. Isa. ix.3 [Heb. 2]); wine really gladdens man's heart (Ps. civ.15) and the cup is really a typical metaphor for joy and salvation (cf. Ps. cxvi.13). But all this by its association with ὀργή is now changed into its opposite. Something similar in the employment of metaphors may be observed elsewhere too in the Bible.

[2] It is a matter of choice whether γῆ is to be understood simply, as in verse 25, of the whole earth or simply of 'the land' (TWNT I, pp. 676, 677), i.e. Palestine as in iv.25 (cf. F. Hauck, *Lukas ad loc.*) In spite of the parallelism which rather suggests the second alternative, I consider the first one to be correct, firstly because verse 25 is so close as to make a different meaning in verse 23 unlikely, and secondly because already at that time 'the land' in the messianic promises was frequently understood in Judaism in a general sense to mean the whole earth.

light; cf. especially I Thess. ii.16 (cf. p. 107), also Rom. ii.5—the Jews primarily are the impenitent ones who despise God's μακροθυμία; and in Rom. iv.15—the Jews primarily are the people of the law which for them ὀργὴν κατεργάζεται.

But by no means only the Jews are concerned. In face of God's wrath all mankind are alike. For they are all born with the same nature: they are all bound to the *desires* and *passions of the flesh* and hence they all lie under ὀργή. Hence all men were originally *by nature τέκνα ὀργῆς* (Eph. ii.3),[1] and it is equally true (cf. pp. 108 f.) that the σκεύη ὀργῆς like the σκεύη ἐλέους, derive *not only from the Jews but also from the Gentiles* (Rom. ix.22 ff.). The book of Revelation presents a particularly full picture of the operations of wrath.[2] Here it comes upon all nations (Rev. xi.18, xiv.8, xviii.3, xix.15), and all classes (though particularly the powerful and the rich, Rev. vi.15 ff.), all mankind (Rev. xiv.19, xvi.1), because they became worshippers of Anti-christ (Rev. xiv.9 ff.), and most of all Babylon, the embodiment of the godless, tyrannical, totalitarian power (Rev. xiv.8, xvi.19).

Now Babylon is associated so closely with the 'beast' (e.g. in Rev. xvii.3) that it itself acquires a share in the character of a power of the next world which resists God. This is the special enrichment of the picture in the book of Revelation—God's wrath is also directed against the devil and all powers opposed to God, as had become evident already in the manifestation of God in Christ (p. 92). Indeed the *dies irae* is intended for them in the first place; and in fact here there is presented

[1] The ἡμεῖς in this passage means either *we Jewish Christians*— οἱ λοιποί are the Gentile Christians—or *we Christians*, then ὡς καὶ οἱ λοιποί means: *as the rest of mankind* (i.e. are still so today).

[2] In the passages of the book of Revelation listed here, ὀργή occurs only in vi.16 f., xi.18, xiv.10, xvi.19 and xix.15; all the rest have only θυμός which is preferred in this book (p. 120, n. 2).

a picture of two powers coming into conflict with each other in wrath. Here the devil is fighting with his θυμὸς μέγας (p. 77)—symbolised in Rev. xii.17 by the image of the furious dragon (καὶ ὠργίσθη ὁ δράκων)— and at his side the nations of Rev. xi.18 raging against God and his kingdom. It is the great eschatological counter-wrath opposing the wrath of God, displayed with colouring from the Psalms, so that the drama of the book of the Revelation can be understood as the conflict between two ὀργαί.

(b) *Its Instruments*

It comes to the point of struggles between the ὀργαί because God himself in his wrath with mankind allows 'the demons to fume and rage'. Hence this means that the powers opposing God become the instruments of the divine wrath against the world.[1] 'The power and rights of Satan and his hosts are derived from the wrath of God.'[2]

The wrath of the devil has reached the position of a servant subordinated to divine wrath by a circuitous route. At the first stage the powers opposing God replace divine wrath independently; not until the second stage is their service made subject to him. The first stage is due to the attempt to remove as far as possible from God the catastrophes which formerly were themselves considered to be indications of divine wrath (pp. 29 f.). The second stage arose out of the concern to close the door against the dualism threatened by the first one. For the first one compare I Chron. xxi.1 with II Sam. xxiv.1 (p. 36); Jub. xlix.4 with Exod. xii.12;

---

[1] An attempt which is scarcely justified has been made to find in Rom. xiii.4, also the idea, in a somewhat different sense, of using the powers of the next world εἰς ὀργήν (cf. p. 102, n. 2).

[2] Althaus *op. cit.* (p. 84, n. 2) II, p. 260.

I Cor. x.10[1] with Num. xiv.34 ff.; Heb. ii.4 with Gen. iii.19b.[2] For the second stage, cf. Ecclus. xxix.28 ff.: *there are winds[3] created for vengeance and in his wrath lay on their scourges heavily; in the time of consummation they pour out their strength and shall appease the wrath of their maker.* The spirits are imagined as God's agents who *in his wrath scourge heavily*; but they will do so because *in the time of consummation*, i.e. evidently in the last days immediately before the final judgement, *they will pour out their strength and appease the wrath of their maker.*[4] Thus here, it seems, is an anticipation of the last judgement as the furious raging of ministering spirits, by which the final paroxysm of divine wrath at the judgement itself will be soothed. A second idea that the devil is assessed and put in his place lies behind the assertions in the NT even where the devil apparently places himself independently beside and in opposition to God. He is never

---

[1] The ὀλεθρευτής is either an angel of destruction (p. 85 ; p. 103, n. 2; cf. p. 64) or again the devil himself (cf. TWNT V, p. 170).

[2] cf. Apoc. Mos. xiv: God's wrath is death (p. 128, n. 1). The divergence in the interpretation of δυνάμενος καὶ ψυχὴν καὶ σῶμα ἀπολέσαι ἐν γεέννῃ in Matt. x.28 (p. 84, n. 1) is due to the conflicting opinions of the Bible itself. The same twofold statements about death are also made about temptation. Conversely God himself takes on the role of accuser in court, which is after all the *opus proprium* of the Satan, i.e. the 'the accuser' κατ' ἐξοχήν (cf. Rev. xii.10); cf. Gen. R. 93 (59b) on Gen. xlv.3 (cf. Wetter, p. 49, n. 1; Str. B. III, p. 220): *How will men one day hold their own before the holy one, . . . who is judge and accuser at the same time?*

[3] It is probably not a question of *winds*—beside the forces of nature enumerated in the following verses—but of *spirits*, i.e. of the personification of these forces described just as if they were persons in verse 31: ἐν τῇ ἐντολῇ αὐτοῦ εὐφρανθήσονται κτλ, i.e. *they rejoice in his commands*, etc.

[4] The transitive use of κοπάζω (*appease*) (mentioned neither by Passow or by Liddell and Scott) seems to be a peculiarity of Ecclus. (cf. in addition xliii.23, xlvi.17 and especially xlviii.10); cf. Helbing, *Kasussyntax*, p. 79.

more than 'God's agent' without knowing or wishing it; he is an instrument of God's wrath, whose function he has only apparently taken over on his own account (cf. I Cor. ii.8).[1]

But at the same time the devil is also the object and victim of divine wrath (pp. 117 f.; also p. 67). Thereby a fundamental law for the divine control of the world is observed, namely that being an instrument of God's wrath involves *eo ipso* being also its victim; a σκεῦος ὀργῆς in the active sense (Jer. 1.25 [LXX, xxvii. 25]) is in itself also a σκεῦος ὀργῆς in the passive sense (Rom. ix.22; p. 108). That was true under the old covenant with regard to the great powers (cf. Isa. x.5-19 with v.25-30 as well as I Chron. xxvii.24 with II Sam. xxiv.1) in relation to Israel. It is true under the new covenant with regard to the Jews in relation to Christ and the new Israel (p. 127), with regard to Judas (cf. Luke xvii.1) and above all with regard to the devil himself, who as the will opposing God is simply the active and passive σκεῦος ὀργῆς of God κατ᾽ ἐξοχήν in relation to the cosmos in this age. At the same time in this matter too the primeval era and the final era are correlated to each other: as the twofold catastrophes at the beginning and at the end of the world's history (p. 111) correspond to each other, so does a judgement of wrath on the devil at the beginning (cf. Vit. Ad. xv f.; Apoc. Mos. xxvi; Jude 6) and another at the end (Rev. xx.10).

Lastly the relationship of the power of the state to the wrath of God must be regarded in this light. The ἐξουσία[2] in Rom. xiii.4 is called: θεοῦ διάκονος εἰς

---

[1] cf. the excursus on 'Die Täuschiung der Geisterwelt durch Christus' (Christ's deception of the spirit world) in H. Lietzmann, *Korintherbriefe* ([3]1931) on I Cor. ii.6.

[2] Although the powers of the next world can play the part of διάκονοι εἰς ὀργήν and of ἔκδικοι in God's service (p. 118), yet to

ὀργὴν¹ ἔκδικος τῷ τὸ κακὸν πράσσοντι. It was considered strange that here the political power appears as the power to execute divine wrath; but it will not do on that account to strike out εἰς ὀργήν which is attested almost

interpret the ἐξουσίαι in Rom. xiii by reference to these powers seems to me very questionable (G. Dehn, 'Engel und Obrigkeit', in *Festschrift für K. Barth* (1936), pp. 90-109; K. Barth, *Rechtfertigung und Recht* (1944), pp. 14-21 (yet in his commentary on Romans, even in the recent edition, K. Barth has not included this interpretation of ἐξουσίαι); O. Cullmann, *Königsherrschaft Christi und Kirche im NT* (1941) pp. 44-48; *Christus und die Zeit* (1946), pp. 169-186 (ET *Christ and Time* (1951), pp. 191-210, where there is on pp. 182 f. (ET pp. 205 f.) a bibliography of this discussion; W. Schweitzer, *Die Herrschaft Christi und der Staat* (1949). In view of phrases like ἕξεις ἔπαινον ἐξ αὐτῆς, τὴν μάχαιραν φορεῖ, φόρους τελεῖτε an unprejudiced reader would always think first of political powers, as Irenaeus already (*Haer.* V.24, 1) perceived correctly. In the NT, especially in the book of the Revelation, it is quite clear that other powers stand behind the politicians, but it cannot be proved, even in spite of I Cor. ii.8, that they are intended to be included in Rom. xiii (cf. G. Kittel, *Christus und Imperator* (1939), pp. 48-54; F. J. Leenhardt, *Le chrétien doit-il servir l'État?* (1939), pp. 36 ff.; E. Brunner, 'Zur christologischen Begründung des Staats', Kirchenblatt für die reformierte Schweiz, 99 (1943), pp. 2-5, 18-23, 34-36; M. Dibelius, *Rom und die Christen im 1. Jahrhundert* (1942), pp. 6 ff.; W. Elert, 'Paulus und Nero', in *Zwischen Gnade und Ungnade* (1948), p. 42, n. 1; H. von Campenhausen, 'Zur Auslegung von Rom xiii; die dämonistische Deutung des ἐξουσία-Begriffes', *Festschrift für A. Bertholet* (1950), pp. 97-113; G. Bornkamm, 'Christus und die Welt in der urchristlichen Botschaft', ZThK 47 (1950), p. 224; TWNT II, p. 562, article on ἐξουσία, which was written, however, before the discussion started by Dehn).

¹ In spite of the usual order of words being better attested, I consider the one just given to be the original one; διάκονος εἰς ὀργήν is parallel with διάκονος εἰς τὸ ἀγαθόν (cf. the same contrast εἰς ἀγαθόν-θυμός II Esdr. viii.22) and it is better to connect ἔκδικος with the dative than with εἰς ὀργήν: *as an agent in matters concerning the working of God's wrath the state administers retribution to the offender.* The order of the words was changed probably because 'God's agent for wrath' seemed to give offence.

unanimously[1] or to find here a reference to the wrath of
the authorities.[2] How many heathen people and rulers
are mentioned in the Bible as having carried divine wrath
into effect (cf. pp. 32 f. with p. 33, n. 2; p. 41). They do so
even when they, like the devil, consciously wage war on
God and his own; thereby they rage unconsciously actually against themselves as διάκονοι εἰς ὀργὴν ἔκδικοι τῷ
τὸ κακὸν πράσσοντι. This is precisely the picture of the
power of the state in the book of the Revelation and this
explains the inner unity between Rom. xiii and Rev.
xiii ff.[3] The ἐξουσίαι can at any time lose their position as
agents, thereby they become agents of the devil instead
of agents of God, as the imagery of the book of the
Revelation shows, and, like their master, they themselves fall all the more into the power of God's wrath,
whose instruments they were chosen to be.

(c) The position of the Christians

In face of God's wrath there can be no one who is not
affected by it (cf. Rom. iii.23); one can only be excul-
pated. This is the peculiar position of the 'third race',
compared with all the others, with Jews just as much as
with Gentiles. Like all the rest it must present itself
before God's judgement seat, but through Christ it is
delivered from the ὀργή (I Thess. i.10; Rom. v.6) and
from κατακρίνεσθαι (I Cor. xi.32; II Thess. i.5 ff.); so

---

[1] Thus Procksch following the Western Test. It is probably not
unwarranted to regard the immediately preceding passage in
xii.19 as connected directly with xiii.4 f.: a power of the state has
been appointed the agent for the ὀργὴ θεοῦ whom the individual
must not on his own account prevent from carrying out his task
(cf. O. Cullmann, Christus und die Zeit (1940), pp. 177 ff. ET pp.
200 f.).

[2] J. Chr. K. von Hofmann, Römerbrief (1868), ad. loc. (pp. 536 f.).

[3] This inner unity is thus not only exhibited by the acceptance
of the so-called ' "christological foundation" of the state' (against
O. Cullmann, op. cit. (n. 1) p. 179, ET p. 202).

that looking back with Christ in mind it can confess: we were never meant for wrath; we were prepared from the first (προετοιμάζω in Rom. ix.23) to be σκένη ἐλέους.

vi. *The reasons for and the effects of divine wrath*

(a) *The reasons for divine wrath*

In the NT, as in the OT (p. 39), all motives for divine wrath can be traced back to one fundamental motive, namely man's contempt of God.[1] Paul demonstrates that the whole world, both Jewish and Gentile, stands under the ὀργὴ θεοῦ (Rom. i.18–iii.20). The reason is ἀδικία and ἀσέβεια; the Gentiles' contempt of God is shown by their disregard of the revelation of his nature (δύναμις καὶ θειότης) through what he has created (Rom. i.18, 21 ff.), that of the Jews by their disregard and violation of his will in the law (Rom. ii.17 ff., iii.19 f.). The wrath of Paul in Acts xvii.16 (παρωξύνετο) is like an echo of this divine wrath: its cause is the dishonouring of God by the worship of false gods, like the ζῆλος of Jesus in John ii.15 ff. The NT message clearly shares with that of the OT the explanation of ὀργή as wrath against evil (Rom. xii.19, xiii.4), against παράβασις (iv.15), against ἀδικία (iii.5); cf. especially also Heb. iii.11, iv.3 with the motivation given in iii.10 (ἀεὶ πλανῶνται τῇ καρδίᾳ) and the parallel passages in Eph. v.6 and Col. iii.6, where the ὀργὴ τοῦ θεοῦ, associated perhaps with a kind of traditional catechism,[2] is followed by a list of vices in which the ὀργή of man is also mentioned. The ὀργή of the ἡμέραι ἐκδικήσεως in Luke xxi.22 f. is explicitly linked with the OT and this happens in other passages where the ὀργὴ

---

[1] That this is in fact the common denominator can be gathered especially from Jesus' parables, e.g. Matt. xxii.11 ff., xxv.24 ff., xxi.37 ff.

[2] cf. E. Lohmeyer, *Kolosserbrief* ([8]1930), *ad loc.*

ἐρχομένη or μέλλουσα (pp. 98 f.) is mentioned; it must 'come' for the very reason that it has been foretold by the prophets whose picture of the future includes the manifestation of wrath as an integrating feature. But the real reason in both passages is always the fact that men are ἁμαρτωλοί, ἐχθροὶ θεοῦ (Rom. v.8, 10, etc.), that they are apostates. The book of the Revelation carries this explanation of divine wrath further, and into another sphere. Wrath is kindled in Rev. xiv by apostasy from God—not only against the created order as in Rom. i, but also against the power opposing God, the 'beast'. Wrath is discharged not only on indulgence in sin, but on apostasy itself; for πορνεία is actually God's wine of wrath (pp. 113 f.), thus his wrath in action which thereby reaches its highest intensification.

The explanation of the ὀργὴ θεοῦ becomes more profound and stern when it no longer springs from ἁμαρτία against God as contempt of his holy will in the law (or in creation), but as contempt of his holy love in the gospel (Rom. ii.4) (p. 39). However in this case it exhibits a parallel in detail to the contempt of God in the law.[1] The line leading to ὀργή is in the OT: νόμος— παράβασις—ὀργή; in the NT it is: ἐπαγγελία—ἀπιστία —ὀργή. The opposite series is in the former ὑπακοή— τιμή, in the latter πίστις—χάρις—δόξα. Contempt of God's kindness, patience and tolerance (Rom. ii.4) is the decisive reason for ὀργή in the NT. Jesus describes the same thing in the contemptuous refusal of the invitation (Luke xiv.16 ff., especially verse 21) which in the Matthaean variant (xxii.2 ff.) rises to hatred and

---

[1] Both can be called ἀπειθεῖν-ἀπείθεια; in the latter case rather in the sense of disobedience (Eph. v.6, in the former in that of lack of faith, John iii.36). The transition, or rather the mingling of the two, is indicated in Rom. ii.8: ἀπειθεῖν τῇ ἀληθείᾳ, πείθεσθαι τῇ ἀδικίᾳ; cf. also i.18: τὴν ἀλήθειαν ἐν ἀδικίᾳ κατέχειν and the close proximity of ἀπιστία and ἀδικία in Rom. iii.3, 5.

murder. So too does Paul in a corresponding 'anti-semitic' picture of the Jews in I Thess. ii.14 ff.: they said 'no' to Jesus and God replied with 'no' in the form of his ὀργή.

Another reason in the NT for ὀργή is that the response to the love of God is lack of love, to his mercy it is mercilessness, which also increases to hatred and murder (cf. Mark iii.5 f.; Matt. xviii.21 ff.; ἔπνιγεν in verse 28). That too is contempt of God and his χρηστότης. In addition to Mark iii.5 and Matt. xviii.34[1] this is the reason for the ὀργή in Rom. ii.5, in so far as judging is also uncharitable and at the same time an expression of impenitence.[2] This passage makes it clear that the two causes of ὀργή—contempt of God and uncharitableness towards our brother as response to the gospel—are fundamentally one and the same; for the ἀμετανόητος is eo ipso merciless. The prototype of both these qualities is the Jews, and especially the Pharisees in the gospel.[3] The NT calls this attitude πρώρωσις τῆς καρδίας (Mark iii.5) or σκληρότης (Rom. ii.5). To this the reply of the ὀργὴ θεοῦ is the 'revenge' (Rom. xii.19) of wounded love in which revenge is at one with his righteousness as a judge.[4]

The line indicated here for the occasion of God's wrath in the NT cuts across a final cause which is hard to understand. Paul seems to know something about the fact that behind all other reasons for ὀργή there stands the really decisive one, the will of God himself.

[1] On the other hand in the parable of the prodigal son, the second part of which is akin to this, only the ὀργή of the uncharitable brother is mentioned (Luke xv.28), and no word is said of an angry reaction, in itself very natural, on the part of the father—in fact just the opposite (cf. verse 31 τέκνον, also Matt. xx.13-15).

[2] cf. Schrenk, pp. 20 f.

[3] cf. J. Schniewind, Das Gleichnis vom verlorenen Sohn (1940), pp. 35-38.

[4] cf. P. Althaus (p. 84, n. 2) on Rom. xii.19.

Here the mysterious possibility of a *praedestinatio ad iram*
appears in the background when Paul (Rom. ix.22)
speaks of σκεύη ὀργῆς κατηρτισμένα εἰς ἀπώλειαν which
God 'wills' to use to demonstrate the power of his
wrath; for κατηρτισμένα means, not that *they had developed, were ready* (for destruction),[1] but that because of
the parallel ἃ προητοίμασεν in verse 23: *they have been
prepared for this by God*. There is evidence for such a
preparation for divine wrath by an indirect statement
in I Thess. v.9: οὐκ ἔθετο ἡμᾶς ὁ θεὸς εἰς ὀργήν, ἀλλὰ
εἰς περιποίησιν σωτηρίας. *God has destined us* (i.e. the
Christians) *to the attainment of salvation;* but us alone; for
the others there is in fact a θέσθαι by God εἰς ὀργήν.
The same thought lies behind Paul's ideas concerning
the law in Rom. iv.15: ὁ γὰρ νόμος ὀργὴν κατεργάζεται,
and for Paul this is not a *parergon* of the law, it is its
opus proprium; it is the purpose of the law to place men
definitely under the wrath, ἵνα πᾶν στόμα φραγῇ καὶ
ὑπόδικος γένηται πᾶς ὁ κόσμος τῷ θεῷ (Rom. iii.19).
Such ideas never occur in isolation, but are always
embedded in statements about ἐκδίκησις and similar
subjects. This means that in such cases always, before
all else, the guilt of man must be perceived. Here
human guilt and God's will form a network just as
inextricable as elsewhere the temptation of the devil
on the one hand and human original sin, with ever
fresh actual lapses, on the other (Eph. ii.2 f.).

(b) The causes and effects of divine wrath are inseparable

We enter into the final impenetrable darkness of
divine wrath when we recognise that the effects which
it produces itself are its most important causes, and that
again all great acts of divine wrath become an equal
number of reasons for fresh discharges of wrath. What

---

[1] Thus von Hofmann, *op. cit.* (p. 122, n. 2), p. 401.

the Jews did and that for which they are blamed so
severely, had to happen in accordance with God's own
plan. Even they, with their hatred of God venting its
furious rage on Jesus, were the instruments of this purpose of love and salvation, and yet on that account
God's wrath fell upon them. The very thing which
caused the anger is imposed on them as a retributory
punishment, namely complete rejection of Christ.[1]
Thus we find ourselves here in a sequence which appears
to human logic as a *circulus vitiosus* of guilt and punishment, and this belongs to the most terrible discoveries
in the Bible. Sin and unbelief, the two main causes of
the ὀργὴ θεοῦ are at the same time its effects. Paul
demonstrates this in Rom. i; it is probably also the
meaning of Rom. ix.22: God reveals his wrath in the
hardening of the σκεύη ὀργῆς (e.g. the Pharaoh) whom
he has long tolerated. This applies also to the Jews.[2]
Here it is impossible to distinguish what is sin and what
is destiny. Divine wrath acts on the divine principle[3]
which requites like with like, which lets the deed recoil
on the head of the perpetrator.[4]

[1] cf. Filson, p. 43.

[2] 'The reality of the hardening shows up the power of God's
wrath which holds sway over man also in his sin (Althaus, *op. cit.*
(p. 84, n. 2) on Rom. ix.17 f.). Without the use of the word
'wrath' the unity of guilt and the fall, as a thing prepared by God,
is expressed with excellent brevity in I Peter ii.8: προσκόπτουσιν
τῷ λόγῳ ἀπειθοῦντες, εἰς ὃ καὶ ἐτέθεσαν, thereby giving what is
fundamentally a description of the effects of his wrath on the
unbelievers (cf. G. Stählin, *Skandalon* (1930), pp. 197 f.).

[3] Without any possibility of being itself this principle, against
Wetter, p. 20.

[4] cf. also Matt. xxvi.52b; xxvii.25. Jewry too recognised something of this, although not in the full depth of the NT discovery;
cf. Ab. 4, 2: *the performance of one duty involves the performance of
another, and one transgression involves another; since the reward of per-
forming one duty is to perform another, and the reward of a transgression
is to transgress again.*

(c) The effects of divine wrath

In what we have just said the most profound reply of the NT to the question concerning the effects of divine wrath has been anticipated. In this reply the non-biblical and the OT world had approached each other in a striking manner (pp. 7 ff., 33 f.), in so far as in all these cases natural catastrophes and those in the nation's life are traced back to God's wrath. The OT (e.g. in Ps. xc.7-11) exposes with particular emphasis the fundamental connection between God's wrath and death[1] and the NT follows in its footsteps;[2] cf. in particular Rom. i.18 ff. (verse 32 ἄξιοι θανάτου) and Rom. xiii.1 ff. (μάχαιρα—ὀργή).

Furthermore, in the picture of eschatological wrath the correspondence of ὀργή and θάνατος is replaced by that of ὀργή and ἀπώλεια (cf. Rom. ix.22; Rev. xiv ff.), the prelude to which is the destruction of Jerusalem as a phenomenon of ὀργή (Luke xxi.23 and an exact parallel in the parable in Matt. xxii.7). But in fact the most terrible form of the eschatological ἀπώλεια is not annihilation, not being snuffed out, but eternal βασανισμός[3] (Rev. xiv.10 f.; xx.10 et passim; also Matt. xviii.34): the judgement of wrath is just as 'boundless' as previously compassion had been (cf. verse 27, 24).

But the most real and characteristic effect of ὀργή in the NT is unbelief, apostasy and what follows from it, just as the NT considers μὴ πιστεύοντες and ἀπολλύμενοι to be equivalent. Thus the very thing generally

---

[1] According to one of the Pseudepigrapha even God's wrath and the universal fate of death are identical, namely when ὀργή is considered to be the *punishment of wrath*. In Apoc. Mos. xiv Adam says to Eve: *What have you wrought in us, and brought upon us great wrath which is death lording it over all our race?*

[2] cf. amongst others Bartholomäi, p. 258.

[3] cf. Wisdom xi.9: *they learned how the ungodly were tormented, being judged with wrath.*

supposed to be the cause of ὀργή becomes its effect. It is this which in Rom. i leads far beyond the OT pronouncements, even though these Pauline thoughts may be called a more penetrating modification of the Deuteronomic pattern of retribution (p. 33). The chaos of ancient immorality, and indeed of all human immorality, is a dispensation of the ὀργὴ θεοῦ according to the revelation bestowed upon faith. That is even indicated formally by the ingenious construction of this section: the threefold (μετ)ήλλαξαν (verses 23, 25, 26) correspond to the threefold παρέδωκεν. Here cause and effect are one and the same; the pattern which consists in linking cause and effect as modern man's view of the world, is shattered by the force of divine wrath.

vii. *Deliverance from the wrath of God*

(*a*) The NT shares with the non-biblical[1] and the OT world[2] the desire to escape from divine wrath, or to avert it altogether.

(*b*) Since in the NT the prospect of the wrath to come dominates the picture, the question how to be delivered from it is asked and answered also at the very beginning, in the preaching of the Baptist. The reply is given in these words: μετανοεῖτε . . . ποιήσατε οὖν καρπὸν ἄξιον τῆς μετανοίας in Matt. iii.2, 8, and the promise of deliverance is baptism, in so far as it anticipates the judgement of wrath as a symbol which is more than a symbol, and by means of the anticipation ensures that the judgement itself will be averted (pp. 111 f.).[3] But this

---

[1] cf. pp. 6 ff.; cf. F. Heiler, *Das Gebet* ([5]1921), pp. 87-89; ET *Prayer* (1932), pp. 33-35 *et passim*.

[2] cf. pp. 42 ff.; also Cr. Kö, pp. 811 f.

[3] The same train of thought—baptism to allay the wrath—is the background already in the legend in Vit. Ad. vi-xi: Adam and Eve undertake in the Jordan, or it may be in the Tigris, their own baptism, which is intended to procure their deliverance from

deliverance is not obtained *ex opere operato*. That seems to be the error of the Pharisees, and the Baptist proceeded against this first heresy concerning baptism with the utmost severity: γεννήματα ἐχιδνῶν, τίς ὑπέδειξεν ὑμῖν φυγεῖν ἀπὸ τῆς μελλούσης ὀργῆς; in Matt. iii.7. As *vipers' brood*, which means *children of the devil*; cf. TWNT V, pp. 566 ff., they are τέκνα ὀργῆς, destined to the eternal fire (Matt. xxv.41). *Who warned you*—if anyone, it can only be the devil—to let yourselves be baptised deceitfully, that means: to pretend to repent and thereby to obtain protection from the judgement of wrath by deceit.[1] It is not the *opus operatum* of baptism which saves—everything depends on genuine μετάνοια, which accepts God's verdict by taking upon itself the judgement of wrath in the symbol of baptism, and which proves its genuineness precisely by the καρπός it bears (verses 8-12). This is the only permissible and the only hopeful way of escape from wrath and even the Pharisees are not excluded from it (verse 8).[2]

divine wrath. The alternative, either to allay the wrath by means of baptism or to be judged instead by means of fire—is put forward in Sib. IV.165, 189, 178. Here the 'baptism' in the river is combined with loud appeals for forgiveness (cf. I Peter iii.21), whilst Adam and Eve (in Vit. Ad.) pray for deliverance silently.

[1] Akin to this is the refusal of a sacrifice from the ungodly for the purpose of appeasing the *ira deorum* in Cicero, *De Legibus* II, 22; cf. p. 9.

cf. T. Zahn, *Kommentar z. Matthäusev.* (²1905), pp. 138 f.; A. Schlatter, *Matt.* 69 ff. On the other hand Jesus relies on the possibility for his own to escape from the doom of wrath during the messianic woes, literally by flight (Luke xxi.21). The sentence 'no deliverance by baptism without repentance' in the sense of the Baptist, as later in that of Jesus and the apostles, carries the same weight as the other, 'no salvation by repentance without baptism'. It may be said that already John's baptism (like the Passover) is a genuine pre-Christian sacrament, in which salvation is effected by means of its being bound up with God's command and its physical performance just as much as with the affirmation of the recipient.

(c) The apostolic *kerygma* links the deliverance from God's wrath with Jesus. Jesus is he who delivers even now (I Thess. i.10). It is Jesus who some day will deliver from the future wrath (Rom. v.9). Only through him are we certain that we are not destined to wrath (I Thess. v.9 f.). Through him we are even now σωζόμενοι just as he is even now the ῥυόμενος. The deliverance is present and future at the same time, corresponding to the twofold temporal nature of eschatology. Why is deliverance from wrath associated with Jesus? Because we are justified by his blood, because we are reconciled by his death (Rom. v.9 f.), that is to say, there is no longer any condemnation for us (viii.1), we are no longer enemies (v.10). Or may we say: because Jesus has tasted God's wrath for us? Attempts have been made to base the affirmative answer to this question[1] on the scene at Gethsemane and the words from the cross in Matthew and Mark. R. Otto[2] would regard the struggle in Gethsemane in the light of the numinous with its *mysterium* and its *tremendum* and show that the nearest comparison to this conception of it is Jacob's struggle at the Jabbok and the attack on Moses at the lodging place (p. 36). He says it was principally

---

[1] An affirmative answer to this question is given, e.g. by J. T. Beck, 'Der Zorn Gottes', in *Chr. Reden* V ([2]1871), p. 200; H. J. Holtzmann, *Lehrbuch der neutestamentlichen Theologie* II, ([2]1911), p. 122: The wrath beneath which the dying (Jesus) seems to be placed has been effectively spent at his death. Similarly Procksch: divine wrath is broken by the sacrificial death of Christ. Also K. Barth, *Kirchliche Dogmatik* II, 1 ([2]1946), p. 444, ET *Church Dogmatics* (1957), speaks of 'his enduring the eternal wrath of God'. A negative reply is given by Ritschl, *Rechtfertigung und Versöhnung* II, pp. 155 f.; cf. also W. Hasenzahl, *Die Gottesverlassenheit des Christus* (1938), pp. 138-148, where admittedly the question of ὀργή is hardly touched upon, and also Althaus, *op. cit.* (p. 84, n. 2), II, pp. 259-261.

[2] *Das Heilige* ([26-28]1947), p. 106; ET *The Idea of the Holy* (1928), p. 88.

a grappling with divine wrath, and the victory over it already means that the decision has been reached. Similarly Procksch considers that the cup for the removal of which Jesus prays (Mark xiv.36) is the cup of wrath (p. 112, n. 2); Jesus shudders at the final depths of being forsaken by God according to the impressive representation in Luke xxii.44. The angel who in the gospel appears only at crucial points in the events personifies the nearness of God in the threatened abandonment by him (verse 43).[1] But Jesus is not spared the extremity of suffering; his prayer was not answered.[2] This is expressed in a deeply moving way by his last cry in Matthew and Mark: *Eli, eli, lama sabachthani?* For to be abandoned by God means to stand under wrath. That is the prevailing view of the OT: he who provokes God to anger is abandoned by him, and vice versa (Deut. xxxi.17, xxxii.19 f.; Isa. liv.8; Ps. xxvii.9, lxxxix.47).

It must of course be admitted that Jesus' passion is never connected directly with God's wrath; at any rate it is never said *expressis verbis* that Jesus stood under wrath.[3] On the contrary it is stated expressly (Luke ii.40, 52; Mark i.11; Matt. xii.18, xvii.5), that εὐδοκία and χάρις rest on Jesus from beginning to end. It is true that the voice from heaven at the baptism can be understood as a sign that Jesus when he accepted baptism, the symbol of the judgement of wrath, submitted himself to it (p. 112, n. 2). That was the πρέπον which the Baptist could not understand, and so the voice said to this Jesus, who though innocent took God's wrath upon

[1] cf. E. Schick, *Die Botschaft der Engel* (³1949), pp. 128-130.

[2] Hebrews v.7: οὐκ εἰσακουσθείς (according to Harnack's conjecture). Gal. iii.13 also says something similar.

[3] Nevertheless perhaps Jesus himself gives a hint in his allegory of the fire in Luke xxiii.31: Even Jesus, although he is 'green wood', will be thrown (i.e. by God) into the fire, i.e. the judgement of wrath (p. 110).

himself, 'not ὀργή but εὐδοκία'. That which was promised to Jesus when he anticipates taking our place on
the cross, is denied him on the cross itself, in order that
just because he bears it, he may take away God's wrath
from us (cf. Rom. v.9 as well as the parallel αἴρειν
ἁμαρτίαν in John i.29).

At any rate it certainly belongs inextricably to the
message of the NT that by Jesus' death deliverance
from the wrath to come is guaranteed and therefore
freedom from the present wrath is granted as well, and
this is decisive; for wrath is the real power which
destroys.[1] In Christ alone a breach is made in eternal
wrath. In him alone can we view as one whole the
scandalising tension between God's wrath and his love.[2]

If deliverance from eternal wrath is granted in
Christ alone,[3] then everything depends on whether a

---

[1] Althaus, op. cit. (p. 84, n. 2) II, p. 260 in a comment upon
Greek theologians and K. Heim. However it seems to me that
the view of the NT taken as a whole attaches equal weight to the
two propositions: 'Christ is the saviour from divine wrath and
condemnation' and 'Christ is the great divine counter-action
against Satan's rebellion', cf. Stauffer, Theologie (²1947), p. 4
(ET, p. 19) and frequently, especially pp. 127-130. (ET, pp. 146 ff.).

[2] cf. Althaus, op. cit. (p. 84, n. 2) II, p. 32; R. Bultmann,
Theologie des NT (1948), p. 283, ET Theology of the NT I (1952),
p. 288.

[3] There are no analogies in the ancient world to the Christ who
as judge is the representative of wrath and yet at the same time is
the only deliverer from it. Three passages come relatively
nearest to the thought of the NT, although in a different way:
(1) Livy 8, 9, 10 (p. 11), where admittedly the thought that the
deity itself sends the propitiatory sacrifice to appease the wrath, is
only a beautiful idea (sicut caelo missus); but the willingness of
Decius to offer himself voluntarily as a sacrifice is a proper
analogy. (2) The offer of Moses to expose himself in place of the
people to divine wrath (Exod. xxxii.32) and (3) the rendering in
the Midrash of Ps. vii.6 [Heb. 7] (p. 85, n. 2) in which God
himself is summoned to fight against his wrath. Cf. in addition also
the interpretation of Num. xxi in Wisdom xvi.5 ff.

man rejects Christ or appropriates what Christ is and brings—or more correctly, whether he lets himself be appropriated. He who rejects him remains under wrath; he who accepts him is free. *Either he must dread the wrath to come or love the present mercy—one of the two* (Ign. Eph. xi.1). Freedom from God's wrath is bound up with faith in Christ (John iii.36). By faith in him we possess the eschatological gift of freedom from wrath as a present reality. By the baptism with water as a preliminary judgement we acknowledge the right of the real baptism of judgement, that of fire; and thus this ἀντίτυπον of the overflowing wrath delivers us from this wrath itself.[1] But the power of the ἀντίτυπον rests on the fact that through it the baptised person has a share with Christ who himself bore and destroyed the wrath. By means of the power of Christ given in baptism we become σκεύη ἐλέους instead of σκεύη ὀργῆς, living persons instead of νεκροί; this interpretation of baptism thus approaches very closely that of Rom. vi. The two interpretations do not exclude each other, they are complementary.

Nevertheless the deliverance from wrath obtained through sheer grace is not a possession which cannot be lost. Even after complete forgiveness, even after admission into the fellowship of God's kingdom, a complete rejection is still possible (cf. Matt. xviii.34, xxii. 13), and then those who are rejected fall a prey to the eternal operations of wrath (p. 106), *where the worm never dies and the fire is not quenched.* This too belongs to the *kerygma* of the NT (cf. Rom. ii.16)[2]; yet its final testimony is not to wrath's sea of fire, but to the fountain of compassion in Christ.

[1] cf. A. Schlatter, *Kommentar z. Matthäusev.* (1929), p. 71.

[2] But cf. now W. Michaelis, *Versöhnung des Alls* (1950), especially pp. 55 f.

INDEX OF REFERENCES

GENERAL INDEX